Precarious Lives

CONTEMPORARY ETHNOGRAPHY

Kirin Narayan and Alma Gottlieb, Series Editors

A complete list of books in the series is available from the publisher.

PRECARIOUS LIVES

Waiting and Hope in Iran

Shahram Khosravi

UNIVERSITY OF PENNSYLVANIA PRESS

PHILADELPHIA

Published by
University of Pennsylvania Press
Philadelphia, Pennsylvania 19104-4112
www.upenn.edu/pennpress

Printed in the United States of America on acid-free paper
10 9 8 7 6 5 4 3 2 1

Library of Congress Cataloging-in-Publication Data
ISBN 978-0-8122-4887-6

For Parvaneh and Nader
My Parents

CONTENTS

NOTE ON TRANSLITERATION AND DATES

The system of transliteration used in this book follows the style of the *International Journal of Middle East Studies*. Transliteration of Arabic words and words in Persian of Arabic origin follows the system used for Persian. All translations are by the author unless otherwise stated.

In the text, dates are all in the Common Era unless they refer to Persian texts. In the text and bibliography, dates are given in the Iranian *shamsi* (solar) calendar and are followed by the corresponding date in the Common Era separated by a slash. The year 2015 is 1394 *shamsi*.

INTRODUCTION

This book deals with nothing other than hoping beyond the day
which has become.
—Ernst Bloch (1996 [1959]: 10)

On a hot day in late June 2014, I was to meet Hamed at 2 p.m. on the west side
of Valiasr Square. In early summer, the day temperature in Tehran can easily
reach 45° C in the shade. Valiasr Square is a central node in Tehran, a busy
business zone, close to major universities. The hot sun did not drive people
away, and the square was as usual crammed with people and cars. This was the
first time Hamed and I would meet; we had spoken only on the telephone a
couple of times, after a mutual acquaintance in Kabul had put us in contact. I
could easily feel Hamed's hesitation—he had changed the time and place for
our meeting several times—but he was too gracious to reject my request for
an interview. I understood his concerns and anxiety. I had asked him for an
interview for an article I was writing on post-deportation because he had been
deported from Sweden a year earlier and I wanted to know what had happened to him afterward. It was already 2:20 p.m., and he had not yet shown
up. I thought that a police car parked on the west side of the square might
have deterred his approach, so I moved from the square to Keshavarz Boulevard. I was right. Hamed had sent a text message saying that he wanted to
avoid passing the police car, and we should go to the southern side of the
square. And there he was, a tall, handsome young man in a white shirt with
small blue flowers hanging over a pair of jeans. A few minutes later we were
sitting in a coffee shop with two chilled bottles of Iran-made nonalcoholic
beer with citron flavor on our table.

Hamed is an Afghan Iranian man, born in 1990 in Tehran to undocumented Afghan parents, who had escaped Afghanistan after the Soviet

invasion in the early 1980s. They started a new life in Shahr-e Ray in southern Tehran, first as welcomed refugees, then as unwelcomed undocumented migrants. The altered migration policy toward Afghans has been significant for the Iranian economy. The legal production of migrant illegality (De Genova 2002) has created a large, cheap, and docile labor force, active mainly in the construction and agriculture sectors. The Afghan presence in the labor market is so firmly established that many Iranians use the word *Afghani* as synonymous with "unskilled worker."

Hamed, like his five siblings, grew up in a condition of deportability, under a constant risk of removal. Despite his youth, he had been exposed to multiple deportations. The first time he was twenty years old. After one month in the notorious Asgarabad detention center south of Tehran, he was taken to the Afghan border by bus—for which he had to pay the fare—and was forced to cross the border on foot. He returned to Iran the following day with the help of *dalals* (literally, brokers, human smugglers), for whom each deportee is a new client.

Back in Tehran, Hamed decided to start a new life by seeking asylum in Europe, unaware that his destiny would be interwoven with deportability. After a long and dangerous journey across several states without documents, he reached Europe, but his asylum applications were rejected in both the Netherlands and Sweden. From 2011 to 2014, he was deported four times, the last time from Sweden to Afghanistan in February 2014. In Kabul, a city he had never visited and knew nothing about, he became the target of bullying and derision because of his Tehrani accent, clothing style, and behavior. Like many other young Afghan deportees, Hamed faced stigmatization in terms of being "culturally contaminated" by foreign cultures. In Afghanistan, he was bullied by being called *iranigak* (literally, one who acts Iranian). After a few weeks in Kabul, he found a *dalal* and crossed the border to Iran to join his family. Reaching this point in the story of his life and his journeys, being back in Iran, the country where he was born and grew up, the only land he has known as home, though hostile and unwelcoming, he said, "Now here we live like animals on the streets. We were born on the street and we die on the street." This state of irregularity affects even the smallest aspects of life for the undocumented. All everyday activities are "illegalized," from housing and work to physical mobility. Undocumented immigrants lack not only the right to health care, education, police protection, and work, but also the right to social relations and freedom of movement in public spaces. As an undocumented person, Hamed cannot even have a telephone contract in his own name. For any simple bureaucratic task such as housing, a contract with a company, transport, school, he needs to pay an Iranian citizen to make his life livable. Hamed embodies the social precarity of Iranian youth, although his lack of documentation makes his condition even more precarious than that of others.

Since early in my career, I have been working in two geographically and thematically different research fields—or perhaps only imagined differently in my mind. One is urban Iran and the youth culture, the other irregular migration and border studies in Sweden. For almost two decades, I have kept them apart. When I arranged a meeting with Hamed, I could not imagine that this book would start with him. However, during the writing process, I realized how much the two fields overlap. Gradually, I saw how the precarious lives of undocumented migrants in Europe resemble the social vulnerabilities Iranian youth are struggling with. In Chapter 2, I write about the condition of "waiting," and how keeping people waiting and turning them into "patients" of the state is the same mechanism as the marginalization and domination of both migrants in Sweden and young people in Iran. To criminalize a particular group (for example, the *arazel owbash* in Chapter 3) to regulate, control, and punish them is also similar in the two fields. The precarious labor condition and informality in the labor market that the undocumented in Sweden experience are not so unlike the conditions that youth, particularly young women, in Iran face. Another interesting similarity is the Agambenian theory of how the system of nation-states differentiates between naked (depoliticized) life (*zoé*) and a political form of life (*bios*) (Agamben 1998). Similar to undocumented migrants, many young, single Iranians (as I develop in Chapter 3) are consigned to the zones of exemption, outside officially recognized rights, rules, and norms, where they are exposed to invisibility, exploitation, exclusion, and violence. In this condition, norms and rules taken for granted by all citizens cease to apply.

In both fields an *othering* process is at work. While in the one field borders target the racialized migrant bodies, in the case of Iran other forms of borders discriminate and exclude young people who do not fit the authorized forms of life. Since the establishment of the Islamic Republic, the official discourse divides Iranian society between those who are inside the religious-ideological community (*khodi*) and those who are outside it (*gheir-e khodi*). A common experience among outsiders is discrimination by the law because of gender, political opinion, ethnicity, class, sexual orientation, or age in a broad range of areas: from education and the labor and housing markets to the public

sphere and political life. As Étienne Balibar (2002) puts it, borders have become invisible, situated everywhere and nowhere. Undesirable people, either
undocumented migrants or defiant youth, are not expelled at the border:
rather, they are forced to *be* the border. The question is not what or where the
border is, but *who* the border is. A comparative approach between my two
fields shows that borders can restrict the rights of noncitizens as well as citizens. In Iran, the young can easily find themselves turned into quasi-citizens
whose rights can be suspended, rejected, delayed, and denied because of their
class, religion, ideological belief, ethnicity, or lifestyle. A young man expressed
the condition in Iran in this way: "we live in an occupied country, like France
under Nazi occupation." The analogy reveals clearly how he, like many other
marginalized people in Iran, experiences the shrinking citizenship, the lack
of, in Hannah Arendt's words, the "right to have rights" (1994 [1951]). The
withdrawal of rights or limiting access to citizenship rights—making rights
available but not accessible—in migration theory, is identified as *denization*.
The term *denization* is from medieval English law, which allowed a foreigner
certain rights, for example, the right of residence, without being a full member
of the society. Reintroduced to migration studies by Tomas Hammar (1990)
the term has been used for noncitizen immigrants with a limited degree of
rights. Denizens are neither citizens nor foreigners; they are included but not
recognized as full members. In short, Hamed's story made me realize that the
core question in both fields has been acts of citizenship and the struggle for
citizenship rights, both for citizens and noncitizens.

Social Precarity

Originally the term *precarity* was used to depict a work condition without
predictability or security in post-Fordist capitalism. It has been used to sum-
marize contemporary neoliberal labor relations in postindustrial societies,
irregular employment, vulnerability, and "flexploitation" (Neilson and Rossiter 2005, in Waite 2008: 416). Following Anne Allison (2012) in her study of
precariousness in contemporary Japan, I use "precarity" to understand how
insecurity in the material condition leads to pathological symptoms that
haunt multiple aspects of contemporary life (see also Molé 2012: 41; Millar
2014). Precarity here moves beyond the labor market and become a defining
feature of society in general. The term, thus, refers to "the process whereby
society as a whole becomes more precarious and is potentially destabilized"

(Waite 2008: 415). One form of insecurity leads to another form, engendering multiple precarities that undermine and desecuritize one's life condition. Precarity, or as Allison puts it, "social precarity" is therefore insecurity in life: material, existential, and social (Allison 2012: 349). Precarity here is used to cover a broad range of social vulnerabilities that Iranians are struggling with: from insecure work conditions and physical insecurity to hopelessness, purposelessness, alienation, and disconnectedness from a sense of social community.

There is a growing sense of exile from home and homeland among the Iranian youth. Incapable of managing the transition to adulthood, to be "productive," to build a family, young people feel they are being exiled from the very life they are supposed to reproduce (cf. Allison 2012: 354). The feeling of being in exile originates not from spatial distance but from a temporal one, in not being integrated into the "national time." Suffering from perpetual suspension (Echeverri Zuluaga 2015) and the predicament of being "stuck," caught in prolonged waiting for job, marriage, or a visa to a Western country, makes young people feel out of sync with others. The sense of being in exile from the home(land) is also reflected in a growing sense of disconnectedness to home and to the family. A rising anxiety among authorities and "experts" in recent years has been the "collapse of the family" (as I will develop in the next chapter). Alongside a soaring divorce rate, there has been a growing rate of domestic violence. *Havades* (literally, incidents) pages in newspapers report shocking family dramas: a man who under financial pressures first kills his wife and then his children before committing suicide; daughters who kill their fathers who had forced them into prostitution; women who in collaboration with their lovers murder their husbands; husbands who kill their wives to marry the women they love. The killing of family members makes up 40 percent of all murders in Iran (Ghazinezhad and Abasian 1390/2011).

Alienation and a sense of exile from one's home(land) trigger a desire for emigration. Each year 150,000 to 180,000 educated young Iranians emigrate. In 2013, more than 600,000 Iranians played the U.S. Department of State Green Card Lottery. Others, who are not "desirable" in Western states because of lack of capital or education, opt for more dangerous ways to reach Australia or Europe by boat without passport or visa. There is a general feeling of detachment, isolation, ineptitude, and defeat among youth as consequences of protracted un(der)employment, being stigmatized, and being bullied as a "burden." Not surprisingly, several of my interlocutors used the term "death" when talking about their lives. Noelle Molé finds Italian workers, who have been subjected to "precarious-ization" in a zombie-like state of being (2012: 39), feeling not fully alive. The movie *Parviz* (by Majid Barzegar 2012), about a man who has been kept biologically alive by his father until he reaches middle age, shows this feeling well. The movie illustrates very well how multiple precarities create bare lives (Agamben 1998), biological bodies deprived of any political rights. Parviz is socially dead, a ghost, half-alive, half-dead.

Recent official statistics on the proliferation of precarity in weak groups are alarming. The official rate of unemployment among young people (fifteen to twenty-four years old) is 25 percent, almost twice the national average. Many experts believe that the real rate is much higher. In early 2015, the deputy minister of labor declared that there were seven million "*allaf*" (a contemptuous term referring to a person who does nothing, a loiterer) in the country and that these *allaf*s are unemployed and do not participate in any education or training program. Claiming that youth do not actively seek a job, the deputy blamed them for not taking responsibility for their lives.[1] But there are many other troubling statistics, such as 5,700,000 educated unemployed in Iran.[2] The Statistics Centre of Iran announced that, as of spring 2014, almost forty million Iranians did not participate at all in the production and economic development of the country.[3] Some groups suffer more than others from unemployment. According to the Iranian Central Bank, in 24 percent of households, no one is employed at all.[4] Another vulnerable group is the elderly. Half of all senior women and 25 percent of senior men have no livelihood. Among senior Iranians, 70 percent have no complementary private health insurance, and 20 percent have no insurance at all. The situation is not much better for those who do work. Irregular employment, short-term contracts, and underemployment have become so much the norm that experts warn that job security could disappear altogether. Job security is already unreachable for the majority of the labor force. Up to 93 percent of all Iranian workers have irregular employment.[5] Every year more Iranians are classified as poor. In 2015, the official sources announced that 40 percent of Iranians lived under the poverty line.[6] Un(der)employment and irregular jobs mean irregular housing conditions. According to the governmental data from April 2015, of urban residents, up to ten million lived in slums and informal settlements.[7]

As expected, all these combined have had an effect on the deterioration of people's physical and mental health. Alarming statistics say that one in four is suffering from a "mental disorder."[8] Depression has become epidemic among middle-class urban youth, and Prozac and Diazepam are nowadays unavoidable words in conversations with young people. Studies show an increased use of antidepressant drugs between 1997 and 2008 (Behrouzan 2010). Social precarity in Iran is multilayered. Different but interrelated forms of precarities exacerbate each other and strike various aspects of life. Alongside financial insecurity, Iranians are facing the worst environmental crisis in modern time. Pollution and drought have become major national concerns. Since 2013, not a day has gone by without alarming warnings on shrinking water levels in dams, dying lakes, and drying rivers. Some scenarios depict Iran as uninhabitable land in the near future. Shrinking water reserves have resulted in pollution of reservoirs, industrial wastes have polluted the soil, and major cities are shrouded in poisonous smog. In the past years, four of the ten most polluted cities in the world have been Iranian: Ahvaz, Sanandaj, Kermanshah, and Yasouj.[9] As if all these precarities are not enough to break down a people, we should add the decade long international sanctions that have had disastrous consequences for ordinary Iranians. Furthermore, the geopolitical position of Iran in the middle of ongoing and horrifying wars and conflicts in Afghanistan, Iraq, and Syria on the one hand and the imminent threat of military attack by Israel on the other have worsened the precariousness of the Iranian people. Almost every day, Iranians read or hear warnings by journalists or "experts" diligently using terms like "social collapse," "silent earthquake," "dreadful statistics," or "invisible tsunami."

Insecurity has led to the proliferation of occult practices and economies that penetrate all levels of Iranian society. Sorcery and witchcraft were used by high-ranking political officials in the government of President Mahmoud Ahmadinejad (see Rahnema 2011; Doostdar 2013). Spells are used in games between national football teams. Young men and women turn to sorcerers to find their spouse or to get rich. Failing to build a future for themselves through education and work, many people turn to magical means: divinations, treasure hunting, pyramid schemes, multilevel marketing, the Green Card Lottery, or sources of metaphysical "positive energy" (see Chapter 7). People turn to occult practices seeking promises of health, happiness, and success, unreachable by other means. Multiple precarities trigger a desire to escape both from here and from now. A longing to be somewhere else (emigration) and some time else (in a future that would replace the untoward presence) is a symptom of the precarious life that Iranians live. The occult economies, that is, making wealth without effort, have engendered speculative practices and betting games. People buy property, cars, or foreign currencies in the hope of a jump in prices in the coming months. A "casino relationship" has penetrated

Iranians' everyday life. The occult economies characterizing "neoliberal culture," as observed in many studies of African societies (Comaroff and Comaroff 1999; Piot 2010; Smith 2007), can also be observed in Iran. Mathieu Hilgers's scrutiny depicts a culture of neoliberalism in which "New forms of enchantment are produced by a casino relationship to the world, in which a nobody can acquire a fortune and a private income with nothing but luck and a lottery ticket" (Hilgers 2011: 353). Listening to endless discussions in taxis, in coffee shops, in private gatherings, or around dinner tables about investments, speculations, swinging prices, risks, the rising or falling value of foreign currencies and gold, losses and gains makes one imagine that Iranian society has turned into a vast casino.

Unlike other terms, such as vulnerability, *precarity* does not only signify subjugation: it also encapsulates political potential for mobilization among those who experience it (Waite 2008). In the past decades, Iran has become the scene for small and big social movements and protests. The major ones have been the student protest in 1999 in Tehran, the One Million Signatures for the Repeal of Discriminatory Laws in 2006, and the Green Movement in 2009. Furthermore, small-scale and local yet significant protests are taking place continually. In 2014 and 2015, the most significant ones were organized by unpaid workers throughout the country; by waterless farmers in Isfahan; by residents of Ahvaz who can barely breathe due to air pollution; by the Bakhtiari ethnic minority who forced the national television to halt the broadcast of an offensive television series; and by street vendors who expressed their precarious lives through demonstrative suicides in Tehran, Tabriz, and Khoramshahr (see Chapter 7).

Needless to say, the multiple precarities Iranians experience today are not specific either to today or to Iran. Throughout this book, references to surveys, reports, and studies of other countries indicate that the precariousness discussed in different chapters is similar not only in other Middle Eastern countries such as Egypt (Ghannam 2013; Abu-Lughod 2005; Ismail 2006; Hasso 2011), Saudi Arabia (Menoret 2014), or Lebanon (Deeb and Harb 2013; see also Dhillon and Yousef 2009), but also in countries such as India (Jeffrey 2010; Chua 2014), Ethiopia (Mains 2012), Togo (Piot 2010), Nigeria (Smith 2007), Japan (Allison 2013), Senegal (Echeverri Zuluaga 2015), Chile (Han 2012), Brazil (Millar 2014), and Argentina (Ayero 2012). Nor do I mean that precarity, in the form of vulnerability and insecurity, is unique to the post-revolutionary era, but, as I will show, precariousness has been intensified and institutionalized since the late 1990s.

Fragments of a Neoliberal Culture

The term *neoliberalism* nowadays is used everywhere and for everything. I do not mean that Iran is a neoliberal state or that neoliberalism is the basis for social and political structures in Iran. However, fragments of the consequences of neoliberalism can be seen in current Iranian society. Following the footsteps of recent excellent studies (Jeffrey 2010; Chua 2014; Mains 2012; Piot 2010; Allison 2013; Han 2012; Auyero 2012; Millar 2014; Molé 2011) of novel forms of social marginalization in other parts of the world, I want to show the precarious-ization of life as a consequence of the recent transformations in Iranian politics and economy. During the past two decades, the valorization of the entrepreneurial individual, a preference for the market over rights, the withdrawal of the state from the service sector, and prolonged un-(der)employment have created new forms of exclusion and subalterities in Iran—all characteristics of what is called neoliberalism (Greenhouse 2010).

After the death of Ayatollah Khomeini and the end of the Iran-Iraq war, social policy changed in Iran. Hashemi Rafsanjani's presidency (1989–1997) addressed economic issues rather than ideological ones. Presenting himself as a pragmatist, he launched the "Reconstruction Era" characterized by expansive privatization, deregulation, and reduction of subsidies, which weakened collective contracts and caused the loss of job security. The welfare state of the 1980s was replaced by policies that "led to economic measures such as devaluation of the currency (which increased the cost of living for the poor), privatization (which left many workers unprotected), and the decline of social services" (Bahramitash 2003: 565). To normalize ties with global finance and to facilitate foreign investments, Iran was required to follow the policy guidelines of the World Bank and the International Monetary Fund (IMF). Subsequently, the Iranian government started to back off from "its earlier commitment to the expansion of the welfare state" (565). During Rafsanjani's first presidential term (1989–1993), imports rose from US$8 billion to US$23 billion and the total debt from US$6 billion to US$30 billion (Menashri 2001: 109). Inflation and unemployment soared. Gradually, a postsocial state with more focus on market economy than welfare replaced the revolutionary state of the 1980s. Nevertheless, the neoliberal policy was still formulated in the religious and ideological discourse of *jihad sazandegi* (reconstruction struggle). *Jihad* means holy war.

The infiltration of war into the economic realm has not only been a matter of jargon but also brought economics and politics together. In the 2000s, military officers became the main entrepreneurs at the national level. The Islamic Revolutionary Guard Corps (IRCC) gradually turned into a multibillion-dollar empire with control over a third of the Iranian economy (see Golkar 2015). Bringing a military ethos and mentality into business fitted well with neoliberal policies, which promote risk taking, adventurous, and strong entrepreneurs. War generals have become "successful managers." Many of the current high-ranking political and municipal officials were war commanders in the 1980s. The involvement of the military in the economy has been motivated by the need of encouraging a "risk-taking spirit" and "*jihadi* mentality" in the field. In the media, many rich businessmen call themselves "soldiers of the system." The most notorious, business tycoon Babak Zanjani, who was detained for corruption in 2013, proclaimed himself an "economic *basiji*" (volunteer militia force). The major engineering "company" of IRCC and one of the largest contractors in industrial and development projects is the Khatam-ul Anbia headquarters. Khatam-ul Anbia, which means Seal of the Prophets, is a name of the Prophet Mohammad. The conjunction of religion, military, and finance is characteristic of Iranian post-revolutionary neoliberalism. Defenders of IRCC involvement in financial activities claim that a "culture of war is beneficial for the economy" and that the experience of managing a war can be used in the managing a company.[10] One of the best-known commanders during the war was Mohamad Bagher Ghalibaf, mayor of Tehran since 2005. Following former mayor Gholamhossein Karbaschi (a close ally to Rafsanjani), Ghalibaf has continued the expansion of Tehran through mobilization and control of surplus production. Urban projects are mainly carried out thanks to capital from private actors, who in exchange are exempted from zoning laws. A consequence has been aggressive privatization of the urban skyline. The commodification and privatization of Tehran's skyline have led to enormous building sector profits and skyrocketing housing prices that in turn have forced deprived groups out of the city. A similar situation can also be seen in other cities. While towering buildings become higher and higher, the slums get larger and more crowded.

Urbanization is expanding drastically in Iran. The rate of growth of urban areas is five times greater than that of rural areas. The migration of the poor to cities means the growth of slums and informal settlements. An official source at the Majlis (parliament) declared in March 2015 that since the Revolution the number of people living in the slums has increased by 17 times.[11] In 2014 the number of urban dwellers living in slums or informal settlements reached ten million.[12] The majority, 75 percent, were concentrated in ten big cities, such as Tehran, Mashhad, Ahvaz, and Shiraz.[13] Using warfare experience as a management tool for a megacity like Tehran could not result in something better. This permeation of the military into the economy echoes larger transformations in Iranian society. Terms such as being a conscious (*agah*), warrior (*mobarez*), and being ready for self-sacrifice (*isargar*), used by the authorities to make good soldiers during the war with Iraq, are now used in the project of constructing good entrepreneurial citizens. Nonetheless, we should see this as not contradictory but supplementary. In early 2014, when international sanctions had become more and more suffocating, supreme leader Ayatollah Khamenei introduced "resistance economy" as a long-term strategy. Resistance economy means that Iranians should learn to endure even more (see Chapter 6). Following the supreme leader, Ali Jannati, chairman of the Guardian Council, declared explicitly that if necessary Iranians should make even more sacrifices: "One meal a day is enough, if sanctions get worse."[14]

I recurrently heard the question, "how do Iranians endure?" a topic I develop in Chapter 6. By studying popular television series, I show how the state uses these programs, mainly from East Asia, as pedagogical tools to teach Iranians techniques of self-development and endurance. The choice of Chinese, Japanese, and South Korean historical television dramas is not accidental. In the East, living for centuries amid enormous upheavals of historical and natural disasters, as Arthur Kleinman states, has made "how to endure" into a core "cultural wisdom" (2014: 119). The neoliberal messages in the television series, modified and dubbed into Persian, cannot be more explicit: individualizing and personalizing poverty. Iranian television not only depoliticizes and naturalizes suffering but also aims to show how people can solve serious social issues through endurance, risk taking, hard work, and belief in individual volunteerism.

While in the 1980s *hezbollahis* (partisans of the party of God) were supposed to sacrifice their lives for God and the people, now they are expected to be financially successful. As a high-ranking official put it in April 2014, "*Hezbollahis* should be rich. If he has no wealth, it is because of his ineptitude."[15] In the 1980s, the main acclaimed figure was "the disenfranchised" (*mahroum*) and "the dispossessed" (*mostaz'af*), whereas, since the late 1990s, the celebrated figure in official discourse has been a "successful" (*moafaq*) individual. The official media broadcast many success stories and interviews with successful people. Official discourse valorizes hardworking, self-developed, responsible individuals as ideal citizens. As in Japan (Allison 2012: 352), "unproductive" Iranian youth are seen as a "burden on the family" (*sarbar-e khanevadeh*), since, de-spite—or because of—the economic crisis, financial success and productivity remain the calculus of social worth. The pressure of life and expectation of pro-ductivity has pushed young Iranians toward a harsh, competitive life, where one is under constant evaluation and comparison. This is part of the global neolib-eralism that aims to replace sociality with "decollectivization, reindividualiza-tion, and insecuritization" (Castel 2003: 43, in Allison 2013: 129). Sometimes the reactions toward success and making wealth fast are a mixture of cynicism and admiration. The notion of *zerang bazi* (playing smart)—or sometimes *irooni bazi* (playing Iranian), which means making success at someone else's expense—encapsulates this peculiar combination of respect and jealousy.

Experiencing life as "under occupation by a foreign power," as an interloc-utor put it, expresses a sense of separation between state and society. A young, educated woman said, "They [the state] do their job, and we live our lives. As far as we keep the distance, everything is fine." Separation and "distance," nev-ertheless, do not mean the absence of the state. Its governmentality affects not only the market but also public relationships, social capital, and the sense of belonging. As Greenhouse puts it, the social effects of neoliberalism are not limited to the vertical relationships between the state and society; they also affect the lateral relationships among individuals, their sense of membership in the public, and the conditions of their self-knowledge (2010: 2). By provok-ing and encouraging rivalry and a culture of competition (*cheshm ham cheshmi*) among young people, exemplified best in the ranking system of uni-versity entrance exams (*konkur*) and a scheme of success grading, neoliberal-ism has deteriorated what Robert Putnam (1995) calls social capital, that is, the feature of social life—norms and trust—that enables citizens to act to-gether effectively to pursue shared objectives. The competitive culture has had a negative effect on mutual trust between citizens. A culture of competition and the decline of social capital have not only reduced mutual cooperation, but consequently led to a growth in conflicts. The backlog of more than fifteen million cases in the judicial system in 2015 and entering several million new cases into the system each year are telling enough.[16]

Bombarding Iranians with success stories (particularly of those who come from underprivileged backgrounds) on television (elaborated in Chapter 6) is an attempt to make them believe that the promises of a neoliberal economy are available to all. Neoliberal policies and the postsocial state, along with the growth of a consumerist culture and the flow of vast wealth into the hands of a segment of the population, have led to the false belief that success is attainable for all. Discrepancies between the needs of the larger society and the individual condition have generated alienation and hopelessness among young Iranians. The lack of the means and chances to reach goals and meet one's own and others' expectations is the hallmark of neoliberal capitalism (Comaroff and Comaroff 2001). Failing to meet the expectations and promises of neoliberal capitalism leads to the aforementioned "occult economies" and anomie among youth. Accordingly, the gap between availability and accessibility of society's goals and promises results in an unequal distribution of hope.

The Right to Hope

The widening gap between the rich and the poor is manifested in the unequal distribution of risk and hope. In the middle of the fourth decade since the return of Aytollah Khomeini, the promises of the Revolution are fading away faster than ever. Iranians, particularly the young generation, are left alone with multiple precarities, such as the high rate of corruption, increasing class differences, family break-ups, mass unemployment, financial insecurity, and gender inequalities. An unequal distribution of hope is characteristic of shrinking societies, "when such inequality reaches an extreme, certain groups are not offered any hope at all" (Hage 2003: 17). In recent years, particularly after the 2009 election, I frequently heard young Iranians—or read in their blogs, Facebook pages, books, and journal essays—make references to minority experiences, interestingly often to the experiences of the Jews in Europe during the first half of the past century. A popular quote used by Iranians comes from Franz Kafka—"there is hope, but not for us"—cynical words from a German-speaking Jew living in Prague, who embodied the continuum of exclusion in early twentieth-century Europe. In the mouths of young Iranians, who are not in a minority in terms of ethnicity or religious belief but feel they live a life like "in France under Nazi occupation," this echoes once again the aforementioned analogy between the predicament of migrant illegality and the precarious life of youth in Iran. Expressing anguish and resentment by quoting Kafka originates from their reflections on the unequal distribution of hope and the shrinking of a state's ability to generate hopefulness for all (see Hage 2003). Young Iranians do not feel hopeless because there is no hope (there is for others), but simply because they lack the entitlement to hope. This makes the issue of hope preeminently a political one. Ghassan Hage (2003) states that hope exists when there are potentialities, practical possibilities for a better future. Needless to mention, class, gender, ethnicity, sexualities, legal status (in the case of Hamed as an illegalized person) shape how potentialities for a better future are distributed. However, it seems that the feeling of unjust distribution of hope is shared by youth from different layers of society and varies more with generation than anything else:

> Hope is about the sense of possibility that life can offer . . . and is not necessarily related to an income level. Its enemy is a sense of entrapment, of having nowhere to go, not a sense of poverty. As the state withdraws from society and the existing configuration of hope begins shrinking many people, even with middle-class incomes, urban dwellers paradoxically stuck in insecure jobs, farmers working day and night without "getting anywhere," small-business people struggling to keep their businesses going, and many more have begun suffering from various forms of hope scarcity. (Hage 2003: 20)

As Marxist philosopher Ernst Bloch framed it, hope is future oriented and toward a possibility that has still not become (1996 [1959]: 7). Bloch's notion of "not-yet" consciousness is based on anticipation of something still to happen. His philosophy of hope is one of dreaming forward. There is a time aspect here. The "not-yet" approach highlights how hope (emotion) and waiting (act) intersect. Waiting, as Pierre Bourdieu puts it, is a way of experiencing the effect of power, "Making people wait . . . delaying without destroying hope is part of the domination" (Bourdieu 2000: 228). To keep people waiting and enduring hardship without ruining their hope is an exercise of power over their time. Unlike Vincent Crapanzano's (1985) approach to waiting time in terms of passivity and lack of agency, Bloch argues that hope for a better life, even in the form of daydreaming, is agentive. Drawing on the works of Bloch and Walter Benjamin, anthropologist Hirokazu Miyazaki reflects on hope in terms of repetition and replication. In his ethnography of hope, Miyazaki writes about the Fijian Suvavou people who incessantly petition the government with claims to their ancestral lands. Hope among the Suvavou is generated in repetition and replication of their claims, despite continuous rejection. Miyazaki argues that hope should be studied as a method, since it can only be defined by its repetitive quality: "The method of hope, in other words, is predicated on the inheritance of a past hope and its performative replication in the present" (2004: 139). Similar to the case of the Suvavou people, hope for democracy and social justice in modern Iran has been replicated time and again since the early twen-

tieth century, from the Constitutional Revolution (1911) to the Oil National-
ization (1950), the 1979 Revolution, and the Green Movement (2009). This
history of repetition and replication of hope argues against representation of
the Iranian society in terms of a "short-term society" (Katouzian 2010) and
against the biased representation of Iran as a series of simple dichotomies:
tradition/modernity, Islam/West, and local/global. In contrast to an essential-
izing approach, we should look at how Iranians' hope has historically been
interrupted, suppressed, and deferred (see Dabashi 2007). In that way, we can
understand how unfulfilled hopes inherited from past failures, alongside a
hopeful sense of "not yet," become "pull" factors and motivations to repeat and
replicate political and social demands, claims, and stands in today's Iran.

Very similar to the continual and repetitive petitioning by the Suvavou
people's claims to their rights, petitions (*arizeh*) to the Iranian government
increased drastically in Iran during the presidency of Mahmoud Ahmadinejad. His office claims that, during his presidency, the government received
thirty-eight million petitions.[17] Like the Suvavou, Iranians keep sending petitions because they continue to believe someone in the government might read
their letters and resolve their problems. The act of submitting letters is often
performative and spectacular. During the president's visits, people tried to
deliver their petitions personally by hand. People running after the president's
car to throw their letters into the vehicle was a usual scene on TV news during
Ahmadinejad's presidency. To keep sending petitions is an enactment of
right-bearing citizens. As Matthew Hull (2012: 94) shows in his study of bureaucracy in Pakistan, the petition embodies the relations between the citizens and the government. Petitioners in Iran, as in Pakistan or Fiji, enact the
same political subject who demands rights and justice. Petitions materialize
hope, although hope as method (Miyazaki 2004) takes place more often in
shrinking societies, under the pressure of social suffering and increasing insecurity. This book is partly an ethnography of hope. The following chapters
illustrate the repetition and replication of hope in various forms: from daydreaming, cinema, music, graffiti, new urban practices and visibilities to social movements and political manifestations.

As I show later, Iranian youth's waiting, hope, and daydreaming, orienting
themselves toward "not-yet" fulfilled promises, are preeminently acts of citizenship, that is, claiming their right to potentialities that make prospects for a better
future possible. Thus the right to hope is a basic political and citizenship right.
While the book is partly about social precarity, it also deals with how Iranians
respond to their precariousness. My aim is not to present young Iranians only

in terms of Agambenian bare life, depoliticized *homo sacers* (Agamen 1998), but as agentive individuals who challenge the police in Jacque Ranciere's meaning by rearranging the distribution of the sensible (see Chapters 4 and 5).

New Urban Practices of Youth

To understand social transformations in contemporary urban Iran, we have to look at the new urban practices by the younger generation. Rather than thinking of "youth" as based on chronological age, youth is seen as an economic and social concept. In his classic work, August Hollingshead defined youth as "the period in the life of the person when the society in which he functions ceases to regard him as child and does not accord him full adult status, roles and functions" (1949: 6). The term thus refers not just to an age cohort but to a stage in the lifecycle between childhood and adulthood. The form and duration of youth are determined in relation to macro social and economic circumstances, and thus vary widely among different societies. As in many other societies, a current trend in the Iranian society is toward prolonged youth. Delayed independence from parents, protracted unemployment, extended education period, and failing to build one's own family are factors making youth a longer phase in life. In this book, youth is used as a term referring to young and young adult Iranians' experiences of concrete historical problems (cf. Mannheim 1952).

Urban mobility—*rahpeymai* (in its double meanings: walking and demonstrating) but also driving, practicing parkour, performing street art, occupying street corners and coffee shops—is an act through which young Iranians reclaim their right to the city and thereby to produce their own city. Young Iranians' new urban practices demonstrate their self-assertion socially and politically, as well as their stress on individual autonomy through their active presence on the streets. In Chapters 4 and 5, I focus on several forms of new visibilities: automobility (driving around), imprinting their presence on walls (graffiti), alternative socialization and public life (coffee shops), and what Asef Bayat (1997) has termed "quiet encroachment" by urban poor. The active presence and mobility of the young people in the city, creating visibility of oppressed groups such as women, *mojarad* (single) people, street children, working-class young men stigmatized as *arazel owbash* (thugs), disclose the social and spatial inequalities these groups are exposed to (cf. Caldeira 2012). How they move around, drive, imprint their presence through graffiti, occupy coffee shops as loci for producing youth culture are all integrated into the process of production and reproduction of the city. In the contexts of these forms of mobility and visibility, Chapters 4 and 5 aim to explore transformations and tensions in the urban landscapes in Iran. *Presence* is crucial here. The ethnographic examples in this book show that the claims of urban youth and poor to their right to the city and acts of citizenship (Isin and Nielsen 2008) are formed by collective presence rather than by collective protests. Asef Bayat identifies these practices in terms of "social nonmovements," which he defines as "collective actions of noncollective actors; they embody shared large numbers of ordinary people whose fragmented but similar activities trigger much social change, even though these practices are rarely guided by an ideology or recognizable leaderships and organizations" (2010: 14).

The practices of urban youth, rather than being well-organized movements with explicit political aims, are struggles for enhancing life chances. They are means to reclaim youthfulness, to achieve individualities, and to struggle for gender equality. Being present, being on the stage, being visible and audible, reconfiguring the partition of the sensible are the core of what Jacques Rancière (2010) means with politics. In his view, the social order (or as he terms it "the police order") is a set of implicit rules and conventions that determine the distribution of roles in a given community and the forms of exclusion that operate within it. This order is founded on what Rancière calls the "distribution of the sensible." He refers to the way roles and modes of participation in a common social world are determined by establishing possible modes of perception. Thus, the distribution of the sensible sets the divisions between what is visible and invisible, sayable and unsayable, audible and inaudible. The urban practices of the young and the poor are preeminently political acts, acts of citizenship, because they make visible what is supposed to be invisible and because they make audible those who are supposed to be silent. In urban scenes in Iran, acts of citizenship are performed in claims of the right to the city as well as of the right to hope.

Writing This Book

This book is the outcome of a long conversation and ethnographic engagement with Iran. The conversation with Iran has been going on throughout my life, first as an ethnic minority Bakhtiari migrant in Isfahan, then as an émigré outside Iran. My ethnographic engagement, however, started in 1999. The engagement and conversation resulted in *Young and Defiant in Tehran* (2008), which examines how young, middle-class Tehranis struggle for identity in the battle over the right to self-expression. I looked closely at the structures confronting Iranian youth and the ways transnational cultural influences penetrate and flourish. Focusing on places of gathering such as shopping centers, the book explored the practices of everyday life, through which young Tehranis demonstrated defiance against the official culture and parental dominance. Such places were sites of opposition, but also served as creative centers for expression and, above all, for imagination. I attempted to show the transformative power these spaces had and how they enabled young Iranians to develop their own culture, as well as individual and generational identities.

This book is different from *Young and Defiant in Tehran* in several ways. Unlike *Young and Defiant in Tehran*, it extends its focus beyond both the middle class and Tehran. The data are collected mainly in Tehran but also in Isfahan and from migrant workers from the rural areas. The case of the Julfa neighborhood in Isfahan, a city wrongly branded for cultural conservatism, depicts a multifaceted city, where daily contestation over urban spaces reflects social changes at large. I also include ethnographic inquiries from my own village in the Bakhtiari region. Many men and women from my village worked in construction or the service sector in Isfahan and Tehran for long periods. Broadening the ethnographic field to cover voices not only from Tehran but also from peripheries, I aim to show the magnitude of precarity plaguing urban and rural Iranians.

Whereas *Young and Defiant in Tehran* focuses more on the spatial relations in everyday life, a main theme in this book is the temporal aspects of Iranians' everyday life: waiting, queuing, imaging a futureless tomorrow, feeling nostalgia, hoping, replication and repletion, and transiting from youth to adulthood. Another difference is that *Young and Defiant in Tehran* was formed in a hopeful time for Iranians. During the reform-minded government of President Khatami (1997–2005), a relatively open political atmosphere emerged. The years around the turn of the millennium were characterized by vivacious student and women's rights movements. Those years were also a time of a dynamic cultural life. Iranian youth started to hope for the future. That hope was dashed soon after Mahmoud Ahmadinejad took over the presidency (2005–2013). Under his administration, respect for basic human rights, especially freedom of expression and assembly, deteriorated markedly. The number of banned newspapers, journals, and NGOs increased dramatically. During the same period, Iran's economic situation was also getting remarkably worse; inflation soared, the unemployment rate reached double digits, and international sanctions on Iran tightened, while state corruption extended drastically. At the same time, the harshest drought in modern time unfolded, and environmental pollution (air, soil, water) started to take over Tehran and many other large cities. Ahmadinejad's presidency, formed and performed, according to a messianic faith in the return of the Twelfth or Hidden Imam (that is, the end of history) combined with nuclear ambitions, ruled the country with apocalyptic politics. During the same period, occult imaginaries and practices, along with state corruption, reached unimaginable levels. Political disappointment and bitter disenchantment intensified among urban youth even more after the crackdown of the postelection protests in 2009.

The current book took its form in these years characterized by multiple precarities, a shrinking of hope, people imaging a futureless tomorrow, home(land)lessness, intense individualism, deterioration of human capital, increasing violence (domestic and public), and growing political incivilities. However, this book explores, at the same time, the daydreaming and hope, intense civility, and solidarity during political protests and street carnivals. The book deals with these paradoxes in Iranians' everyday life.

When they came of age and became first-time voters, the post-Revolution generation brought the popular reform-minded Mohammad Khatami to the presidency. Since then, young Iranians have participated in elections with hope but without optimism. They repeat, despite defeats. Needless to mention, it was the young people's vast engagement in the presidential election in June 2013 that led to Hassan Rohani's victory. They voted despite having experienced the failure of former reform-minded presidents. They voted because they hoped—because they *needed* to hope. Not accidentally, Rohani in his election campaigns presented his government as a "government of hope." Repetition of political engagement, despite low expectations and despite unceasing political disappointments in the past decades, signifies hope.

This book aims to show the complexity, disintegration, and contradictions in Iranian society. If forced "immobility" is imposed on the young, they have become a generation of mobility. If they are made invisible by legal and political processes, they are the most visible generation ever. This book is an attempt to reconcile these paradoxes in today's Iran. It displays how Iran is preoccupied with a crisis of modernity: disintegrated and contradictory. Insecurities, unstable lives, shaky institutions, constant disruptions all indicate a crisis of modernity, when, in Karl Marx's words, "all that is solid melts into air." These transformations can mean deterioration of democracy but also emergence of new acts of citizenship.

Methodological Challenges

My story about the contemporary transformation of Iranian society is based on fieldwork of small things and events: waiting, endurance, walls, streets, television series, driving, walking, hope and lack of hope, strolling, divorce, thuggery, bullying, repetitions and replications, and wounds. This book is partly filled with stories people told me about their lives and partly with information I gathered from other sources. Writing it has been arduous and challenging in many ways, not least methodologically. Iran is not an accessible field for researchers who are not affiliated with Iranian universities or research institutes. What and how to write about Iran have been sensitive issues for a long time, but the situation got worse after the 2009 election protests. Many Iranian scholars in the fields of social sciences and humanities were arrested, accused of espionage or *siah namaee* (literally, blackening, illustrating a bad image of Iran). Moreover, control over information became harsher, and there has been secrecy around information on social issues.[18] During this time, scholars abroad got directives not to write theses about Iran.[19] Facing slim chances of conducting conventional and formal fieldwork, having to deal with tightly controlled access to information, and not getting official research permission, I have practiced flexible methods, what Hugh Gusterson termed "polymorphous engagements," that is, "Interacting with informants across a number of dispersed sites, not just in local communities, and sometimes in virtual form; and it means collecting data eclectically from a disparate array of sources in many different ways" (1997: 39). Sources are chosen carefully. Statistics used are primarily from official organizations such as the Statistical Centre of Iran and the National Organization for Civil Registration. Other sources used are well-established Iran-based news agencies and newspapers. The statistics and other information used have been cross-checked multiple times from different available sources. The book relies also on secondary sources, such as media accounts and academic works by Iranian scholars inside Iran and published in Persian. However, the most insightful and interesting works that have guided me in understanding the current transformations are nonacademic works by young intellectuals, artists, filmmakers, writers, and journalists. I owe so much to them.

An accurate perception of Iranian society requires long fieldwork. Metaphorically put, instead of touristic snapshots (dominating recent journalistic documentation of the life of young Iranians), I follow nineteenth-century English art critic John Ruskin's advice for the practice of drawing to learn how to see better details and subtleties of Iranians' life. In the shadow of an Iranophobic misrepresentation by the Western media and politicians, observing details becomes even more significant. Following Antonius Robben, who called for an anthropological perspective on a war-torn Iraq, I believe that an anthropological perspective capitalizing on an ethnography of everyday realities of people and of how they are affected by political forces beyond their reach offers an opportunity to "show that their lives matter within the larger framework of geopolitical forces, ideological and religious conflicts, international oil interests, and global military strategies" (2011: 5).

Political Challenges

This book arose also from concerns about an absence of anthropological voices among the myriad academic and nonacademic voices who define, represent, and analyze Iran and Iranians at a distance. It aims to offer an anthropological understanding of Iran. I write in an Iranophobic atmosphere supported by a huge apparatus of "mediawork" that has been producing anti-Iranian sentiments in the West. Hamid Naficy (1995) uses the term *mediawork* to describe the combined and complex operations that not only involve the mass media but also operate through cultural industries and financial forces that design, commodify, and market the Other. Iranophobic mediawork attempts to naturalize and depoliticize values and views in everyday discourses. Searching *Iran* on Amazon.com provides a long list of foreign policy studies on nuclear issues and military and political conflicts, as well as endless titles in the *Not Without My Daughter* genre written by Iranians (almost entirely women) living in Europe and the United States who, through an internalized orientalist lens, have intensified sentiments against Iranians (see Whitlock 2007). Mediawork functions through a logic of simple dichotomies: traditional, patriarchal religious Iran versus the modern, secular, women-friendly West. This misrepresentation of Iran has resulted in a grotesque caricature of Iranian youth, as a sort of *mimic men*: disoriented, depoliticized, and colonialized subjects, with an inferiority complex, whose will it is to identify themselves with the empire. These journalistic caricature-esque representations dehistoricize Iranian youth and, as Hamid Dabashi writes in his critique of Azar Nafisi's *Reading Lolita in Tehran*, "strips them of their moral intelligence and their participation in the democratic aspirations of their homeland."[20] Dabashi correctly draws attentions to the political implications of these misrepresentations.

Here is one example from October 2013. Israeli prime minister Benjamin

Netanyahu in an interview with the BBC said, "I think if the Iranian people had their way, they'd be wearing blue jeans, they'd have Western music, they'd have free elections."[21] This "caring and saving" concern comes from a head of state who more than any other politician has been trying to convince the West to commence a war with Iran. In line with Iranophobic mediawork, he propagates for war, that is, killing many young soldiers, to liberate them for the sake of enabling them to "wear blue jeans." In this atmosphere, I found writing about Iran challenging, politically as well as ethically. How to write about social injustice, structural violence, political oppression, and domestic violence and not contribute to the Iranophobic discourse? How to write about the victimhood of Iranian people yet avoid victimizing them, not depicting them as agency-less and voiceless objects? How to write about gender inequalities and patriarchal family relationships without reproducing the dominant image of Iranian/Muslim men in terms of "primitive masculinity" (see Khosravi 2009)? Experiences from long fieldwork and previous writings have made me more sensitive about how to write about Iran in order to avoid contributing to the othering discourse in the West toward Iran and the Middle East. I share Farha Ghannam's concerns, in her book on Egyptian urban masculinity, about "how to write [about Middle Eastern societies] in a way that is intellectually honest and politically responsible" (2013: 26).

This book project was born during the post-election protests of 2009—more exactly on Saturday 20 June 2009, around 5 p.m., on Valiasr Street, just before arriving at the Vank Square (see Chapter 4). Participant observation of the powerful emotional, intellectual, aesthetical, and political forms of expression during the Green Movement, experiencing the streets pregnant with historical events, and being overwhelmed by the images that evoked the 1979 Revolution left me with many stories that I found too heavy to bear alone.

Stories

> Death is the sanction of everything the storyteller can tell. He has borrowed his authority from death.
> —Walter Benjamin (2006 [1936]: 151)

This book is made not out of other books, but out of walking and listening. I took long walks along the streets with Iranians and hung out in squares and on street corners all night long. We drove aimlessly throughout Tehran and Isfahan. I walked along walls to see what people write and paint on them. And during all these days and nights, I listened faithfully to their stories. Walk any day or any night in Tehran, and you will hear and witness a story. And if not a story, then a joke, a rumor. Multiple precarities, all-pervading shadows of death, pervading corruption, rising occult activities, unequally distributed hope, demand stories, jokes, and rumors (cf. Piot 2010). Jokes that sarcastically depict the authorities' ignorance and incompetence, rumors about their cease-less thirst for wealth, and nostalgic stories about the past and future far from the inauspicious present circulate every day in public taxis, in workplaces, in coffee shops, at parties, in schools, or through new communication channels such as short messaging services (SMS), Bluetooth, or Facebook. Though they are *only* jokes or rumors, they have both a deep philosophical meaning and a revolutionary power (Bakhtin 1984: 66). They express the social consciousness of the people and uncensored opinions that deride the forged virtue and de-cency of the authorities and unmask the hypocrisies (Kaur 2008).

In Iran, storytelling is a method and a way of life. In Tehran, you barely get into a taxi and you receive a story. In my village in Bakhtiari, life is conceptu-alized through stories. The dissemination of religious and political messages in stories (*hadith*) on state-run television and radio programs; the huge national ritual of the narrative of the Karbala tragedy and the drama performance by a theatrical representation (*ta'ziyeh*) during Ashura (see Khosravi 2008); *naqali* (the oral storytelling of ancient Iranian fables, myths and epics practiced in public places); illicit popular television series as seen on satellite TV; nostalgic stories about the "golden age" of the past and stories about a romanticized fu-ture in *kharej* (abroad, refers often to the West); the stories written in millions of petitions sent to the government expressing the petitioners' needs; all the complaints and *dardodel* (literally, pain of heart, speaking from one's heart) told and listened to in taxis; diaries in hundreds of thousands of blogs (making Iran one of the most active blogging nations); poetry (Iran is said to be a nation of poets); and cinema—all this has made Iran a land of stories and of storytell-ers. Charles Piot, in his compelling and eloquent ethnography of the post-Cold War Togo (2010), wondering about the reasons behind the proliferation of stories in an era of insecurities and necropolitics, makes me ask a similar ques-tion: where does the need and passion for storytelling come from in today's Iran? Piot finds the answer in Walter Benjamin's 1936 essay "The Storyteller." In his reading of Benjamin, Piot states that "death demands explication—and here elicits competing stories—attempting to render meaningful the inchoate, snatching life from death, offering laughter alongside melancholy" (2010: 19).

Death, along with corruption, occult economies, environmental disasters, political and existential insecurity, involves the mysteries and silences Piot argues necessitate narrations. As in West African societies, Iranians face the mushrooming of death and necropolitics. Death has become omnipresent. Walls are covered with the death announcements of private individuals. Calendars are full of official anniversaries of deaths of imams or political leaders. During the war, 300,000–500,000 Iranian soldiers were killed. Libraries, bridges, and other public spaces bear their names. The murals of their faces decorate urban landscapes. Memorials of martyrs are broadcast every day on state-run media. Unnatural death is so frequent it has become naturalized. Iran has become necropolitical, preoccupied with death. With the highest rate of executions per capita in the world (at least 753 executions in 2014);[22] the highest traffic fatality rate (20,000–28,000 per year) (Moradi and Rahmani 1393/2014); the world's highest cancer growth rate;[23] and an increase of suicides by 63 percent in 2013,[24] death seems to be irrepressible. This observation by a woman is telling:

So many people die every day that we cannot mourn anymore. So many die, even young ones. Funeral ceremonies have become simpler. The period of mourning is much shorter too nowadays. How could people have time for so much death otherwise? . . . Do you remember you asked me why we were joking and laughing at the mourning ceremony for Naser? I tell you. We do not cry anymore Shahram. Who can? We have cried so much that there is no tear left.

The ubiquitous presence of death elicits storytelling. In a similar way, the absence of political transparency and censorship begets rumors and stories. For instance, who is attending whose funeral has become a way to trace conflicts and tensions among high-ranking politicians. Sitting in a taxi, you can hear how people speculate about coming changes on the political scene by narrating the most recent funeral ceremony of a relative to a politician. Attendance of Supreme Leader Ayatollah Khamenei at the funeral of President Rohani's mother in late March 2015 has been interpreted as his full support of the current government. Similarly, his conflict with former president Khatami was believed to have been intensified when the leader sent condolences to Khatami's mother and not to him when his sister passed away the same month.[25] Iranians are a nation of storytellers, not only because of their long and rich literary traditions but primarily because they live in the shadow of an out-of-control economy, occult activities, bottomless state corruption, and financial and social insecurities, and are surrounded by the secrecies and mysteries of ubiquitous death. Paraphrasing Piot (2010: 19) I would say that, like Togo, Iran is a terrain wired for drama and affect. Thus, not surprisingly, storytelling fills everyday lives.

Methodological and political challenges aside, writing this book made me face several ethical challenges as well. One has been how to write about the prevalent hopelessness among Iranians while trying to generate hope, as expressed in the epigraph by Bloch at the beginning of this introduction. Following Miyazaki (2004), I understand repetition as a method of hope. Telling and retelling stories, rumors, and jokes "predicted on the inheritance of a past hope and its performative replication in the present" (2004: 139) constitute a hopeful practice. Storytelling engenders hope, so here comes my story.

CHAPTER 1

THE PRECARIOUS FAMILY

Between the family and the state, there is only a bare wasteland.
—Omid Mehregan (1388/2009: 16)

At the close of March 2015, Iranians were celebrating Nowrouz, the Iranian New Year, a time they gather together to praise the family and family kinship. The intensive ritualized practice of "see and resee each other" would strengthen family affections and bonds. While the ancient tradition and rituals were at work to guarantee the stability and continuity of family values, a shocking family drama reminded Iranians about current social changes, the break and discontinuity of family values and norms that are supposed to be transcendental. The murder on the Italy Street in Tehran was soon all everyone talked about, mixed with worries and horror during the Nowrouz rituals.

The news reported that a twenty-seven-year-old man first strangled his sister to death and then cut his father's throat. Afterward he spent the whole night meeting friends and going to the theater to see a movie. This is only one among many news stories, reports, and rumors that reveal the crisis within the family. A panic over the "family crisis" and "collapse of the family" has entered not only the daily life of ordinary people but also official discourse and public debates. In this chapter, I explore how the family has been drastically weakened by structural transformations such as the political turbulence after the Revolution, the eight-year war with Iraq (1980–1988), mass emigration, long-term economic hardship, controversial family policies, and discriminatory politics that have particularly targeted women.

Revolutions and the Family

The Islamic Republic values the family as the core foundation of Islamic society. Since the Revolution of 1979, the main focus of the state, on both a rhetorical and a practical level, has been to promote and strengthen the family as an institution. In official discourse, the ideal Islamic family is crucial for a harmonious social order; a "healthy society is built on a healthy family."[1] The Iranian Constitution, in the Preamble and Article 21, praises the family as "the fundamental unit of society and the main center for the growth and edification of the human being" and mandates that the government protect and support the family.[2] The family thus has become a central focus of legislation and regulation in post-revolutionary Iran (Osanloo 2012). The new Republic aimed to recreate the society built on the fundamentals of Islam, according to the pattern of the charismatic community of "early Islam." The lifetime of the Prophet appears in post-revolutionary political discourse as a temporal frame of reference, against which the present is measured. The original Muslim community led by the Prophet is seen as the most authentic form of an Islamic community. Since the Revolution, the regime has made attempts to legitimize its policies by utilizing the myth of the early Islamic era. Based on Quran verses and *hadiths* (reports of statements or actions of Muhammad), the official discourse endorses "a true family" (*khanevadeh oswah*; *oswah* is an Arabic word that means symbolic and true representative). One historical feature of Shiite Islam is the family tie between the first imam, Ali, and Fatemeh, the daughter of the Prophet Muhammad. Their marriage has been used as an allegory of an ideal family in school books, official sermons, and the media by the Islamic Republic. Indeed, the birthday of Fatemeh became Mother's Day, and the birthday of Ali became Father's Day. In the manifest of the state-run Family Studies Association, a true family is presented with a heterosexual, patriarchal family structure in which the man is the breadwinner and head, while the woman is responsible for the education and upbringing of the children.[3] A huge propaganda apparatus has sent patriarchal and heteronormative messages through the mass media and educational system to maintain and support the ideology of the Islamic family. State-sanctioned television series, weekly magazines, films, radio and television talk shows, as well as the school curriculum, have all been used as means "to strengthen the family system." However, over the three decades since the Revolution in Iran, the family as an institution has never been as weak and fragile as it is now. Iranian families are struggling with enormous crises. In the official discourse, the crises have re-sulted in an escalating divorce rate, fewer marriages, a generation gap, "run-away girls," "sexual anomie," an increasing number of street children, and domestic violence. Rapid political and social changes have created huge chal-lenges for the family, gradually resulting in structural changes of this institution.

The Revolution

Revolutions weaken the family. There are several historical examples, from the French and Russian Revolutions to the Chinese Revolution. Not an exception, the Iranian Revolution of 1979 changed family structures in Iran as well. Power relations within the family shifted enormously as a result of the rapid social changes. Ideational changes and changes in cultural goals followed the Revolution. Some unintended consequences of the Revolution have been more autonomy in terms of choice of spouses, higher demand for gender equality within the family, controlled fertility, increasingly independent nu-clear families, emergence of new forms of partnership, and children challeng-ing their fathers' authority.

A good example of the impact of revolutions on the family is the Russian October Revolution of 1917. "Bolshevik feminism" transformed the family and liberated women from the bourgeois patriarchal household. The Code on Marriage, the Family, and Guardianship in the Soviet Union in 1918 aimed to improve women's legal and social situation. Simple divorce was an outcome of the code, resulting in an accelerating divorce rate. In less than a decade the divorce rate soared and by 1927 two-thirds of all marriages ended in divorce (Goldman 1993: 297). Improved childcare facilities contributed to the en-trance of more women in the male-dominated industries. The Bolshevik emancipation of women even had an impact on urban planning and architec-ture. For instance, small apartments were built for single people. The radical transformation of the family in the Soviet Union meant that a huge number of children were forced to the streets. Poor and neglected by both the family and the state, homeless children became a phenomenon. The growing number of homeless children (*besprizornost*) and single mothers, as well as the so-called "sexual anarchy," reached alarming levels in the second half of the 1920s. As this chapter shows, similar "social harms" succeeded the transfor-mations of the family that occurred in post-revolutionary Iran. Although entirely opposite in their approach to the family and women's roles, there are similarities in the changes of the family structures after the 1917 October Revolution and the 1979 Iranian Revolution.

Revolution, however, is always a protest by young people against what they perceive as the old. Therefore, a generational conflict is inherent in revolution. In general, revolutions deflate the family. They demand loyalties. A revolutionary state requires total loyalty from its citizens; it should stand above all other kinds of loyalties such as ethnic, religious, or familial. I myself have experienced this. One year after the Revolution, my father was arrested, accused of anti-revolutionary activities. I was fourteen years old and a zealous devotee of the Revolution. When my mother told us that my father had been arrested, in a time of political chaos and mass execution, my reaction surprised everyone. I just said, "he is probably culpable." For me at that time, the newborn revolution came before my family. In the presence of the charismatic symbolic father of the Revolution, my own father's authority faded away.

The leaders of revolutions usually turn into father figures and become the father of the nation, such as Mao and Stalin. Theodor Adorno used the term "fatherless society" to explain how, both in Nazi Germany and later in socialist East Germany, the state entered family life and took over the father's (and mother's) roles (Adorno 1969, quoted in Abazari 1381/2002). Drawing on Adorno's argument, Iranian sociologist Yousef Abazari believes that, in post-revolutionary Iran, a "patriarchy without father" emerged. The state replaced the father. A consequence of emergence of the state as a powerful father has been the "child-becoming" process of the nation (1381/2002). As I have discussed elsewhere, the art of government in Iran is characterized by connecting the father's government of the family to the science of ruling the state, continuity and transmission running from the family to the state. The art of government is thus the extension of the "pastoral power" of the father over his household and wealth into the organizing technicalities of the state (Khosravi 2008).

The replacement of household fathers by the state affected the relationship between parents and children. Loyalty to the state weakened family ties. Children were asked to report on their parents, and zealous revolutionary parents assisted police to arrest their children, who were persecuted because of their political opinion. The Revolution politicized the whole nation. Conflicting political ideologies within families, particularly between children and parents, caused families to split, something that also happened among the highest ranks of power.

The War

Beside conflicting ideologies, another factor that destabilized the family drastically was the eight long years of war with Iraq (1980–1988). More than half
a million young Iranian men are estimated to have lost their lives in the war
(Amani 1992). Hundreds of thousands of young war widows with small children faced serious social and economic difficulties. Furthermore, the war radicalized revolutionary young people to break with their families. The war
propaganda apparatus encouraged young men, often teenagers, to go to the
front with or without parents' permission (see Golkar 2015). One of these was
Mohammed Hossein Fahmideh, a thirteen-year-old boy who joined the *basij*
at an early stage of the war. In October 1980, while the Iraqi army was on a
forward march and the border city of Khoramshahr was besieged, Fahmideh
jumped under an Iraqi tank and pulled out the pins of grenades. His self-
sacrifice became a legend, and Ayatollah Khomeini called him "the true leader
of the Revolution." Fahmideh was turned into iconic propaganda of total loyalty to the Revolution, commemorated in official ceremonies and textbooks.
His portrait appears in murals in almost all cities, and a postage stamp in his
memory was issued in 1986. Choosing the Revolution before his parents, he
responded to the call by the authorities, rather than asking his parents for
permission. Prioritizing the revolutionary state before the family has been
part of all revolutions, which need legends like Fahmideh who choose the
state over family. The revolutionary state of the Soviet Union created its own
legend: Pavel Trofimovich Morozov. Like Fahmideh, Pavel was a thirteen-
year-old boy; he collaborated with the authorities to arrest his father, accused
of antisocialist activities in 1932. The father was executed; later Pavel was
killed by his own grandfather. The Soviet state declared Pavlik a national hero:
a thirteen-year-old boy who sacrificed his family and himself for the Revolution. As an icon of a true revolutionary, statues of him were erected in cities,
streets and parks were named after him, and books, songs, and even a sym-
phonic poem have been written about him.[4]

The war caused enormous pressure on Iranian families. Over 2.5 million
people were forcedly displaced, which meant families splitting, the loss of
properties, economic pressures, death of family members, and psychological
stress. Consequently, the number of families breaking up soared. During the
war, the divorce rate among displaced families was about 40 percent higher
than the national rate (Aghajanian 1990). The war also accelerated the mass

emigration from Iran following the Revolution. Hundreds of thousands of young men escaped the country to avoid military service, resulting in family members dispersed throughout the world.

Economic Pressures

The family as a unit was severely struck with enormous economic hardship following the Revolution and the war. Financial insecurity affected a majority of households. High double-digit inflation, lack of foreign investment, the U.S. embargo, and later the international sanctions against Iran have resulted in the drastic deterioration of the household economy. Iranian sociologist Yosuf Abazari (1381/2002) believes that the newborn Republic, busy with various political conflicts that emerged soon after the Revolution and the long and devastating war with Iraq, left families to manage on their own. Furthermore, there were few independent civil organizations to assist families with their problems. The family, then, had no choice but to take over the responsibilities of the state. One example of this is education, which is free in Iran from the elementary school to university level, at least according to the Constitution. Nevertheless the huge burden of education has been and still is put on Iranian families themselves. In reality, a large part of the household budget is invested in children's education. Due to the economic pressures, even public schools, not to mention private ones, demand that parents pay school fees. The poor quality of education in public schools has been the main cause for growth of private schools in the large cities. Upper-middle-class families send their children to private schools, which demand fees unaffordable by lower- and even many middle-class families. The poor education standards in public schools push parents to provide extra tutoring and activities to prepare their children for the annual university entrance examination. The competition for limited seats at state universities is fierce. In 2011, only 10 percent of the 1.3 million people who took the *konkur* were admitted to free universities. Others try to find a place at semiprivate Islamic Azad Universities, to which students have to pay high fees. All this has resulted in the explosion of the private education sector in the past two decades. The documentary *Countdown* (by Khatereh Hanachi, 2008) is about an eighteen-year-old woman struggling with the demands for and expectations of educational successes. The film illustrates not only the severe psychological and emotional pressure on young people facing the *konkur*, but also the devastating consequences of such a burden on the household.

Investing a huge amount of money and time in children's education with no guarantee of employment or a job matching the education causes emotional and financial crises within the family. The family, supporting their children through education, military service, unemployment, marriage, and frequently even after marriage, are bent under the financial and social burdens. Young people are sent back and forth between the state and the family. Betrayed by the state, the young see the family as the only source of support and hope. Parents, meanwhile, believe that the younger generation is too demanding, careless, incompetent, materialistic, and indolent. There is a similar discourse blaming young people for being lazy, demanding, careless, and superficial in Egypt and the United Arab Emirates (see Hasso 2011). Not many families, however, can afford to support their children for a long time, and this causes additional tension. Children, disappointed and failing to achieve full adulthood (that is, marriage and employment), blame their parents for their situation.

Pir Pesar (Reluctant Bachelor, by Mehdi Bagheri, 2011), a documentary film about the director himself, illustrates how economic pressures on families damage this core institution and result in mutual mistrust between parents and children. The film conveys frankly the director's conflicts with his father. Bagheri, a thirty-year-old man from a low-income family, lives in a suburb of Tehran. He is educated but has only temporary jobs. Underemployed, reluctantly single, and unable to build an independent life, he blames his father for his "failures" in life. The father, a hardworking man in his sixties, is disappointed with himself for not being able to assist his son but also with his son for being ungrateful. I screened this film for a group of middle-aged parents and young people in October 2012; afterward, we had a general discussion about it. The parents generally blamed the son and his group of friends for being indolent and demanding assistance and service without making any effort themselves. The overall feeling was that young people's expectations have been raised. Comparing their children's lives to their own youth in the 1960s, the parents claimed that young people themselves bear responsibility for their situation: "What did we do when we were their age? We worked hard and did not expect so much from our parents. We stood on our own feet." The young people in the audience mentioned that the time when a young generation "could stand on their own feet" is gone. One young woman said: "even if we work hard for ten years and save all our salaries, we still cannot build a life for ourselves. Nowadays money has no value." A young man said that his parents' generation, "instead of condemning us all the time, should take their own responsibility for the revolution they made." Unlike their parents' generation, for whom education and hard work would guarantee relative comfort and a secure life, the socioeconomic environment in today's Iran is far different (cf. Allison 2013: 88–89).

Family Policies

One of the main factors contributing to the precariousness of the family has been the erratic family policy. Family policy in post-revolutionary Iran has gone through dramatic changes during the past three decades. At an early stage, the Islamic Republic, taking a pronatalist ideology, dismissed the family planning of the shah, which encouraged fewer children. In general, birth control, abortion, and preventive methods were seen as non-Islamic. The theocrats forbade contraceptives as well as abortion, and encouraged people to have more children. Moreover, the war and the Revolution "needed" children. In the mid-1980s, population growth in Iran had reached 4 percent. In the postwar era, particularly after the death of Ayatollah Khomeini, the pragmatic government of president Hashemi Rafsanjani launched a new family planning initiative in 1989 to lower population growth. The program aimed to "encourage families to delay the first pregnancy and to space out subsequent births; to discourage pregnancy for women younger than eighteen and older than thirty-five; and to limit family size to three children" (Roudi-Fahimi 2002). Free consultation and services for contraceptive methods were offered throughout the country. A large (indeed, the only) condom factory in the Middle East was built in Iran. According to reports, up to 80 percent of women used family planning.[5] The program was successful; by 2011 the fertility rate had dropped to 1.9 percent. Moreover, the many divorces and rising average marriage age contributed to the falling fertility rates. Between 1985 and 2000, fertility decreased by 70 percent, making the demographic transition in Iran one of the fastest in history (Ladier-Fouladi 2012: 140).

However, President Ahmadinejad's government (2005–2013) regenerated Ayatollah Khomeini's demographic vision. Using a discourse based on the concern for the "vanishing" of the nation, in his first year of presidency, he introduced a plan to increase the population from 70 million to 120 million:

I am against saying that two children are enough. Our country has a lot of capacity. It has the capacity for many children to grow in it. It even has the capacity for 120 million people. Westerners have got problems. Because their population growth is negative, they are worried and fear that, if our population increases, we will triumph over them.[6]

In Ahmadinejad's plan, women would stay at home and be devoted to the holy "mother duty." He glorified the "momentous and precious function of motherhood." In her study of the family after the October Revolution, Goldman (1993) describes similar patterns. Soviet authorities, facing the rocketing rate of abortion in the early 1930s, changed their "feminist" discourse and praised the "honorable duty of motherhood." To encourage the birth of more children, they declared motherhood was not only a "private affair but an affair of great social significance" (1993: 333). Just like the Soviet context, love, sexuality, and reproduction according to the Iranian authorities are no longer private and biological issues, but rather belong to the public and political spheres.

Ahmadinejad's government adopted a new policy to encourage population growth that included benefits and subsidies for families with several children. Young people were offered incentives to marry early (see Abbasi-Shavazi et al. 2008). The president also promised at that time to pay about US$1,000 to families for every new child, a promise that never materialized in the end. Furthermore, during Ahmadinejad's presidency, the compulsory course "The Glory of Having a Spouse" replaced the course "Population and Family Regulation" in the curriculum at all educational levels. A fundamental difference between the courses is that the "Glory" course (over)emphasizes the role of women as mothers and housewives. In October 2013 supreme leader Ayatollah Khamenei criticized birth-control programs, stating that, according to "scientific and expert studies," Iran would face an aging and reduced population if the birth control policy continued and that the optimal population size for Iran was double the current number. Ali Reza Mesdaghnia, deputy health minister in 2012, also said, "In our culture, having a large number of children has been a tradition. Previously, families had five or six children. . . . We should go back to our genuine culture."[7] State propaganda launched a promotion of larger families. Colorful cartoon-style images were on billboards along the highways in Tehran in December 2013, encouraging Tehranis to have more children. One of these images depicted a happy father with several sons and a daughter on a bicycle. The mother was absent. The slogan under the image read, "One flower does not make a spring. More children, a happier life."

However, despite all efforts, the Iran Statistics Center announced at the end of September 2012 that Iranian families had become less willing to have children compared to before. In 1355/1976, the average number of children in a family was three; today it is 1.5.[8] Surveys show also that the young generation are less willing to have children.[9] Another survey conducted in four provinces in 2002 indicated changes in attitudes toward the ideal family, from what the authors call "traditional" (with several children) to "modern" values (Abbasi-Shavazi et al. 2008: 228). Despite the confusing plans and contradictory family programs, the rate has constantly dropped. The National Organization for Civil Registration announced in mid-December 2013 that one-third (33 percent) of Iranian families have only one child, and more than 14 percent have no child at all. In rural areas, 16 percent of families have only one child.[10] As Ladier-Fouladi puts it, the fertility transition, rather than a result of state programs, is a consequence of the transformation of social positions of women who have taken control of their fertility (2012: 141).

Drastic and rapid changes in population policies have had unexpected consequences, for example, an imbalance in the sex ratio at marriage age. On average, most Iranian men marry women around five years younger than themselves. Men born in the 1970s (when birth rates were falling) would marry women born in the 1980s (the decade when the birth rate increased). A high rate of population growth in the 1980s and the fact that women marry older men resulted in an imbalance in the sex ratio at marriage age. Thus, there are fewer men than women in the marriageable age. In 2011, there were up to one million more women between fifteen and thirty-five than men between twenty and forty.[11] This imbalance will change again in the near future. Men born in the 1980s will marry women born between the early 1990s and the mid-2000s (when birth rates were falling). Therefore, in the next decade, there will be more men than women at marriage age. The 20 percent shortage of men in 2010 is expected to change to a 40 percent shortage of women by 2020. This imbalance will probably change the traditional pattern of marrying younger women. The increasing age imbalance in the marriage market during the last decade has likely contributed to the rising age at marriage, especially for women. This in turn is related to major changes in the pattern of life for many Iranians: 1) men will have a greater chance of finding wives in their own age group; 2) there will be lower fertility; 3) there will be more education for women; 4) accordingly, men with lower education will marry more educated women (see Salehi-Isfahani and Egel 2009: 56).

Rapid radical changes in family politics in the short term have caused confusion and trouble for Iranian families. One of the state interventions has been state-sanctioned polygyny. The current law allows men to have up to four wives and an unlimited number of temporary wives, called *sigheh*. *Sigheh* is a form of marriage between an unmarried or married man and an unmarried woman for a limited period of time (one hour to 99 years). This practice has been endorsed by the state to encourage young people to enter temporary marriages, and, as a result of offline and online brokerage firms, the procedure has been established. Temporary marriage is presented as a "morally" and "ethically" acceptable solution for unmarried young men to meet their sexual needs. Temporary marriages increased 10 percent in 1391/2012 and 31 percent in 1392/2013.[12] The promotion of temporary marriages has played a central role in destabilizing family ties. The so-called Family Protection Bill, first proposed by Ahmadinejad in 2007, became a hugely controversial issue in the parliament and among women's rights activists. The bill would have facilitated polygyny even more for Iranian men. Article 22 aimed to authorize temporary marriage without registration, thereby abolishing financial and legal protections of women in temporary marriages (Osanloo 2012: 52).

Fundamental Shifts in Gender Relations in Iran

Gender relations have been significantly shifted and rearranged since the Revolution. The change has fundamentally reshaped family structure. The situation of women has been affected by different and sometimes contradictory processes during the Islamic Republic. On the one hand, women have been subjected to structural gender inequality in sociopolitical arenas. They have suffered from exclusion and discrimination in the labor market and public sphere. They have been systematically robbed of their rights to mobility, choice of lifestyle, and control over some aspects of daily lives such as their body and sexuality. On the other hand, there have been structural social transformations that have improved women's social position.

Revolution means, after all, the presence of bodies on the streets. Women participated in political movements throughout the twentieth century, from the Constitutional Revolution of 1906–1911 (see Afary 1996) to the Green Movement of 2009. However, the massive presence of women in the Revolution of 1979 started a new political visibility for them. The vast, active presence of women in the Green Movement three decades later indicates once again their crucial participation in political life. While in 1979 women in black veils became the symbol of the Revolution (Hoodfar 1999: 41), the subversive symbol of the Green Movement is women in green headscarves. The icon of the post-election protests of 2009 was Neda Agha-Soltan, a twenty-six-year-old woman shot to death during the demonstrations. Women's struggle for gender equality and sociopolitical rights has had an extensive impact on the power relations within the family. Education too has played a significant role in this transformation.

The rate of literacy among women tripled from 26 percent in 1976 to 75 percent in 2005. Prior to the Revolution, a majority of women between fifteen and forty-nine spent only 0.93 years in school (2.2 years in urban and 0.10 in rural areas). After the Revolution, thanks to expansion of the education infrastructure, there has been a rapid increase of literacy among Iranian women. In 2006, women in the age group fifteen to forty-nine spent 3.4 years in school (4.9 in urban and 1.3 in rural areas) (Ladier-Fouladi 2012: 141). Since 1998, more women than men have been admitted to universities, a percentage that peaked in 2001 when 61.4 percent of all admissions were women (Azadarmaki 1389/2010: 80; see also Bahramitash and Salehi-Esfahani 2011: 102–3). In 2012, the rate was still slightly over 60 percent. Even in areas that have traditionally been identified as "men's fields," like mining and engineering, women are dominating. Moreover, throughout the 2000s, there has been a 269 percent increase in the number of women in doctoral programs (Shahrokni and Dokouhaki 2012). Generally, the gender gap in higher education has diminished. Women more often complete their education than do men. In 1390/2011, the number of women with higher education degrees and enrolled in higher-education programs (5,024,000) was not far behind the number of men (5,478,000) (Statistical Center of Iran 1391/2012).

Higher education does not, however, open the doors to the labor market for women. While the number of women finishing university is almost double the number of men (Bahramitash 2013: 89), the unemployment rate for women is twice that for men.[13] Unemployment among women in urban areas in 2006 was 2.3 times more than that among men (99). Even compared to that of other countries, Iranian women's labor force participation rate is low. The 2006 census showed that the rate of female participation in economic activities was only 16.6 percent (Hosseini-Chavoshi and Abbasi-Shavazi 2012: 113). Behdad and Nomani's study of women's marginalization in the urban work force between 1976 and 2006 shows no drastic change in women's participation in the labor market after the Revolution (Behdad and Nomani 2012). The defeminization of the urban labor market had a worse effect on working-class women than on women with access to capital, skills, or education. Unlike upper-level working women who had achieved some significant gains by

2006, lower-level working women have not been able to improve their position in the labor market after the Revolution. Systematic discrimination of women in the labor market has pushed them into the informal labor market, as evidenced by some sources that show that the presence of women working outside the home is increasing (Salehi-Isfahani and Egel 2007), particularly in the informal sector.

However, longer schooling and higher education have had three significant consequences for women. First, their chances to gain higher status jobs have grown. Second, subsequent employment has resulted in a rise in marriage age, particularly among women. Between 1966 and 2006, the average marriage age for men increased by 1.2 years, while for women it increased by 4.8 years (Table 1; see also Bahramitash and Salehi-Esfahani 2011: 104). Interestingly, the change is almost similar in rural and urban areas (see Table 1). Similarly, marriage under age twenty has decreased drastically. While 41 percent of all women between fifteen and nineteen were married in 1956, the figure was only 2.6 percent in 1996 (Azadarmaki 1389/2010: 102).

Third, higher education means the domestic migration of a huge number of young people. Migration to other cities in search for education has transformed the pattern of choosing one's spouse, and finding a partner in one's own group has become less important than formerly. Long-term separation from family means new networks and independence. More important, social and geographical mobility among women has meant decreasing arranged marriages in Iran. Studies show that, while 82.5 percent of all marriages in Tehran were arranged by parents until the 1960s, the figure had decreased to 32 percent in the 1990s (Azadarmaki 1389/2010: 127). Higher mobility and education of women affect their status and the power structure within the family. This is shown by the fact that women are less likely to be housewives. While in 1976 as many as 80 percent of married women were housewives, the number dropped to 65 percent in 1996. Furthermore, the national census shows that families in which women are the breadwinner and head have almost doubled since the Revolution and reached slightly above 12 percent in 2011 (Statistical Center of Iran 1391/2012; see also Aghajanian and Thompson 2013). The emergence of individualism and self-actualization in the form of increasing voluntary female household headship indicate fundamental changes in different aspects of the family (2013).

Not unexpectedly, changes to power relations within the patriarchal family have triggered anxieties among conservative forces, who perceive the increasing active presence of women in the public sphere to be threatening. Ayatollah

Table 1. Average Age for First Marriage, Men and Women, 1966–2006

Year	Men (nation)	Women (nation)	Men (urban)	Women (urban)	Men (rural)	Women (rural)
1345/1966	25	18.4	25.6	19	24.4	17.9
1365/1986	23.6	19.8	24.2	20	22.6	19.6
1385/2006	26.2	23.2	26.5	23.2	25.5	23.4

Source: Statistical Center of Iran, *Year Book*, 1388/2009.

Ahmad Jannati, a member of the Guardian Council and an influential senior clergyman, declared in September 2013, "Universities destroy properly veiled girls."[14] Noorullah Heidari, a member of the Majlis Commission of Education and Research, believes that "Education of women is not a problem per se, but education induces desire for employment and this damages the family."[15] Women's employment is believed to be linked to the increased unemployment among men; women are simply blamed for "stealing jobs" from men. The authorities explicitly declare that the "imbalances" between the sexes in education and, subsequently, in the labor market will lead to a "social crisis" (Shahrokni and Dokouhaki 2012). Moreover, the presence of women in public life generates anxieties about endangered masculine identity. For instance, one article stated, "in the shadow of modern women . . . men are no longer the men they were. They have almost been transformed into a third gender, floating between manhood and womanhood. . . . [Men are] marginalized and submissive" (quoted in Shahrokni and Dokouhaki 2012).

The attacks on women's activity in the public sphere have been pointed. The official media use terms such as *hamleh* (attack) and *hojom* (invasion) when referring to women's entrance into education and the labor market.[16] The state-run magazine *Hamshahri Javan* published in mid-September 2012 (issue 376) included a long report on young women's success, titled "Young Women's Invasion to All Young Men's Social Positions." The cover of the issue shows Judy Abbott, a character in the popular Japanese animated series based on *Daddy Long Legs* written by Jean Webster. In the series, Judy, an orphan, gets a chance to go to school thanks to the support of a man she calls Daddy Long Legs. In the illustration on the cover of *Hamshahri Javan*, she has an outraged face and a machine gun in her hands, expressing her aggression toward her male benefactor.[17] The illustration is austere, depicting women as unappreciative, greedy, and offensive. Women are thus seen as the offenders rather than victims of prevalent anti-woman politics, legislation, and daily discrimination. Through combined and complex operations, which involve not only the mass media but also politics, popular culture, and academic writing, the patriarchal mode of seeing remakes the public presence of women into something dangerous, threatening the well-being of the family and society.

The notion of *zanzalil* (literally, being subjugated and humbled by a woman) is significant in this context. A diatribe and sexist jargon used by men to tease other men and humiliate women, *zanzalil* is used, mainly by men, to refer to a husband who is "submissive" to his wife, an idea prevalent in jokes and popular culture (television, cinema, pop music). There are innumerable examples. For instance, the television comedy series *Char Khone* (in 107 episodes), which debuted in 2007, is about a middle-class Tehrani family in a multiunit apartment building. The parents, Mansour and Shokouh, share a flat, and their two daughters live in their own flats with their husbands. *Char Khone*, which quickly became very popular among Iranians, is based on the simple dichotomy between *zanzalil* men and dominating women. Shokouh, the mother, is the family's decision maker. A physically large woman with a coarse voice, she embodies the authoritarian defeminized Other. The other two women, the daughters, also dominate their husbands. The three male protagonists are all depicted as weak and ridiculous, embodying the *zanzalil* man. They are perceived as the oppressed, the ones in need of compassion. The box-office success *Vorood-e aqayan mamnoo* (No Man Allowed, by Rambod Javan, 1390/2011) is another example of the "othering" practices depicting women as oppressor and men as oppressed.

The notion of *zanzalil* became a research topic for Buik Mohammadi, a sociologist at Tehran University. In 2009, he published a book titled *Zanzalil* that claims this problem is widespread in Iran. Mohammadi rejects the idea that Iranian families are patriarchal, claiming instead that a majority of Iranian wives are authoritarian. The author states that the destabilization of families in Iran is due to the imbalance in power relations between authoritarian wives and *zanzalil* husbands. Scientifically poor and methodologically questionable, the book aims at nothing other than demonizing women and presenting them as the cause of chaos and instability in families. The cover image reveals very well the message inside the book: it depicts a man bent under the heel of a woman's shoe. The book was criticized by feminist scholars but defended by other male sociologists.[18] The rhetoric that depicts Iranian men as *zanzalil* serves a dominant consensus that normalizes and routinizes sexism and anti-women policies.

The anxieties about the presence of women in public life are not only expressed rhetorically but also in policies. In 2012, a new regulation banned women from seventy-seven academic fields at the graduate level in the country's thirty-six universities.[19] The ban was partly lifted later during the presidency of Rohani. Another attempt to restrict women's social mobility is a bill presented by the National Security Committee of the Iranian Parliament in late 2012 to restrict women's migration and mobility.[20]

However, education, late marriage, and mobilities have triggered engagement, participation, employment, and a higher demand for gender equality, independence, and social justice, which have resulted in changes in women's attitudes and behaviors. The legal rights women have obtained since the Revolution are results of new civil and legal institutions mobilized by women's social movements (see Osanloo 2012). Besides their success in education and presence in the public sphere, one historical victory for Iranian women undoubtedly has been the fact that they have won control over their fertility, despite the still powerful patriarchal family structure and state interventions. Women's rights campaigns have been the most influential and powerful social movements in the past two decades. The campaign "One Million Signatures for the Repeal of Discriminatory Laws," organized and run by young Iranian feminists in the mid-2000s, is one example. This campaign has been successful and received national and international recognition. The women's rights movement also cast light on discrimination and general social injustice against other marginalized groups such as street children, homeless people, and undocumented Afghan immigrants.

Crises

The radical transformations of the family in the short period after the Revolution resulted in various forms of crises, such as a drastic increase of divorces, "runaway girls" (see Moazami 1382/2003), street children, and domestic violence (Tizro 2012). Almost 600,000 street children were identified in May 2012, and up to 2.5 million other children were identified as in danger of ending up on the streets.[21] The number of so-called runaway girls increased 15 percent in 1390/2011.[22] According to official statistics from 1385/2006, of 13,250,000 children between ten and eighteen, 3,600,000 or 27 percent were outside the education system. Another source shows that there are 1.8 million working children.[23] Street children and "runaway girls" testify to broken families, abuse, drugs, and domestic violence. Domestic violence is extensive, and women and children have been the main victims of violence within the family. In her study, Zahra Tizro (2012: 16–17) claims that more than 60 percent of women suffer violence by their husbands. Not only has domestic violence increased, but it has become more brutal. From 1988 to 2008, family-related murder increased by 2.5 times. A study showed that of all murders in 1367/1988, 15.7 percent were murders within the family, while this number increased to 40 percent in 1388/2009 (Abdi and Kalhor 1388/2009:164; Ghazinezhad and Abasian 1390/2011). [24]

Almost every day one can read stories about family-related homicides in Iranian newspapers. In its issue from the first week of June 2012 (17 Khordad 1391), *Tapesh*, a weekly special entirely devoted to crimes and "social damages," reported that, of eight crime reports, four dealt with murder within family: a drug addict killed his wife; an old man was killed by his "temporary" wife, a poor divorcee with three children, who had become his temporary wife for money; a young man was killed by his wife's lover; a man was killed by his wife and her lover. [25] Polygyny and temporary marriage have been recurrent causes for domestic murders within families. A well-known case that aroused strong emotions in Iran was the case of Shahla Jahed.

Shahla Jahed was born in 1970 into an underprivileged family. She started working very young as the caretaker of elderly women. She loved soccer and was a fan of the popular team Perspolis. Her idol was Naser Mohammad Khani, who played for Perspolis and was a striker in the national team. Somehow, they met, and she fell in love with him. A beautiful and cheerful woman, Shahla was easy prey for him, and she became his temporary wife in 1998. Naser was thirteen years older and already married, the father of two children. In 2002, Naser's first wife was mysteriously murdered in her apartment. Shahla was arrested the following day. Naser was also arrested under suspicion of complicity but released when Shahla "confessed" that she alone had committed the murder. She was sentenced to death in 2004. Later, she retracted her confession, but the court did not accept it. Her case became controversial both inside and outside Iran and was discussed in the newspapers for several years; a documentary about her was made, *Kart-e ghermez* (Red Card, by Mahnaz Afzali, 2006). Despite all inconsistencies in the case and the lack of technical evidence, Shahla Jahed was hanged on 1 December 2010 at 5 a.m. after eight years of imprisonment. Attending her hanging were Nasser, his son, and his murdered wife's parents. Minutes before the rope was fastened around Shahla's neck she pleaded for her life. In vain.

Hamsar koshi (spousal killing) is the main form of family-related homicide. The rate of wife-killing is still much higher than murdering of husbands. The former made up 16 percent of all murders in 1388/2009, the latter only 6 percent (Ghazinezhad and Abasian 1390/2011:78). Spousal killing, conventionally a male crime in Iran, has recently become prevalent among women. The rate of husbands being killed doubled in 2009 (78). In Tehran, 18 percent of imprisoned men were sentenced for killing their wives, whereas 22 percent of imprisoned women were sentenced for killing their husbands. The pattern is similar in the rest of the country.[26]

The main reason behind the increasing number of murders by women is undoubtedly their extensive legal vulnerability. Post-revolutionary family policies have reinforced the patriarchal family structure and undermined women's rights in terms of legalizing polygamy and facilitating temporary marriage, limiting women's legal protection from their husbands' violence and abuse. It is also difficult for women to file for divorce, and they would automatically lose custody of their children after a divorce. A lack of citizenship rights and protection has resulted in individual and family crises (Aliverdinia and Pridemore 2009). Women who have murdered their husbands usually mention brutal physical and psychological violence, infidelity, abuses, and forced marriages as the main motives. In one survey, 67 percent of women who had killed their husbands mentioned infidelity, and 33 percent mentioned their husband's violence as the reason for murder. (Moazami and Ashouri 1384/2005).[27]

Divorce

One of the reasons for the drastic transformations of the Iranian family has been the soaring divorce rate since the mid-2000s. Annual statistics from the National Organization for Civil Registration show that registered divorces in Iran rose 120 percent between 2004 and 2014, increasing from 73,882 (in 1383/2004) to 163,569 (in 1393/2014). The rate is highest in large cities, and Tehran alone accounts for almost 25 percent of all divorces.[28] However, divorce in rural areas has recently displayed a dramatic growth rate as well. In recent years, the growth of the divorce rate in rural areas has gone from one to five per thousand marriages, while the rate in urban areas has increased from five to fifteen per thousand marriages.[29] The highest divorce rate in 2011 was found among men between twenty-five and twenty-nine and women between twenty and twenty-four, indicating that marriages are failing early. Thirty percent of divorces occur in the first year of marriage and 50 percent in the first five years.[30] The request for divorce is higher among women, despite the fact that women's legal rights for initiating divorce are much more restricted than for men. In 2002, 85 percent of all requests came from women.[31] This rate had risen to 90 percent in 2010.[32] The increase of divorce has several reasons, but the main one, according to reports and surveys, causing more than 50 percent of all divorces, is "sexual problems."[33] Anxieties are also expressed over what experts call "emotional divorce" (*talaq attefi*) or "hidden divorce" (*talaq-e penhan*). "Emotional divorce" is a new term to describe a situation in which couples live in the same house but separately. It is said that "emotional divorces" are twice as common as official divorces.[34] A survey conducted by the Social Worker Association in 2012 shows that verbal and emotional communications among the family members had fallen to the "alarming" level of fifteen minutes per day.[35]

The high rate of divorce and falling rate of marriages (see Table 2) have caused panic among the authorities, who regard this as "threatening the bases of the system [the state]."[36] Panic among authorities became so intense that they even sometimes forged the statistics of divorces and marriages

Table 2. Declining Rates of Marriage, Increasing Rate of Divorce, 2004–2014

Year	Number of marriages	Number of divorces	Ratio of marriages to divorces
1383/2004	723976	73882	9.8
1384/2005	787818	84241	9.4
1385/2006	778291	94039	8.3
1386/2007	841107	99852	8.4
1387/2008	881592	110510	8
1388/2009	890208	125747	7.1
1389/2010	891627	137200	6.5
1390/2011	874792	142841	6.1
1391/2012	829968	150324	5.5
1392/2013	774513	155369	5
1393/2014	724324	163569	4.4

Source: National Organization for Civil Registration, 1394/2015.

(presenting the rate of divorce to be lower and the rate of marriage to be higher than they actually were) in order "not to disturb public opinion."[37]

In the official discourse, the high divorce rate is the result of the "cultural invasion" (*tahajom-e farhangi*), which has been orchestrated by the Western states against Iran since the emergence of the Islamic Republic. The family and young people are believed to be the new main target for the invasion and are under attack by Persian and non-Persian satellite television channels and digital media such as the Internet and Facebook. The main aim of the attack is claimed to be an attempt to make free sexuality, infidelity, and anti-family values normal.[38] Targeting the family is regarded as targeting the heart of the regime, hence a security issue. In recent official discourse about the family crisis, terms such as *jebhe* (frontier), *sangar* (trenches), *NATO-e farhangi* (cultural NATO), and *jang-e narm* (soft war) have recurrently been used. Unlike the officials' conspiracy theory, experts, such as psychologists, family therapists, social workers, and sociologists, identify financial difficulties, infidelity, abuses, polygyny, drug addiction, and domestic violence as main factors behind the divorces (cf. Hasso 2011).

The damaging effects on relationships within families due to temporary marriages and polygyny are huge. Infidelity is undoubtedly encouraged by temporary marriage, which is seen by men as an opportunity to have sexual relationships with other women. Although, due to its bad reputation, temporary marriages are usually hidden from others, the practice increased in 2014 and 2015. Despite its significant effect, the issue of infidelity (including *sigheh*) and its consequences on the family has been neglected in public debates. Cinema has been the only medium that has brought this issue into the public eye. During 1390/2011 alone ten films were produced with the theme of infidelity.[39] The most popular films in recent years—such as *Zendegi-ye Khososi* (by Mohammad Hossein Farahbakhsh, 2011), *Chahrshanbe Souri* (by Asghar Farhadi, 2006), *Barf roye kajha* (by Peyman Moaadi, 2011), and *Saadat Abad* (by Mazyar Miri, 2011)—depict the collapse of the family because of infidelity.

Dispersed Families

Another factor that has had a crucial impact on the instability of the urban middle-class family is emigration. While other factors have been studied and discussed, the effects of emigration as a catalyst for divorce have not received much attention. The mass emigration since 1979 has forced many families to split. The 1979 Revolution and the outbreak of the war between Iran and Iraq caused a huge emigration of Iranians. The Iran-Iraq war served to accelerate the exodus when hundreds of thousands of young men escaped from Iran to avoid military service. Furthermore, many young people left to escape the increasingly dominant religious culture of everyday life. Gradually, a huge Iranian diaspora has emerged, stretching from Sydney and Dubai to Los Angeles and Toronto. In September 2012, statistics from the National Organization for Civil Registration revealed that more than three million Iranians live in the United States, Canada, UK, United Arab Emirates, and Europe.[40] Transnational families, or rather scattered families, are a consequence of the migration. Furthermore, migration has also had an impact on marriage instability. Facing huge difficulties to obtain visas and to immigrate to Western countries, many Iranians leave the country alone, often irregularly, and some in the hope of getting asylum. This kind of migration means long-term separation between couples. Another form of migration among middle-class Iranians has been where only one member of the family stays in Iran: the wife and children migrate to Europe or Canada, while the husband stays behind to work and send them money. The main rationale for this kind of migration is to secure good education and a better future for the children, but marital disruption brings painful consequence for children as well as for the couples.

Long-term separation between couples generally means changes of preferences, meeting new people that may lead to a higher risk of divorce. Furthermore, relatively women-friendly family laws in Western countries facilitate divorce. At the same time, for many men left behind, this distance offers opportunity for a second marriage. The impact of migration on the family, neglected by academics, has been a recurrent theme in the popular culture, especially in the cinema during the past two decades. Some of the best-known films are *Banoy-e Ordibehesht* (by Rakhsahn Banietemad, 1998); *Zan-e Dovoum* (by Sirous Alvand, 2008); *Shab-e Yalda* (by Kiumars Pourahmad, 2001); *Santuri* (by Daruish Mehrjui, 2007); *Kanaan* (by Mani Haghighi, 2007); and *Be omid-e didar* (by Mohammad Rasoulof, 2011). The most famous, however, is undoubtedly the Academy Award-winning movie *Nader and Simin, a Separation* (by Asghar Farhadi, 2011). Titled *Jodaeiye Nader az Simin* in Persian, the film is about the dissolution of a marriage. It opens with a scene in a divorce court, the couple, Simin and Nader, looking straight into the camera, addressing it as the judge. Simin, who has decided to emigrate with their daughter, is seeking a divorce, the main reason being to save the daughter from the gender inequality in Iran. Nader insists on staying in Iran to take care of his elderly father. Simin, waiting for a divorce, moves to her parental house. In the absence of Simin, Nader hires Raziyeh as housekeeper and caretaker of his father, who suffers from Alzheimer's. After an incident that results in Raziyeh's miscarriage, the film dwells on the complex legal, religious, and ethical issues. The film illustrates the challenges urban families face. Poverty is destabilizing Raziyeh's family. Her husband suffers from long-term unemployment, debt, and depression. Despite the financial hardship, her husband's patriarchal values do not allow women to work outside their homes. Therefore Raziyeh keeps her work hidden from her husband. In the film, the family and the *home* as a safe place for the family have collapsed. In the absence of intermediate institutions, such as elder care or a functioning education system, the home is turned into both a school and a nursing home. Nader hires a nurse to take care of his old father and a private tutor to teach his daughter at home, turning his home into a semiprivate space. The family of Raziyeh is also scattered, and her home is disturbed because of poverty. In the only scene that takes place in her home, at the end of the film, we see that her home is full of male moneylenders who have come to demand their money back. The ending scene, like the opening one, is at the family court, where Nader, Simin, and their daughter Termeh are forced to bring out private issues and emotions. The home is no longer a private sphere but part of the public one. The film was criticized, ignored, and rejected by the hardliners. It was accused of being an "anti-Iranian" movie because it depicts a "false" and "incorrect" picture of the Iranian family.[41] In general, films that focus on family crises are seen as "political films," and several have been banned, such as *Zendegi-ye Khososi* (by Mohammad Hossein Farahbakhsh 1390/2011).[42]

A general comment I frequently heard both in public debates and in private was that the *qebh* (ugliness/shamefulness) of divorce is gone. As a way to express anxiety about proliferating divorce, this means that divorce is no longer stigmatizing and that divorce does not bring shame on the whole family any longer. As an "expert" put it, divorce in Iranian society has gone from "shamefulness" to be "shamelessness" (*veqahat*).[43]

Anti-Divorce

Calling his government a "government of compassion," President Ahmadinejad saw his main goal to promote marriages and fight divorce among youth. Ahmadinejad's government launched several plans and provided facilities to encourage young people to marry, such as subsidies in the form of "marriage gifts" (up to US$3,000), subsidized dowries, mass marriage ceremonies financed by the state, and interest-free loans.[44] Moreover, a huge campaign for "building up the culture of marriage" commenced. The anniversary of the marriage of Imam Ali and Fatemeh became Marriage Day, and the third week of Aban (around mid-October) became Family and Marriage Week.[45]

Furthermore, conferences and seminars on the "goodness" of marriage and "immorality" of divorce have regularly been convened. The government established family consultations to offer free services to couples. Film producers, news agencies, and the press received financial support to "endorse" marriages. For instance, in December 2010, an exhibition titled "The Iranian Lucky Couple" opened in Tehran.[46] Ahmadinejad's government also showed an interest in arranging mass wedding ceremonies. The government arranged these events for young people who could not afford a wedding party. The ceremonies were often covered by national media and took place at spectacular public places. For instance, in July 2006, when the Resalat Tunnel on West-East Resalat Highway in north Tehran was officially inaugurated by the president, a mass wedding for hundreds of young couples was also arranged in the tunnel. The ceremony was broadcast by the state-run television.

A News Vignette

The Marriage and Family Planning Bureau of the Ministry of Sport and Youth announced at the end of October 2012 that the project for a national symphony of marriage had been started: The symphony would contribute to strengthen the status and value of marriage in all segments of society, especially among the youth ... and to create a common national language for planning conscious, timely, easy, and stable marriages.[47]

One basic obstacle for young people to build up a *khanevadeh* (family) is the difficulty obtaining a *khane* (house/home). According to the Centre for Strategic Studies, housing is up to 55 percent of living costs of families.[48] Housing costs in large cities in Iran have soared in the past two decades. High inflation, an insecure financial market, and increasing demand due to the tradition of investing in real estate among Iranians have put housing costs beyond reach for young people. According to one report, "Real estate prices surged by more than 100 percent in 2007, after rising by about 65 percent in

2006 and by more than 50 percent in 2005."[49] Similarly, average rent prices throughout the country rose by 60 percent in 1390/2011.[50]

To assist young people, the Ministry of Housing and Urban Development launched *Maskan-e mehr* (literally, house of compassion) in the late 2000s. It was a huge national housing project committed to providing small, inexpensive apartments to low-income groups in large and small cities throughout the country. The minister of housing stated in June 2010 that "the main goal of the *Maskan-e mehr* project is to facilitate young people's marriage and to strengthen the family institution."[51] Buildings would be built on state-owned lands in a 99-year contract for free. Moreover, young couples would receive beneficial loans. The project, interesting and well organized on paper, seems less successful in reality due to the fluctuating inflation and an unsteady market, in which the prices calculated by government agencies do not match actual prices in the market. In the official discourse, the housing problem of youth is often linked to their sexual needs. The government sees part of its duty (just like traditional parents' duty to help their children get married) to manage the nation's sexuality. In the discourse of official experts, there is concern about what is called *enqelab-e jensi*, "a sexual revolution."

The idea about "a sexual revolution" among Iranian youth is also discussed outside Iran in *Passionate Uprisings* (2009) by Pardis Mahdavi and *Lipstick Jihad* (2005) by Azadeh Moaveni. Both authorities' anxieties and exiled academics' jubilation over what Mahdavi and Moaveni identify as a sexual revolution are wrong conclusions drawn from the proliferation of sexual practices among Iranian youth. Almost all young feminists I talked to in Iran criticized the term "sexual revolution." In their view, free sexual relationships do not necessarily lead to women's emancipation. Contrary to what Mahdavi and Moaveni present, objectification of the female body and sexual abuses have not been declining. The two authors compare young Iranians' "sexual revolution" with sexual liberation in the West during the 1960s and the 1970s, believing that young Iranians are experiencing a similar sexual emancipation. What they neglect is the fact the sexual liberation in the West was interwoven with other progressive movements such as the anti-Vietnam war protests, class struggles, the civil rights movement, and feminism. The so-called sexual revolution in Iran is isolated from other acts of citizenship rights; thus describing it in terms of a "revolution" would be misleading. The authorities are concerned about "pervasive uncontrolled and unmanaged" sexual activities among the young, so the "management of sexuality" (*modiriyat-e jensi*) has become one of the main missions of the government.

Administration of Sexuality

The "un-administrated" sexual life of young Iranians has been described as a *bomb-e shahvat* (literally, lust bomb, bomb of uncontrolled sexual desires). Warnings by politicians and "experts" for the explosion of this "bomb" are recurrently heard in the public debate.[52] According to the official view, signs of the imminent danger of the "lust bomb" or "sexual revolution" are "growth of sexual imagination among young people, increasing number of divorces, gang rapes, infidelity, sale of sex toys [in the black market], sexual [verbal and nonverbal] harassments in public places, cougars, and a 100 per cent increase of HIV."[53] Asghar Mohajeri, a professor at Tehran University, claimed, in March 2012 that his research showed that "eroticism has increased a hundred times in the past three decades."[54]

Although we should be careful with the numbers and statistics in the quotes above (since it is not clear what they are based on), they reveal the officials' concerns. The main focus in the patriarchal discourse is a regretful anguish for the vanishing of *qebh* (shamefulness/ugliness) toward sexual behavior among young people, particularly among young women. Fear of female sexuality is explicitly palpable in the official discourse. Ebrahim Fayaz, professor at Tehran University and a well-known "expert" on youth issues, highlighted this fear in an interview on 27 May 2012: "Unfortunately nowadays women demand sexual relationships and this means a dangerous sexual revolution."[55]

The fear of the lust bomb and uncontrollable sexuality has caused a sort of sexual paranoia among officials, who rummage for traces of sexual expression everywhere in the society. Since the 1979 Revolution, Iranians of opposite sexes in the company of each other have been forced to explain/confess to the "morality police" what kind of sexual relationship (authorized as married or unauthorized as unmarried) they have or do not have. In the authorities' views, the first and perhaps only relationship between an unrelated man and woman cannot be something other than sexual. Their imagination, however, goes far beyond young people walking on the street. They see signs of sexual desire in urban planning, football games, architecture, or a newspaper logo. For instance according to a social commentator: "The open kitchen of modern architecture is an icon of prostitution. There is no privacy. Nothing is covered. There is no chastity in architecture any more. Such architecture is in its essence sexual."[56] In one striking example, the logo of the newspaper *Tehran-e Emroz* ignited a big national controversy in 2011 when officials claimed the logo depicted an erotic image of a female body and had to be changed. Similarly, the recorded female voice used in elevators announcing floors was criticized for being "too erotic."[57] Not surprisingly, even the post-election protests in 2009 were described as "extremely erotic."[58] Referring to female protestors, it was claimed that sexual incitements were the main factor in the protests.

While the state identifies pre-marriage sexual relations among young people as anomic, it turns a blind eye on the extensive growth of prostitution and the fact that temporary marriages are regularly used as legal covers for selling and buying sex. The only form of sexuality that is harshly controlled and penalized is the one between young men and women before marriage. Labeled as *biband o bari jensi* (sexual anomie, licentiousness), unauthorized sex is seen not merely as a sin/crime but also as part of the "soft war" driven by the Western states and therefore a severe threat to the stability of the family institution and thereby to the state. According to official surveys, sexual dissatisfaction is the primary reason for almost 50 percent of all divorces in Iran.[59] Thus, to rescue the family, the authorities have emphasized the urgent need for the "administration of sexuality." A huge niche for manuals, instruction booklets, and educational guidance on sexuality and sex life has emerged. A large number of these publications are published by governmental organizations, but individual clerics and religious institutes are also producing them. People's sexual instincts are seen as a potential factor for family building, a divine gift, which should be stimulated, even encouraged, but at the same time administered and controlled. Sexual activities are described as a holy *jihad* for men and a holy *duty* for women. Unauthorized sexual activities are, however, seen as a destabilizing factor on the family and the society. Not surprisingly, controlling and administering sexuality in a form of patriarchal heterosexuality has been on top of the agenda among the theocracy. Accordingly, only a single and utilitarian locus of sexuality is acknowledged: the fertile heart of every household, that is, the married couple's sexuality. All other forms of sexuality have been rejected and repressed in terms of both sin and crime. When *sharia*, Islamic law, became the civil law, the distinction between the unlawful and the sinful disappeared; subsequently, crime and sin became synonymous. Sin thus is a violation not only of divine rule but also of society's well-being. Thus a sinner is subjected to criminal law.

In a Foucauldian perspective, Iranians' sexual activities become a matter for the policy makers. Policing sexuality has been handled through "useful," "healthy," "natural"—biological reproduction—discourses. Concern for the size of the nation in terms of political issue, birth rate, and fertility of the people conflates with religious discourse on legitimate sexuality. The "administration of sexuality" requires knowledge and education in order to understand, catalogue, and identify any "distortion" that needs to be controlled and "cured." Experts called for *mardomshenasi ye jensi* (an anthropology of sexuality).[60] The result has been an explosion of discourses—in politics, medicine, psychiatry, education, and the media—about sexuality. To administrate the sexuality of young Iranians and to discipline an appropriate sexual subjectivity, a large knowledge production has been launched, what Michel Foucault (1990) has called *scientia sexualis*.

Clerics and various kinds of experts, such as sexologists and psychologists, have been engaged to instruct how to maximize the sexual gratification for young couples with respect to Islamic rules and values. Thus, the science of sexuality in Iran aims not only to manage and administer sexuality but also to intensify sexual pleasure within the authorized relationship. Therapeutic speeches about healthy and gratifying sexuality have become common in the state-run media, given even by conservative religious forces. For instance, Hasan Dehnavi, a well-known clergyman, is recognized for his public speeches on the "Art of Love Making," also available on DVD for purchase.[61] The state-run television has increasingly been broadcasting educational programs in which sexual topics, such as premature ejaculation, sexual foreplay, or female orgasm, are addressed.

The most controversial product of this governmental sexual management has been the DVD *Ashna-ye mahboub* (The Beloved Companion). In the summer of 2011, the DVD, produced jointly by the Ministry of Health and the media company Namava, was released and has been distributed through pharmacies in Iranian cities.[62] Targeting young couples, it is an educational video about sex and sexuality. The main expert figure is Dr. Mohammad Majd, a professor of medical science at Tehran University. Combining the science of sexology with Islamic values, for more than two hours he describes in detail the sexual anatomy of men and women and gives instruction on what he considers to be good sex. Although it targets both men and women, men are considered the primary audience; perhaps the reason is the religious quotes that are more oriented toward men's sexual needs.

The video starts with the famous flower sequence from Pink Floyd's music video *The Wall*. The animation shows two flowers flirtatiously swirling around each other and ends with a symbolic penetration. Then, one flower encapsulates the other. The next scene shows swimming sperms. Pink Floyd's "What

Shall We Do Now" is replaced with Richard Strauss's symphony *Thus Spoke Zarathustra*. Soon after the flower scene, a quote from the Prophet Muhammad appears, saying that a wife should make herself pretty for her husband and be prepared for sexual intercourse; later, a quote from Imam Jafar Sadegh, who emphasizes foreplay in intercourse, appears on the screen.[63]

There has been a shift in the official discourse on sexuality, going from regarding sexuality as biological reproduction to celebrating love and sexuality, albeit still between married, heterosexual couples, as the growing number of state-sanctioned projects for educating people in maximizing sexual gratification indicates. In the new discourse, sex is no longer only a holy burden or a social duty (reproduction of the nation) but also a bodily pleasure. The authorities' strategy to "administrate" the nation's sexuality is an attempt to rescue marriages that are suffering from sexual dissatisfaction.

Conclusion

Islamic family values and ethics have been vital features of the "art of government" in the post-revolutionary Iran. However, an unintended consequence of the Revolution has been the weakening of "traditional" family forms. Political turbulence, the war with Iraq, mass migration (both domestic and international), economic hardship, swift demographic changes, and a repressive apparatus concerning youth have had a significant impact on the family structure. Furthermore, state interventions in family policies—for example, encouraging polygyny and temporary marriage, rapid and drastic shifts in family planning programs, and gender discrimination against women in the labor market and other public areas—have changed the Iranian family pattern forever. A huge discourse on "family crises" has been produced by state officials, politicians, the clergy, the state-run media, social workers, and official experts and academics. Moralizing the family as being in crisis is a nation-building project (cf. Hasso 2011). The Iranian state legitimizes its interventions into the private life of the nation by claiming that the "family crisis" destabilizes the society.

In the official discourse, "family crisis" is part of a "cultural invasion" or "soft war" imposed by foreign states' anti-Iranian policies. The "predicting-catastrophe" discourse about how the family crisis will lead to national insecurity has encouraged state interventions in regulating family formation, administering sexuality, or recommending the optimal number of children.

Here, state power penetrates into the private sphere of the individual, for instance, by making marriage a condition for employment, mobility, education, and career advancement. Needless to mention, anxiety about the "family crisis" is a patriarchal heteronormative concern and what are presented as causes of crises can indeed be liberation attempts by women and youth.

Consequently, home and the private sphere of the family have moved into the public discourse. The administration of sexuality within and outside families, the numbers of permanent and temporary wives, the marriage age, and divorce are a few examples of the recurrent themes discussed by politicians in the Parliament, by governmental officials, and by experts in public debates. The administration of sexuality, not only as a patriarchal moral concern but also as a political concern for the reproduction of the nation, has become an imperative. *Home* is no longer a "protected" private sphere for the family, but an arena for state interventions.

While the state has left families alone in raising children into adulthood, families have become sites for severe tensions. An increasing crime rate within the family, a soaring divorce rate, a declining marriage rate, domestic violence, a growing number of runaway girls and street children, generational conflicts, and addiction—all are somehow the consequences of the crisis of the family. Furthermore, the weakening of the family for socializing the young known as "the 60-generation" (Alikhani 1382/2003) is crucial in the transformation of the family institution. Statistics from the early 2000s show that in both urban and rural areas, the average age of schooling among young people is in general higher than among their fathers, which challenges the patriarchal hierarchy within the family (Ladier-Fouladi 2012: 156).

Furthermore, structural transformations, such as a more educated and mobile generation, the entrance of more women into the public life, urbanization, and the impact of media consumption, have resulted in a shift in desire for and expectation about the form of family among young people. A growing desire for individualism, independence, personal freedom, more mobility, residential autonomy, and marriages based on romantic love is changing the cultural ideal of family life. The ideational changes have caused behavioral changes in family formation. Marriage at an older age, more autonomy in the choice of spouse, a higher demand for gender equality within families, controlled fertility, single-parent households, an independent nuclear family (from the ideal extended one) are factors that disassociate the new family constellations from the traditional ideal "familism." Related to the ideational change is the change in attitudes toward divorce, marriage, and sexuality. One significant feature of the change is the vanishing of the "shamefulness" of divorce and new forms of partnerships. Contrary to state expectation and intended policy, the young generation's ideal family form is a nuclear family, independence from kinship groups influence (Ladier-Fouladi 2012: 143), fewer children, easy divorce, and more gender equality.[64]

Left alone by the state and in the absence of a well-established civil society, the Iranian family is more precarious than ever. As I will show in the next chapter, the weight of precarity is put on the shoulders of the young generation.

CHAPTER 2

THE 1360 GENERATION

The country is at war with its own youth
—Anne Allison (2013: 47)

Friday, 19 June 2009, was my first day in Tehran after the notorious presidential election. In the Friday Prayer that day, the supreme leader, Ayatollah Khamenei, gave his support to the victory of Mahmoud Ahmadinejad. The ayatollah emphasized the legitimacy of the election, calling it a "divine assessment." He also declared that protests would not be tolerated and would have severe consequences. It was a menacing and fierce warning from the most powerful man in the country. I expected that protests would drastically weaken after his speech. He had stated the same thing in 1999 during the student uprising, and his warning then, in effect, put an end to the clashes and protests. It was a gloomy and sad day, as the whole city of Tehran was mourning, harassed with the bitter taste of failure. The supreme leader's support for Ahmadinejad was not unanticipated, nor was it expected to be so explicit. His speech was a slap in the face for young people, who had hoped that the symbolic father of the nation would, at least publicly, stay neutral.

In the late evening that day, I went to Borj-e Sefid, a high-rise building and center of commerce in a middle-class neighborhood of northeastern Tehran. Its tower is famous for the revolving restaurant on the top floor. Under the restaurant, there is an outdoor coffee shop on a large terrace, offering a panoramic view of a large part of the city at night. Tehran is more beautiful at night, when the infamous air pollution that envelops the city in dust and lethal exhaust emissions from millions of vehicles on the streets is unseen. From the cab driving me to Borj-e Sefid, I had seen mobs of paramilitary forces in plain clothes at every major intersection, ready to attack protesters. During my fieldwork in 1999, I used to come here at nights to look at the city and meet those I would interview. In that summer a decade ago, after the crackdown on the student uprising, just like now, a feeling of public disenchantment had been in the air. Now, while I was sipping my tea, staring at the lights of the city, I heard a voice from below. We were so high up that I could not hear well. The voice was hazy and unclear but rose in volume and strength so that, in the end, its message was audible at the top of the high-rise building: *Allahu Akbar* (God is great)—the sound of protest. A striking and gripping scene in the dark, it brought to my mind images from the Revolution of 1979 when I was thirteen and had accompanied my mother or sisters, who also chanted "Allahu Akbar," to protest against the shah. I wondered, "Has nothing changed since? Are we back to the same point where we were, three decades ago?" However, chanting "Allahu Akbar" in post-electoral protests in 2009 differed from "Allahu Akbar" in 1979. While, in the latter, it was a central slogan in an Islamic ideologized revolt against a monarchy that was seen as secular, in the former, it did referred not to religion but to the visions, promises, and expectations of the 1979 Revolution. It was not a repetition but a replication. Replicating protests, slogans, and tactics from the 1979 Revolution signified the hope.

In the coming nights, for the more than two months I was in Iran during the summer of 2009, the chant "Allahu Akbar" at ten o'clock every night became a major feature of the political behavior of Iranians. The scene of this nightly call to God was spectacular. People gathered on the rooftops of houses or apartment buildings, old and young, even children, chanting "Allahu Akbar" for about twenty minutes. On the roofs, one could see the silhouettes of human beings, scared to be seen, identified, or shot by snipers. This dramatic sight was captured by photographer Pietro Masturzo, who won the 2010 World Press Photo prize for his picture of three women on a rooftop in Tehran, chanting. The chants of "God is great" echoed from roof to roof. Afterward, people phoned each other to check how the chanting session had been in different parts of the city. Voices of people on rooftops rang the bells of "Death of the Father," the social death of the source of political authority. This demise happens when there is a consensus among the people that all vital functions of political authority have ceased (Borneman 2004). The scream of a generation, now liberated from the authority of a symbolic father, occupied the sky of Tehran at nights.

The symbolic father in the Iranian political context should be understood in the context of the *morad/morid* relationship rooted in Sufism and the aesthetics of self-abasement (see Khosravi 2008). The *morad/morid* relationship is a generational hierarchy that allocates power to the elders, a system that aims to school young people in total obedience to the patriarch. *Morad* is the master, and *morid* is the disciple. The master is also called *pir* (literally, old) in Sufism. To find the right path in life, one needs a master, a *pir*. The master is not only a leader but himself the goal (*morad* literally means "goal"), a beloved role model for youth. The disciple should love his or her master. The pattern of obedience and loyalty embedded in the *morid/morad* relationship resembles the relationship between a father and his children. The master replaces the father. In this relationship, total obedience to one's father is transformed into total obedience to one's master, leader, and goal. Translating this into the political relationship, *morid* is not a citizen but a submitting subject.

The simple but sharp central slogan of the Green Movement—"Where is my vote?"—challenged the expected obedience and loyalty to the *morad*/master/father/state. The demand for being counted, included, seen, and recognized echoes in the word "my" in the slogan, which revealed the emergence of a new political subjectivity. The slogan "Where is *my* vote?" symbolizes the clash between the hegemonic discourse and aesthetic of self-abasement (total submission to the father) and self-assertion (demonstrating political subjectivity and individual autonomy). The assertion of political subjectivity is also manifested in the huge and decisive participation of young people in the presidential elections in 1997, 2009, and 2013.

A few days before the presidential election in June 2013, Iranians were engaged in a heated debate on the participation or boycott of this election. Disappointed by the election fraud in 2009, many middle-aged people were ambivalent about whether to vote. Younger people showed greater enthusiasm to participate, however, not because they had forgotten what had happened four years earlier but because they used any chance, no matter how small, for a peaceful change. They repeat and replicate to generate hope, despite constant political defeat. The long and passionate discussions just before the election of 2013 can be summarized in the words of Reza, a twenty-three-year-old IT student at a top university in Teheran:

> What is the option? Boycotting the election means we close the door for peaceful changes from inside. What is the alternative? Another revolution? No thanks, our parents made one, and it is more than enough for generations to come. Another revolution and it will be like this again thirty years from now. Or should we ask the Americans to

invade Iran to liberate us? Like Iraq? Like Afghanistan? No. It may be naïve of us to think our votes can change something or if our votes will be read at all. But this is the only way we know. . . . What we need is hope, even if it would be short-term.

The political subjectivity of the young generation, unlike former generations who made the 1979 Revolution, goes beyond political ideologies and concentrates on the citizenship rights, manifested in the slogan "Where is my vote?" Absence of ideologies increases the chance for diversity, tolerance, and pluralism, all reflected in the slogans, political behaviors, performances, symbols, and references among youth in the post-election protests of 2009. In this chapter, I draw a portrait of this generation, *daheye shastiha.*

Portrait of a Generation

Daheye shastiha (literally, of the 1360s, henceforth the "60-generation") is a term used for those who were born in the 1360s (1981–1990) in Iran, currently somewhere between twenty-five and thirty-five. Its self-image is that of a generation who has failed in its transition into adulthood and is stuck in an infinite position of *not becoming,* a prolonged youth. Iran faced a huge demographic change after the Revolution. The Iranian population increased drastically, from almost thirty-three million in 1976 to almost eighty million in 2016. The number of people born in the 1360s (the decade when birth rates increased) was 21,954,053, that is, about 23 percent of the present total population. *Daheye shastiha* is an emic generational classification that emerged in the mid-2000s when this generation started to come of age. In the late 1990s, the emic term *nasl-e sevoum* (the third generation) was used by young Iranians generally to refer to the post-revolutionary generations (Khosravi 2008). Today, the post-revolutionary generation is divided and fragmented, categorized and labeled in terms of decades: the 1360s generation and the 1370s generation.

A number of factors make it possible to group them as a generation: they have had no direct experience of the 1979 Revolution; their first years in life were spent during the eight years' war with Iraq. Although they do not have any direct memories of the war, their parents' stress and fear are always mentioned in interviews. However, those born in the early 1360s remember the times they had to rush to the basement when Iraqi missiles hit Iran's large cities. This generation spent its formative years in the postwar era, character-ized by a liberal market economy, consumer culture, and access to new com-munication technologies (such as satellite television channels, cell phone, and the Internet). Digital access to the outside world without reach of state control played a significant role in shaping the identity of the 60-generation. When they were in their mid-teens, the 60-generation experienced the Second of Khordad (23 May 1997, the election of President Khatami) and subsequently the "Reform Era" (1997–2004). During these years, Iranians enjoyed freedom of the press (to some extent) and a flourishing cultural scene. The numbers of newspapers, journals, and books published soared. Cinema, theater, and music also boomed. During the Reform Era, Iranians gained more access to the outside world. Iran, people used to say then, was on its way toward global-ization, aiming to put an end to its political and cultural isolation. Foreign tourism increased, and the government made it easier for Iranians in the di-aspora to return, make visits, and invest in the economy. The historical climax for the 60-generation was undoubtedly the Green Movement in 2009, devel-oped, formed, and carried out by this generation. Altogether, these historical events shaped a generational sensitivity among the young Iranians.

"Generational objects" (Bollas 1993) are collectively lived experiences that signify a generation's identity. Lived experiences of historical events and crises shape generational consciousness, which forms social and political behaviors, sexuality, everyday communication, symbols, rituals, and language. In a soci-ety like Iran where historical events occur within short intervals (the Revolu-tion, war, the Reform Era, the counter-reform period of Ahmadinejad, and the Green Movement), the generation cycles become shorter. A generation cycle in Iran has decreased from a period of thirty to ten years (Sohrabzadeh 1388/2009). Not surprisingly the 60-generation see huge differences between themselves and those born in the decades before and after, that is, the 1350s and 1370s. There are also many in the 60-generation who make an internal distinction between those born in the first half and in the second half of the decade. This internal division is mainly based on the experiences of the war by those born in the early 1360s. However, those born in the late 1360s grew up with digital technologies, and by the time they reached school age the In-ternet had entered the country.

"Generational objects" among Iranians differ depending on which histor-ical event they have experienced. The 1360s was a decade of revolution and war, characterized by an idea of self-sacrificing, martyrdom, aesthetics of modesty, planned economy, and scarcity of basic needs. The 1370s, the decade after the war, known as the "Reconstruction Era" was characterized by a market-driven economy, an increasing class gap, consumerism, and technocracy. The Reform Era (1997–2005) began during these years and made the second half of the decade a time of cultural openness, political pluralism, media diversity, reconciliation with the outside world, and student movements. This hopeful time ended in the 2005 when conservative forces took over the presidency. After Mahmoud Ahmadinejad became president, life in Iran was characterized by populist revolutionary rhetoric, messianism (state propaganda for endurance and waiting), censorship, oppression of social movements and NGOs, political isolation, financial insecurity (soaring unemployment, capital flight, international sanctions), and mass migration of well-educated young people (putting Iran at the top of the list of countries where "brain drain" has been most prevalent). This decade, however, was also the time of expansion of social media among youth, rage, and groundbreaking political mobilization, manifested in the Green Movement.

What makes those born in the 1360s a generation is not only shared historical and social experiences (Mannheim 1952) or having shared the problems of the time, but significantly also the "responses to these shared problems" (Borneman 1992: 48). The characteristic differences between the Revolution of 1979 and the Green Movement thirty years later are the responses to same problem (that is, political oppression). While the former was highly ideologized and violent, emphasizing localism, the latter was nonideologized, characterized by nonviolence, gender consciousness, and pluralism. The 60-generation claim that their generational identity was constructed in opposition to their parental generation's identity, ideals, and values. The responses by the 60-generation to rapid social changes and radical political events have somehow created a ground for the 60-generation's demands and identity-making process.

Furthermore, the social organization of any generation in post-revolutionary Iran is built on the objective conditions of access to information. Thanks to new communication technologies, the 60-generation (and even more the 70-generation) has had much better access to transnational flows of information than any other previous generation. They easily navigate through the global youth culture, operate means of access (digital devices), and have more foreign language proficiency. Needless to mention, differing access to information is not only a question of generation but also shaped by class. Unlike former generations, the identity of the 60-generation is formed publicly, either actively—protests, street life, new urban practices (see Chapters 4 and 5)—or virtually, on the Internet. Cyberspace has become a public sphere for intense civil engagements (Lotfalian 2013; Mottahedeh 2015). Despite harsh censorship, Iranian bloggers have made Persian one of the top five languages in the global blogosphere. The crucial role of the new social media in the formation of the 60-generation is clearly expressed in the words of a twenty-five-year-old woman who believes her generation was "rescued" by the Internet:

> We were forced to learn by ourselves. We learned from our own experiences and from no one else. We learned about the life in chat rooms. There was one called Tehran Chat Room. It was very good. We had free discussions about everything. We learned to talk, to protest against traditions. We abandoned the traditions and even changed them, like marriage, Chahrshanbeh Souri, and Ashura. The Internet rescued us.

On innumerable blogs, Facebook pages, and chat rooms, 60-generation members express themselves mainly through diaries recording personal anxieties, grief, anguish, or sexual desires, but they also write about a wide range of topics, ranging from cinema, politics, or sexuality to unemployment. Young Iranians have found a new device to tell stories. As I have discussed elsewhere (Graham and Khosravi 2002), the Internet can enable people to be politically active in pursuit of a common cause, but it can also provide opportunities for very public, but also anonymous, interaction in which individual users can reveal or conceal as much about themselves as they choose. On the Internet, people can openly discuss topics not addressed by the official media.

> Cyberspace is a growing reserve of alternative, sometimes conflicting ideas, including alternative blueprints for cultural and social ordering, hence our use of the term heterotopia to describe it. It is a topos where submerged, subjugated, and excluded knowledge are increasingly accessible and where often private and semi-private opinion can become more available for much larger publics. Cyberspace reorders access to information through reconfiguring the division between public and private information. In doing so, it can reveal a degree of cultural and social heterogeneity among Iranians that was either unknown or only suspected. (Graham and Khosravi 2002: 242–43)

The 60-generation's self-image is associated with being "forgotten," "sacrificed," "burnt," or "fucked up." A young architect and blogger known as Sheikh-e Shahr expresses his anguishes about his generation this way:

The Revolution Generation

We are a foul generation. A generation that had to compete for everything. A generation of Konkur. . . . A generations who sees but does not have, wants but is not able to do anything. . . . We are a generation with unrealized dreams. . . . A generation forced to choose between bad and worse. A generation who suffers from not being seen, not being read, not being heard. . . . We are a generation of tears, whining, cries. We are the generation of the Revolution.[1]

A young woman of the 60-generation and an active blogger known as Leng Deraz describes her own generation in these words:

We the 60-generation are called without identity and without ideology. They say we are thoughtless and careless, that we do not have gods, or heroes, that we do not know *Reza Motori* [a cult movie from 1970], Che Guevara, or Fidel Castro. It is correct! We are this way. We have no legends. We change our minds and interests fast. . . . The 60-generation became the reckless figures in the cinema of Kimiai and Farmanara [two filmmakers both born in the 1940s]. The 60-generation is not like former ones. They ridicule everything. . . . I have seen how the 60-generation has been humiliated for long time. . . . Visit Evin [the notorious prison in Tehran]. There are many of us there. Visit the cemeteries. There are many of us there. From those born in 1360 to those born in 1369 . . . students, workers. They were alive until June 2009. Then they were killed one by one. . . . One day they went to the streets and never came back. . . . They did not go for death [like the martyrs] but for life. This is why after their death what remain are their Facebook pages and not testaments.[2]

Of course, Iran had a young population prior to the Revolution, too. Traditionally, however (and through the conventional structures), young people were immediately incorporated into the sphere of adults. Then, in the context of the Revolution and the war, both carried on the shoulders of young people, the "youth" category was recognized as a social category (Ladier-Fouladi 2012). However, it was not until the mid-2000s that the "problems of generations" began to circulate in the wider society. President Mohammad Khatami was perhaps the first high-ranking official who mentioned this issue, using the words *gosast-e naslha*, "generational break" (Azadarmaki 1389/2010: 79). The issue of young people became highly politicized after the student unrest of June 1999. The "generational gap" or "generational break" soon became a heated issue among politicians, scholars, and experts. An issue that was a political taboo, ignored and denied, became a central theme in public debates in mass media and other public spheres. Officials launched a huge apparatus of knowledge production and organized innumerable television shows, academic and nonacademic seminars and conferences to address the issue. Scholars began to carry out research (Azadarmaki 1389/2010: 81) and included generation studies in academic curricula; translations of theoretical and empirical studies on generations from other countries were published. Various state organizations conducted systematic "research" and "surveys" mainly to observe, correct, and "cure" youthful "divergent" behaviors. These studies were conducted by trusted insider researchers, but the results were inaccessible to outsiders. Youth studies have been politically sensitive and have been a risky field for non-insider researchers. The habit of concealing knowledge expanded during Ahmadinejad's presidency. In February 2010, a letter was sent to the heads of universities by the head of the security unit of universities commanding that information, statistics, or other data could not be released to nonofficial and independent researchers.

What the officials want to suppress and dismiss is "generational conflict," depicted in many independent studies. A nationwide survey conducted among students in twenty universities shows that young Iranians are "less religious, less fundamentalist, and less traditional" (Farastkhah 1392/2013). Another study claims that empirical data show that the young Iranians are not religious in their behavior, that is, do not perform religious duties (for example, fast, pray, go to the mosque) compared to their parents' generation (Azadarmaki 1389/2010). Another anxiety for the authorities has been the fact that the legacy of the war and the Revolution has significantly faded for the 60-generation. According to a quantitative survey, the 60-generation's attitude toward the Revolution and "traditional beliefs" differs immensely from their parental generation (Sohrabzadeh 1388/2009). At the same time, surveys and studies indicate a lack of religiosity among youth, new forms of spirituality are emerging, for instance, an increase in the popularity of Zoroastrianism,

Buddhism, New Age, or occult practices. This transformation can also be seen in how the youth transform Islamic rituals, such as the Ashura ritual. Young people in large cities have created new ways of performing this ceremony, different from those performed by previous generations, resulting in transforming the holy mourning ceremony for Imam Hossein into something else. The new forms of performing Ashura have the characteristics of a carnival, performed with modern musical instruments, stylish clothing, or choreographed collective breast-beating (sin-e zani). Sarcastically, the new form of collective mourning of the imam is called a Hossein Party, a symbolic parody of the convention. The 60-generation has learned how to survive and even be rebelliously vociferous. It has created its own counterculture (music, literature, painting, multimedia, graffiti, animation, photography, and cinema) that is vigorous, dramatic, and elucidatory. Music, visual art, literature, and cinema are means by which the 60-generation construct, discuss, and reconstruct generational identities.

At the Movies—Cinematic Vignette

Since the late 1990s, films about generational conflicts have become a popular genre in Iran. The films shed light on taboo subjects such as love, teenage crisis, generational conflicts, drugs, and youth culture from the patriarch father's gaze. In the mid-2000s a new wave of films on the youth issue made by the 60-generation began to emerge. Unlike the previous films, they approach the young generation from a different angle, without blame or condemnation but by looking at Iranian society through young people's eyes. One such film is described in the following review:

Mahi va gorbeh (Fish and Cat, by Shahram Mokri, 2013) is a unique cinematic experiment in Iran. Shot in a single 130-minute sequence, the film tells the story of a group of students who have traveled to a remote Caspian region to camp. A couple of serial killer cannibals terrorize the students. The movie shows the isolated youth stuck in waiting. They wait for something that never happens. Meanwhile, they are chased, killed, and eaten. The film is about generational conflict but also the precarious situation of young Iranians. Mokri chose the horror genre to illustrate a dark society in which young Iranians are waiting for the next catastrophe.[3]

Another film is *Boghz* (Hatred, by Reza Dormishian, 2012). It is about the 60-generation; indeed, the film's subtitle is "the 60-generation's film." *Boghz* also means "lump in the throat," which refers to young people's silenced grief and agony. The film tells the story of a desperate, rebellious young couple in transit in Istanbul, struggling to find a way to the United States. The young man, Hamed, uses graffiti to express his frustration, and both embark on a self-destructive spree of drugs, crime, and betrayal. They are stuck and find themselves without any salvation or means to escape. The film was shot in Istanbul because the Ministry of Islamic Culture and Guidance found the screenplay "too dark." In the ministry's view, the "dark" society illustrated in the screenplay "could not be Iran." So the director, himself a member of the 60-generation, relocated the setting from Tehran to Istanbul. He believes the relocation exemplifies how the "60-generation do not find a place inside Iran for themselves and young people live in exile in their own homeland." The film illustrates the generation's desperation and anxiety. In the words of the director, "desperation, delusion and rebellion are typical for the 60-generation who see no future and are constantly suppressed."[4] Dormishian also made the controversial film *Asabani nistam* (I Am Not Angry, 2014), which I come back to in Chapter 7. *Asabani nistam* is the 60-generation's manifest, disclosing the extreme political and social precariousness Iranian youth face, particularly after the 2009 election.

The youth cinema genre of the 1990s sought compromise and consensus between generations. By taking the parental generation's side, these films argued that the solution was to return the rebellious young to *aghosh-e khanevadeh-e pedari* (the embrace of the patriarchal family). But the youth's own wave of films is pessimistic and uncompromising and accuses the parents' generation sharply. The films are radical in their approach to taboos such as HIV, drugs, sexuality, and subcultures. While the earlier films illustrated the youth as shallow and their crisis "trivial," the new films depict a deepened understanding of this generation and their issues of concern: identity, control over their bodies and lives, the economic situation, and social harms. The characters in the films are pariahs, outcasts, defeated, and exiles in their own homeland. In almost all these films, there is a sense of home(land)lessness. Young men and women are in an exile-like condition, detached from the parental home and the homeland. Not surprisingly, in many films emigration is presented as the only option for young people who do not see having a chance for a future in Iran.

Rebelling Through Music—Music Vignette

The iconoclastic counterculture of the 60-generation is also reflected in contemporary Iranian rock and rap music. Musicians like Mohsen Namjoo, Kiosk, Sayeh Sky, Hichkas, and Shahin Najafi not only write political lyrics and songs, but also challenge the inviolable conventions and traditions of their parents' generation. Namjoo, an avant-garde fusion musician, satirizes social codes and norms. Sayeh Sky is a lesbian rapper who sings against the heteronormativity and homophobia in Iran. Kiosk is a rock band known for its critique of the double morality, corruption, and duplicity in society. The most iconoclastic is undoubtedly the rapper Shahin Najafi, who has given voice to the agony and resentment of his generation. He sings against the patriarchal, "young-oppressive" culture. For instance, the music video "Taraf-e ma" (Our Foe) illustrates what it was like to grow up in the 1980s and to come of age in 1990s, portraying a terrorized generation trapped in a melancholic society, torn apart by war, poverty, social suffering, patriarchy, and state terrorism. In the video, we see a group of young men who are beaten and put down first by their fathers, then by their teachers, and finally by policemen. "Ma mard nistim" (We Are Not Men) is Najafi's manifest against the sexist Iranian culture. In this song, he challenges and ridicules society's masculine identity, where *mardanegi* (manliness) is a metaphor for courage, generosity, honor, humanity, and rectitude. Making a parody of Iranian manliness, the song is about Iranian men's failure and incompetence. Even Rostam, the mythical legend of ancient Iran and the allegory of Iranian masculinity, is parodied. Najafi sings that, if Rostam were alive today, he would probably be a "drug addict," a "taxi-driver in exile," a "cowardly conservative," or a "traitor." Interestingly, the young visual artist Siamak Filizadeh also creates a parody of the epic hero Rostam in his collages of photography and graphic design in *Rostam 2: The Return*, showing a Hollywoodish caricature of the epic legend and an allegory of Iranian manliness.

Biband o bari

A frequently heard term used by the older generations when they talk about the 60-generation is *biband o bar*. The term literally means "without bond" and "without belonging." The term refers to licentiousness, disrespect, abandonment, and rejection of cultural values and norms by young people. In the official discourse, the term is used synonymously with anomie, such as "sexual anomie," "ethical anomie," or "social anomie." *Biband o bari* of youth, associated with the "ethical crisis," is seen as an indicator of self-alienation and inauthenticity. While the officials blame the West for misleading and intoxicating the minds of the young, the parental generation blames young people for incompetence, irresponsibility, egoism, arrogance, and laziness.

Like anomie, the term *biband o bari* is related to a lack of norms and absence of clear-cut standards. The 60-generation has grown up with double normative ethics and value systems, which in most cases oppose and conflict with each other. They are caught between two institutions, the state and the family, both of which impose their own norms and values. The state interferes not only in the education but also in the upbringing of children to construct an ideal citizen according to an Islamic model. The school and the family transmit contradictory norms. The interpretation of Islamic values, norms, and rules by parents is often quite different from the official one. Thus, urban middle-class young people have lived a double life: one "inside," situated in the domestic sphere, and the other "outside" in accordance with the reigning social order. Consequently, the state has created a break, a clash between what children learn at home and in school (Azadarmaki 1389/2010: 160). The school thus became a battlefield for the state and the family over children's identity and loyalty. Parents taught their children the dichotomy between indoor and outdoor cultures, their different roles, and the importance of keeping the distance between them. Parents and children assisted each other to lie, to conceal, to say and do something else in public.

A twenty-six-year-old female student recounted:

My father often drank Whisky but he never mentioned its name for us, he called it *noushabeh* [soft drink]. When we got older he told us that he did so because he had heard that teachers used to ask kids in schools about what their parents did at home. We have been instructed to lie to everyone. We are a liar generation. We have been taught to lie in school to our teachers to protect our families.

A twenty-three-year-old male engineer had a similar story:

Our problem is that we cannot trust anyone. We are suspicious and cynical about everything. This comes from the duality of our lives. We pretend all the time. We are all the time preparing lies to avoid problems.

And a young female art student said:

You should always change things, names, everything to protect yourself. You have to hide things from others and keep your personal life separate from your social life. You have to always be vigilant. It gradually becomes a habit.

The 60-generation has carried the burden of the mutual mistrust of the family and the state. They became a field on which the dichotomization of the public and private could be played out. Many parents I talked to believe that this dichotomy makes the young "confused" and makes them *dou shakhsiati*, have dual characters. The term frequently heard in conversations is *dou roie*, "two-facedness." A young man told me in a sad voice, "Here no one is what you see." Almost all the young people I talked to mentioned this dichotomy as a major cause of stress and anxiety in their daily lives. They felt not only the responsibility of keeping the distinction between the public and the private accurately and carefully but also the burden of bearing the feelings of duplicity and hypocrisy. As one of my interlocutors put it, "We do not believe in anything anymore. Our generation doesn't have any norms. The old norm is gone, and nothing replaced it."

Women in Art Vignette

The so-called *biband o bar* youth are stereotypically represented not only in the official discourse but also by young writers and artists. Homa Arkani, born in 1983, is an artist whose pop-art paintings illustrate young women's "identity crisis." Her exhibition "Share Me" (2011) depicts the young generation's "dreams and agony." In Arkani's paintings, young urban women are "unauthentic," grotesque, and ridiculous figures, lost between local realities and global norms. Saghar Daeeri and Shirin Aliabadi are also artists who focus on young women's "identity crisis" in their paintings and art photography. I will discuss Daeeri's interesting grotesque illustrations of young women in the public spaces in Chapter 4. Born in 1973, Aliabadi presents in her series *The Miss Hybrid* (2007) cartoonish images of young women caught between

Western ideas of female beauty and the local aesthetics of female modesty. The young women pose in dyed blond hair, wear light-colored contact lenses, and have band-aids on their noses, indicating plastic surgery. Both Arkani's and Aliabadi's art show the hybrid and unfixed character of young women's identity. While the young women in their works are viewed as artificial, grotesque, and absurd, their art also illustrates the suppressed desires, frustration, anxieties and hopes of the 60-generation.

Lack of trust in others leads to vanishing social capital among Iranians. The young generation has lost trust in the state and is disappointed in the family. What is referred to as *biband o bari* is a consequence of decreased social capital, eroding family influence, and rejection of official moral codes. An anomic situation, in Durkheim's view, is the consequence of rapid social changes, which break down social norms and values. Neither the norms designed and dictated by the state nor those by the family match youthful desires and goals. This mismatch is how Robert Merton defined anomie. According to him, anomie emerges when there are discrepancies between what the larger society requires and the individual condition: "Anomie is then conceived as a breakdown in the cultural structure, occurring particularly when there is an acute disjunction between the cultural norms and goals and the socially structured capacities of members of the group to act in accord with them" (Merton 1968: 216). Merton saw the paradox of the American Dream, a cultural structure that encourages people toward upward social mobility, hindered by the social structures. This is what young Iranians are facing.

First, the cultural goals of the Revolution are out of reach for young people. They have grown up with images and imagined lifestyles throughout their years in school, broadcast by the media promising welfare, a stable life cycle, equal distribution of wealth, and social justice. More than three decades after the Revolution, the promises have faded away. The young generation are left to their own devices, and, far from the promises of the Revolution they face a precarious society with a high rate of corruption, increasing class differences, family breakups, mass unemployment, social injustice, financial insecurity, and gender inequalities. The class gap has never been so wide, conspicuous, and visible as it is today. Moreover, the expansion of higher education created expectations for good job opportunities. Among young Iranians there is a situation similar to what Pierre Bourdieu calls "diploma inflation": "The disparity between the aspirations that the educational system produces and the opportunities it really offers is a structural reality" (Bourdieu 1984: 143). Second, young Iranians are exposed to "global cultural goals," depicting "the right to youthfulness," transmitted by digital media and diasporic or other connections. While the cultural goals, either of the Revolution or from transnational sources, seem to be available, they are inaccessible to a majority of young people.

The normlessness and the failure of the society to regulate desires, goals, and goal-achievement push the society into "dejection and pessimism," as Durkheim wrote: "To pursue a goal which is by definition unattainable is to condemn oneself to a state of perpetual unhappiness" (1951: 248). Anomie, as result of the conflict between value systems, leads in some degree to uneasiness and a sense of separation from the society. A huge survey in 2007 among young Tehranis between fifteen and twenty-nine showed an "alarming" high degree (54 percent) of anomie among young people. The survey claimed that in this situation young Iranians feel a break between themselves and society (Shiyani and Mohammadi 1386/2007). In the official discourse, the main "threats" due to the normlessness are "intense individualism," "nihilism," "monetary mentality" (success at any cost), and "purposelessness" (Azadarmaki 1389/2010: 163). In contrast to the official discourse, which attempts to individualize social problems, what is called *biband o bari* is a consequence of the structural discrimination of young people in the labor market and in political life, reinforcing their alienation and distance from mainstream society.

Life in Literature—A Literary Vignette

Pochgarai, nihilism, is believed to be proliferating among young Iranians. Nihilism, alienation, and aimlessness are reflected in a new literary genre, known as *adabiyat-e apartemani*, (apartment literature), written mostly by young writers. The genre focuses on relationships between women and men in a middle-class, urban setting. Older generation literary critics have criticized the novels for their poor language and literary quality. However, the genre, popular among young readers, portrays characters and a predicament many young people recognize and identify with. Novels such as *Yekshanbeh* by Araz Barseghiyan (1390/2011), *Shab-e momken* by Mohammad Hassan Shahsavari (1388/2009), *Bazdam* by Anita Yarmohammadi (1393/2014), and *Negaran nabash* by Mahsa Mohebali (1388/2009) are the most interesting and controversial examples of this genre.

Mohebali's short novel *Negaran nabash* deals with 60-generation's Tehran. It depicts a city constantly shaken by small earthquakes, with the looming threat of a major quake any time soon. The city is drowned in chaos and people are desperate to escape. The main character, Shadi (which ironically means joyfulness), is a young woman and also a drug addict. While her family prepare for evacuation, Shadi walks through the streets of the city in search of drugs. She is a rebel without a cause; she represents a group that rejects what her parents' generation stood for. Unlike the previous generation who fought for an idea, her generation have no plan or political aim other than to take over the city, claiming their rights to it. To avoid having to wear a veil and to be able to move freely in public places, she cuts her hair and dresses like a man. Following Shadi around the city, the reader experiences Tehran through constant shocks and collisions. The story also depicts the bizarre relations between children and parents and between brothers and sisters. Like the city, the institution of the family is collapsing. And while Tehran collapses, the police are trying to pretend that nothing has happened, declaring on the loud-speaker, "Do not be afraid! Everything is under control." Those in power pretend they are in control of the situation. However, they know very well that the young generation will change everything and that it is too late to stop or control this mass. And when the young take over, nothing will be the same. In addition to the metaphor of the youth revolt, the novel hints at a bleak reality. Tehran is one of the world's most earthquake-threatened cities. According to experts, the city will in the near future be almost totally destroyed by an earthquake of magnitude 7 or higher. With constant references to an expected earthquake, *Negaran nabash*, literally "don't worry," is a worrying read about a Tehran moving into battle against an inevitable apocalyptic future.

Anita Yarmohammadi's *Bazdam* is another short novel that portrays a group of friends who belong to the 60-generation. In their early thirties, they all are struggling with existential precariousness. Their destinies are exile from home(land), death, failure, divorce, infidelity, and self-destruction. One is asylum seeker in Europe, one has committed suicide, one isolates himself and becomes drug addict, one suffers from her marriage, one is preparing to migrate. The novel illustrates the predicament many young Iranians find themselves in: detachment from family and homeland, lack of future prospects in Iran, and damaged social capital.

Delayed Adulthood

One aspect of "normlessness" and "purposelessness" is disruption in the stable and safe transformation from youth to adulthood. For a majority of the

60-generation, adulthood has been suspended and postponed. The 60-generation has been forced into a prolonged transition from school to work and family formation. Protracted unemployment, underemployment, delayed marriage, and financial dependence on their parents have resulted in a delayed transition from youth to adulthood. Not being able to start an independent life, young Iranians experience powerlessness. The state, social institutions, schools, universities, labor market, and family have failed to assist young people in their transition. More and more, Iranian youth are caught in "waithood," a period between adolescence and adulthood; the prospects of leaving this situation look very bleak. The basis for this delay is young people's financial insecurity.

During the first half of the 2010s, the Iranian people have experienced a critical economic situation. Highly dependent on oil export, the Iranian economy is vulnerable. International sanctions, which have drastically intensified since the late 2000s, reached a climax in the fall of 2013. Women and youth were hardest hit by the economic crisis and the international embargo. Foreign investments were reduced drastically, and capital flight from Iran has been massive. According to an official source, "as much as $300bn may have left the country since Ahmadinejad was elected" (Mather 2009: 73). Furthermore, internal challenges such as high inflation , unemployment, and domestic economic mismanagement have caused a severe financial crisis. Like other countries, poor and young people suffer the most from the economic downturn. The high inflation of more than 29 percent in 2008 (official data from Iran's Central Bank, quoted in Mather 2009: 67) has hit Iranians who struggle with the rising cost of basic needs in their daily lives. Other independent sources declare that the real rate of inflation is slightly over 40 percent.[5] In the second half of 2012, Iranian currency lost its worth by more than 100 percent against hard currencies. The increase of foreign currency affects all other costs inside the country. While I write these words in June 2016, international sanctions are lifted, but there are no hopeful prospects for a better economical situation in near future.

The situation for young people in the labor market is critical. While the working age group (fifteen to sixty-four) increased from 56 percent in 1375/1996 to 71 percent in 1390/2011, job opportunities have not increased. In 2010, twice as many entered the labor market as a decade ago (Salehi-Isfahani 2010: 9). Unemployment has soared, particularly among young people. Youth unemployment has been double the general unemployment rate since the mid-2000s. According to official statistics, overall unemployment in

2011 was slightly over 12 percent, while for young people it was 26.5 percent. The gap between general unemployment and youth unemployment increased in 2010 and 2011.[6] Up to 70 percent of all unemployed people are under thirty. In urban areas, unemployment of young people is up to 35 percent. Unemployment has hit women hardest: the number of unemployed women fifteen to twenty-five is double that among young men in the same age group.[7] Indeed, the unemployment rate for young women has reached 50 percent (Salhi-Isfahani 2010: 12).

Nor is the situation better in the case of educated young people. The number of unemployed educated youth was reported to have reached four million in the fall of 2013, and the absence of an active and targeted labor market policy could result in doubling number in the near future.[8] But the official statistics can be misleading. To keep the apparent rate of unemployment low, the definition of "employment" was changed during Ahmadinejad's presidency: according to this new definition, an employed person is an individual who works at least one hour per week. Of course, lower-income groups suffer even more from increasing unemployment. While the rate of unemployed young people from the middle class has remained more or less unchanged, it has increased by 50 percent among lower-income groups (Salhi-Isfahani 2010: 16). To have access to social capital, be skilled, and have the "right" cultural capital have been crucial in surviving the crises in the labor market. Educated young people with an urban middle-class background are reluctant to take jobs seen to be "low" status. Undesirable jobs are unskilled, poorly paid, or manual occupations usually carried out by stigmatized groups, such as migrants from the rural areas or from Afghanistan. A "decent" and "honorable" occupation is more about social relations than the salary. Being associated with "low-status" workers is what makes a job undesirable in the eyes of educated, middle-class young people.

Nader is twenty-six. With a degree in civil engineering from a four-year university program, he moved from Shiraz to Tehran in the fall of 2012 for a temporary job in a construction company because seeking jobs in his hometown was a waste of time. He had tried for two years until his grandmother found a temporary job for him through her cousin who was a manager in a construction company. His employment is informal, meaning he is not insured, gets no pension, and is not protected by a labor union; nor is his work officially documented. Nader is, however, pleased to have a job because "Being at home day and night and waiting makes you crazy! Here I am at least busy and do not have negative thoughts." Nader's salary is around US$350 per month, in his words "not even US$100 more than what an unskilled worker earns." Half his salary goes for rent. He can barely make ends meet without his parents' almost monthly economic assistance. To be twenty-six and dependent on his parents is embarrassing for him, particularly since he has two younger brothers at home whose university studies put a huge financial burden on his parents' household. Nader's mother is a housewife and his father is, like himself, an engineer. But unlike Nader, the father could build a relatively comfortable life for his family of five. Nader's parents own a large apartment, have a car, and have been able to pay for all their children's education. What his father has managed to achieve with his salary is unthinkable for Nader. When he was twenty-six, Nader's father had his first child, Nader. What remains of Nader's salary after the rent is paid is barely enough to survive in the megacity of Tehran, let alone put aside money for savings or marriage. To own a place to live or a car or to pay for his own marriage is an unreachable dream for him and a majority of young Iranians in his situation. The case of Nader is an example of downward class mobility among middle-class children who cannot afford the life their parents had. Nader complains all the time about how his quality of life has deteriorated since he moved to Tehran. He says that he now is forced to share a flat with people from the "lower" classes. Downward social mobility among middle-class youth is not uncommon. There is a large group of educated young people caught in protracted unemployment or underemployment, for whom the standard of living they grew up with in their parental home is beyond reach.

The endless waiting for the first job in the mainstream job market pushes many young people into the informal labor sector. Estimates of the total size of the informal labor market vary depending on how this market is defined. Iranian scholars believe that it comprises between 30 and 35 percent of total labor market (see Amuzegar 2003; Bahramitash 2013). The informal labor market becomes the only option for young people, particularly in rural areas like my village in the Bakhtiari region, a small village with not more than sixty households. Throughout my fieldwork (since 1999), not a single young person living in the village has had a job in the mainstream labor market. Everyone has been irregularly employed or been working in the informal sector. In many households, not only young people but also their parents have been working in the informal sector throughout their lives. Generally, employment opportunities in the informal labor market are short contract jobs, and dismissal without notice is a constant danger: a common tactic by employers to keep wages down while limiting the employee's possibilities for protest or negotiating better conditions. This situation restricts young people's mobility. Working in the informal sector simply entrenches their marginalized status. Informal work means that the individuals are generally isolated from the mainstream labor market. As seen with Nader, they are not insured or members of labor unions, leading to increased vulnerability. They do not benefit from an employee pension either. Furthermore, since their work experiences remain undocumented, employers do not give them references. It also means they will be marginalized from the networks that are necessary to find permanent employment in Iran. The precarious situation of the 60-generation in the labor market and their financial insecurity means a "delay" in marriageability. Statistics show a slowdown in the increase of the rate of marriage and even a decrease in marriage rates since 1390/2011 (see Table 3).

The cohort of the unmarried is increasing in number. The percentage of unmarried young people between twenty-five and twenty-nine has increased from 20 to 40 percent for men and from 8 to 25 percent for women. The difficulty of starting an independent life disturbs the transition from youth to adulthood. "Adulthood" has been reconstructed. While adolescents are treated as adults by the law, young adults are treated as children since they are seen as socially dysfunctional for failing to build a family, to be "producers," and subsequently to be optimal consumers. Accordingly, the conventional linear notion of the transition from adolescent to adulthood is interrupted.

The proportion of men between twenty-five and twenty-nine who lived with their parents increased from 50 percent to 75 percent between 1984 and 2005. Among women of the same age, the figures increased even more in the same period: from 20 percent to almost 50 percent (Salehi-Isfahani and Egel 2007: 7). Not being able to leave their parental home, one of the crucial events

Table 3. Statistics of Marriage, 2007–2014

	Number of marriages	Increase or decrease (%)
1386/2007	841107	
1387/2008	881592	4.8 increase
1388/2009	890208	1 increase
1389/2010	891627	1 increase
1390/2011	874792	2 decrease
1391/2012	829968	5 decrease
1392/2013	774513	6.7 decrease
1393/2014	724324	6.5 decrease

Source: National Organization for Civil Registration, 1394/2015.

in the transition to adulthood (Billari et al. 2001), postpones young people's emancipation. They are stuck between two social positions, between two stages of life. The protracted transition from youth to adulthood has pushed them into the predicament of "waithood." The consequence of protracted unemployment, an unmarried lifestyle, *belataklifi*, suspension, the dependence on one's parents is that the time of being "young" has become longer. Youth seems to be no longer a transitional stage but an indefinite position of *not-becoming*. Parviz, the central character in the film of the same name, embodies the protracted *belataklifi*. *Parviz* (by Majid Barzegar, 2012) is a film about the tragedy of the long-drawn-out liminality in today's Iran. Parviz is a middle-aged man who still lives in his father's home in a residential complex in Tehran. He has never been employed, never married, and has no social network. He is an asocial type who spends his days doing nothing except some housework. We often see him alone in *belataklifi*, in situations of uselessness, purposelessness, and idleness. He seems stuck in an endless waithood. But waiting for what? The real tragedy begins when his father decides to marry, and Parviz has to move out. Unable to cope with the difficulties he is faced with in his new life outside his father's house, Parviz becomes an outcast. The rest of the film is his revenge on society. It is a dark film that excellently depicts the devastating consequences of being caught in prolonged liminality that causes a disconnection between individuals and the larger society.

A Waiting Generation

Throughout my fieldwork, every young person (between eighteen and thirty) whom I interviewed "was waiting." They were waiting for employment, *moafi* (exemption from military service), marriage, emigration, a good business, or political change. Like young educated men in India (Jeffrey 2010), Iranian youth imagine themselves as "just waiting." The most common answers I got from young people to my question of what they were doing were "I wait now to see what happens later" or "What else can we do but wait?"

There are two words for waiting used by Iranians, *entezar* and *sabr*. Originally an Arabic word, *entezar* has connotations of expectation, anticipation, waiting with hope. In Shiite Islam, *entezar* is used in relation to the "messianic waiting" for the return of the Twelfth or Hidden Imam. Twelve Imam-Shiite Muslims believe that the final imam has been in occultation since the ninth century. The Imam Mehdi, also known as the "the ruler of time" (*sahib-e zaman*), is the ultimate savior of humankind. In Shiite theology, the time we live in is called the era of waiting: waiting for redemption. Thus *sabori*, the noble act of waiting and suffering, is regarded as a characteristic of a good Shiite. This messianic waiting is linked to *sabr*, also an Arabic word meaning patience, endurance, self-control and forbearance. *Sabori* means suffering patiently, and *sabor* is the one who endures pain and suffering. Similarly, the word *patience* comes from the Latin word *pati*, which means "to suffer, to endure" (Auyero 2012). *Sabori* (waiting while suffering) is valued, praised, and noble in the Iranian culture. In *Young and Defiant in Tehran* (Khosravi 2008), I wrote about the notion of *dard* (pain) among Iranians and how it is associated with inner purity, conscience, and responsibility. In a similar way, *sabori*, patience, and endurance have connotations of self-sacrificing, generosity, and virtue. Waiting is praised and encouraged in Iranian culture and Persian classic literature. Common sayings and expressions such as "Gar sabr koni ze ghore halva sazi"; "Sabr khob chiziye"; "Shahnameh akherash khosh ast"; "Jojeha ro akhar-e paiz mishmarand"; and "In niz bogzarad" all underscore the value and significance of waiting.

Since the Revolution of 1979, waithood has become politicized. The Islamic state promotes a "culture of waiting" (*farhang-e entezar*) of the Shiite messianic worldview. Moreover, to keep people waiting hopefully has been part of the mechanism of domination. The authorities have encouraged young people to practice the noble act of waiting (*sabr va sabori*). Youth usually is associated with lack of *sabori* and an inability to wait; young people have no patience.[9] The religious and political officials, however, endorse waiting and endurance.[10] Moralizing and politicizing waiting are usually intensified during religious rituals; "Ramadan is the best time for strengthening young people's patience."[11] To keep people waiting with a sense of hope became the main characteristic of Ahmadinejad's presidency, a period of "promises": eliminating unemployment, *Maskan-e mehr* (a housing project for young people), distributing wealth in form of "justice shares" (*saham-e edalaat*), and a flourishing economy. He always included the promise of a better future in his official speeches. However, by the summer of 2013, the last year of his second term in office, few of Ahmadinejad's promises had been fulfilled.

Waiting in Queues

However, the politicization of waiting goes back to the early 1980s, when the lives of Iranians were organized by and with queues (*safs*). A scarcity of almost everything during the war forced people to stand for long hours in various queues (lines) to get subsidized items and rations. Standing in long, slow-moving, tedious queues became part of daily life in Iran. The 60-generation grew up seeing adults around them spending a large part of their free time in queues for various necessities: food, petroleum, clothing, or other household items. People conceptualized life as the logic of queues. Queues have become one of the main elements in forming Iranians' post-revolutionary subjectivity. Waiting, whether for a trivial thing or an important decision, produces "the subjective effects of dependency and subordination" (Auyero 2011: 8). The queues also manifested the state's sovereignty and people's dependence on the state. Patiently waiting in queues, Iranians became "patients of the state." While queues became gradually shorter and shorter after the war, the 60-generation today are still waiting, primarily in queues, for university admission, employment, housing, loans, marriage, or emigration.

Farhad, a twenty-five-year-old man who suffers from chronic physical ailments, has been struggling to get his exemption from military service for more than two years. Encountering inefficient bureaucracy, he has spent countless hours in queues and has been sent back and forth between different offices:

> No one gives you an answer. They just say, "Come back tomorrow or next week." They just want to take bribes. I am upset because I have all the documents they ask for, but they still send me around. You cannot complain. They can just put your dossier under hundreds of others, which means several years waiting.

The policy of waiting generates corruption. Keeping people waiting is a common tactic used by bureaucratic gatekeepers for extortion. Connections and bribes can move a file to languish in "negligence or intentionally withheld from circulation file" (Hull 2012: 156). In their encounters with the state, young Iranians do not act as citizens with rightful claims, but as meek clients waiting for the state's mercy. Waiting for something coming from the state (education, loans, jobs, exemption from military service) young Iranians are turned, in Auyero's words, into "patients of the state" (2012).

Waiting is an inescapable part of life in modern societies. The act of waiting is also a common feature of bureaucracy; when in contact with organizations, individuals wait for their turn and officials' decisions. In the context of this study, waiting is a particular experience of time. It is a manipulation of other's time. Waiting is expecting something coming from others. Waiting, as Pierre Bourdieu excellently puts it, is a way of experiencing the effect of power (Bourdieu 2000: 228). Waiting is usually something for the less powerful groups in society. In his ethnographic study of poor people's waiting practices in Buenos Aires, Javiar Auyero (2012) shows how waiting—for a trivial thing or an important decision—produces the subjective effects of dependency and subordination. Marginalized and unprivileged groups, to use Vincent Crapanzano's words, "wait for something, anything, to happen. They are caught in the peculiar, the paralytic, time of waiting" (1985: 43). Waiting generates feelings of "powerlessness and vulnerability" (45). Another consequence of waiting is the feeling that one is not fully in command of one's life. To be kept waiting for a long time "is to be the subject of an assertion that one's own time (and therefore, one's social worth) is less valuable than the time and worth of the one who imposes the wait" (Schwartz 1974: 856).

In modern societies, people approach time in terms of how it can most efficiently be used. Time is associated with success and money. Hence, waiting symbolizes waste, emptiness, and uselessness. There is a discrepancy between the common social goals in modern societies (speed, mobility, the idea that "time is money") and the reality of the lives of individuals forced to a prolonged act of waiting. Consequently, prolonged waiting among the young, like the experience of waiting for other marginalized groups such as the poor, the unemployed, or asylum seekers, can result in a weakening of the individual's ability to connect to the larger society. Waiting is usually an experience equaling what Victor Turner (1969) calls liminality. Waiting is inherent in liminality (Sutton et al. 2011). Liminality is the transitory stage between two social positions, between two stages of life. People are caught in a position of betwixt and between structures. Accordingly, the individual's liminal status is socially and structurally ambiguous. The loss of social status and role in society results in social invisibility, which in turn generates vulnerability. For Turner, there are similarities among liminality, marginality, and inferiority. Liminal persons are usually in an inferior position and are socially and economically marginalized. When liminality is turned into a protracted waiting, the very structure of social life is temporarily suspended. Accordingly, young find themselves in a situation Ghassan Hage calls "stuckedness" (2009: 7), characterized by invisibility, immobility, uncertainty, and arbitrariness. The ambiguity about the duration of waiting generates a sense of uncertainty, shame, depression, and anxiety. Waiting "is demeaning, reeks of helplessness and shows we are not fully in command of ourselves" (O'Brien 1995: 177, quoted in Auyero 2012: 27). Young people express their feelings of being stuck in "waithood" in terms of agony, hopelessness, and dependence. When youth are shaped by waithood, there is a widespread sense of the absence of youthfulness. A common complaint by young people is that they have not enjoyed their youthfulness. They have missed the chance to "do youthfulness" and instead "got aged fast." Time for many young people is as experienced broken.

The broken time and feeling of stuckedness are best reflected in the emic term *belataklifi*, protracted liminality. *Belataklifi* or to be *belataklif* is the most common word used by young people when they describe their situation. It is difficult to translate this term literally. The prefix *bela* means without and *taklif* means purpose, duty, or function. The term expresses a feeling of uncertainty, suspension, rolelessness, and purposelessness. It also expresses boredom. *Belataklifi* is very similar to what marginalized young people in the Philippines experienced, encapsulated in the emic term *buryong*, a predicament of uncertainty, boredom, and waiting for nothing. Steffen Jensen in his study of youth in the Philippines uses the local term *buryong* as the symptom of a present projected hopelessly into the future (Jensen 2014). *Belataklifi* can also be compared to *tufush* among Saudi youth:

> Rather than a psychological void or ennui, *tufush* suggested a feeling of social impotence that overwhelmed ordinary Saudis when they recognized the incommensurable distance between the economic opportunities of Riyadh and their own condition of unemployment or low income, broken families, and poor housing. (Menoret 2014: 58)

The feeling of being stuck with no prospect to realize their dreams has led to frustration and boredom. Rather than having to do with monotony or lack of inspiration, boredom strikes when "something expected does not occur" (Spacks 1995: 5). Like young urban Ethiopians (Mains 2007), Indian youth (Jeffrey 2010), and Filipino youth (Jensen 2014) young Iranians are stuck in *belataklifi* and suffer from modern boredom. Drawing on Goodstein (2005), Mains describes modern boredom as a "sense that the actual reality of life is not equal to what one had imagined. Boredom is the feeling that one not only has too much time but also that that time is not meaningful because it is not passed in the progressive manner that one has come to expect" (2007: 667).

A related term to *belataklifi* is *allaf*, a contemptuous term that refers to a person who does nothing, a loiterer. Declaring that there were millions of *allaf* in the country, the government in 2015 blamed youth for their own *belataklifi*,[12] A large survey conducted in Tehran and several other cities in 2013 among 8,740 young people between seventeen and twenty-six claimed that "67 percent of young people have no clear aim for their future and are in a sort of behavioral *belataklifi*." The researchers concluded with a moralizing warning that *belatakilfi* could be a threat for the future of the country since it could cause a decline in ethical norms, the law, and religion.[13] *Belataklifi* is also associated with the absence of rules and order. Due to their position, liminal individuals are unmanageable. They are invisible, and therefore regarded as dangerous, inauspicious, and polluting (Turner 1969: 108). The stigmatization of the 60-generation as an uncontrollable, unmanageable, and unpredictable mass threatening the purity of the social body and the well-being of the nation, as will be elaborated in the next chapter, was followed by the strategy to govern the young by criminalizing them.

Waiting is costly. Not all young people can afford to wait. To cope with suspension, young people from middle-class families spend a lot of money on courses (language, music, art, sport, or computer), travel, or just hanging out. Attending university is also a way to avoid *belataklifi*. A large number of waiting youth pay high fees to attend the semi-private universities run by the Free Islamic University. Hundreds of thousands of students are trapped in a game of education, which means high costs for the family and low prospects for finding a job since a university degree does not automatically guarantee employment. One of every twelve unemployed Iranians holds a university degree. There is an increasing number of unemployed educated young people, almost four million in the fall of 2013. Protracted education (obtaining several university degrees, for those who can afford it) is the only option to avoid *belataklifi*. I have heard from many students at different levels that they are at university because there is nothing else to do. Waiting is usually considered a sign of passivity and lack of agency. However, in contrast to what young people told me about their "passive waiting," I understood them to be relatively active in their waiting. Studying at university, hanging around on street corners, going to coffee shops, networking, engaging in endless discussions about life, politics, education, emigration, and jobs, they were not only creating their own youth culture but also performing citizenship.

Balataklifi has become a theme in art and literature. It is best illustrated in Mitra Tabrizian's staged photography "Tehran" (2006). The huge photographs show people in an urban setting who "appear to be going about their daily activities. . . . their direction uncertain, their purpose blurred . . . waiting for something to happen but it never does" (Irving 2009: 44–45). The novel *Betallaat* by Ehsan Norouzi (1386/2007) tells the story of the predicament of waiting. Difficult to translate, the title signifies meaninglessness, emptiness, and vacuity. Belonging to the 60-generation, the author tells the story of his peers. The novel is set in a university in an unknown city covered in smog and with trash. In a surrealistic style, it depicts a melancholic ambiance of waithood. Young men stand in queues for exemptions from military service, and the only reason they go to university is to postpone that compulsory duty. Stuck in waithood, their time and life is wasted. *They* are wasted. The novel is apocalyptic; *betallaat* is omnipresent and has penetrated every aspect of life. There is no rescue.

Suspension and Precarity

In the liminal state of *belataklifi*, in which one has nothing to do but kill time and loiter, the individual's status is socially and structurally ambiguous, resulting in invisibility and vulnerability. Wishes and plans are deferred. The nation's young are marginalized spatially, temporally, and socially. A survey among twelve thousand young Tehranis in 2009 indicated that almost 50 percent of them experienced "social rejection." Conducted by the Ministry of Sport and Youth, the survey showed that the most vulnerable individuals were those between twenty-five and twenty-nine, particularly young women. "Social rejection" includes exclusion from the labor market and social participation. These young people do not have access to "their civil rights such as rights to education, marriage, housing, health, cultural activities, and social participation."[14] Unemployment, the inability to start a family, and boredom generate disappointment and frustration. Many young people, particularly men who are supposed to support not only their wives and children but also their elderly parents, see themselves as failures. Navid, a twenty-eight-year-old man, educated but unemployed, lives with his parents who still provide him with pocket money. Finding himself in this situation means not being seen as a human being but as burden: "Here you are nobody. They look at you not as a human but as a load."

While *belataklifi* generates shame and a sense of guilt for some, it also more seriously engenders despair and *pochgarai*, nihilism, causing anti-social behavior among young Iranians. The dependence on one's parents, protracted unemployment, a failure to form a family, poor prospects for a better future, political instability, an international embargo, and the risks of war have reduced young people's self-confidence and have resulted in mental depression. A recurrent warning in reports and surveys is the rise in the number of young Iranians who suffer from depression and "mental disorder."[15] According to the Mental Health Office of the Ministry of Health, some 24 percent of the total population suffers from "mental disorders."[16]

The number of suicides has increased, as has drug addiction, crime, and violent behavior in public spaces. The rate of suicide showed an increase almost five times between 1984 and 2004.[17] Furthermore, official sources estimate that there are over 3.6 million drug addicts in Iran.[18] Almost half of them are under twenty-nine, the average age being twenty-one.[19] The UN World Drug Report mentions Iran as having the highest proportion of opium addicts in the world (UNODC 2010). Similarly, consumption of alcohol has reached an alarming level among young people, according to a police announcement in the summer of 2012.[20] Another social issue is increasing public violence. Experts state that young Tehranis have turned into "a bomb of violence."[21] They relate the expansion of public violence to unemployment, police violence, joylessness, and "mental disorder."[22] Criminality and prostitution have also been increasing drastically. In 2012, it was estimated that more than 250,000 individuals were imprisoned every year in Iran and that the prison population increased by 20 percent annually.[23] Poverty is the preeminent reason behind increasing criminality among young people. While robbery constitutes 47.4 percent of the offenses committed by male delinquents, "prostitution" is most common among female delinquents. A report from 1388/2009 showed that half of those who received a prison sentence were between fifteen and twenty-nine. The same report showed that between twenty-seven thousand and thirty-three thousand young people between nineteen and twenty-five entered prison every year.[24]

In an attempt to decrease violent behavior in public places and other youth-related problems, the State Welfare Organization of Iran (Sazman-e behzisti-ye keshvar) launched a new project in 2011 called Ozhanse ejtemai (Social Emergency). Established in about 150 cities, the service includes several vans manned with staff and a telephone hot line for mobile social services driving around cities. Psychologists and social workers offer mobile assistance to young people with "social problems."[25] Interestingly, the authorities attempted to depoliticize the issue and blamed both the increases in depression and violent behavior among young people on air pollution in large cities, particularly in Tehran.[26] On the other hand, there is a consensus among Iranians that the main reason behind increasing criminality among young people is *belataklifi* and *bikari*. *Bikari* means both "unemployment" and "idleness" and is believed to cause either *biarri* (indolence) or *bimari* (ailment).

Young Iranians are caught in a radical precarity. Political and social chaos, financial hardship, violence against women (verbal and physical harassment in public places, domestic violence, gang rapes), police brutality, corruption, social injustice, threats of war, living in a "state of exception" since the Revolution—all these problems more or less make the present unbearable. Not surprisingly, people find themselves between a nostalgic past and a utopian future. For young Iranians, the present is absent, forgotten. They are both waiting for something to happen in the future and looking nostalgically back to find relief in accounts of the past. Paradoxically, under the theocratic rule, a pre-Islamic Persian renaissance has emerged among young people, who increasingly express an interest in pre-Islamic Iran, a time in history when the country was a great empire. The increasing interest in pre-Islamic Persian culture and pre-revolutionary times indicates a conscious dissociation from the present situation in Iran, understood in the global context as "isolated," "backward," "belittled." Pre-revolutionary time is often nostalgically "glorified." I heard this joke frequently in Iran in the summer of 2012: After the Revolution, we have now four tenses in the Persian language: past, present, future, and the Shah's time. The "Shah's time" refers to the nostalgic and "imagined" time prior to the Revolution, particularly the late 1960s and the 1970s—a period of oil dollars, flourishing urban popular culture, and a hopeful future. It appears to young people as a time of joyfulness, with people living the "good life." Hoping for rescue in the future and finding pleasure in past memories, the young lose their sense of the present. As Nadeem Malik shows in his study on waiting in socially unstable Pakistan, "the present is absent and this absence is felt as helplessness, as an inability to set things right. People become indifferent to the present" (2009: 64).

Longing to Be Anywhere But Here

In the eyes of many young Iranians, for whom the future is somewhere else, migration has become the only way out of *belataklifi* for many young people. A recurrent topic discussed by youth is the question of leaving or staying. A survey conducted in the Fars province among 770 young people between eighteen and thirty showed that over 90 percent had a high interest in emigration (Moghadas and Sharfi 1388/2009). According to a report from the International Monetary Fund, between 150,000 and 180,000 young, educated people leave Iran each year, putting the country at the top of a list of ninety-one countries experiencing a brain drain (see Torbat 2002; see also Karimi and Gharaati 2013). Every year around half a million Iranians play the U.S. State Department Green Card lottery. Educated women make up 40 percent of those taking their chances. After the crackdown on the Green Movement, the emigration of the 60-generation intensified. Almost forty-five thousand left the country and sought asylum between 2009 and 2011.[27]

Kharej literally means "outside" or "abroad" but is mainly used to refer to the West. *Kharej* and its adjective form, *khareji*, carry connotations of high quality and standards. Consequently, this "geographical" hierarchy has put its mark on how to refer to the quality of commodities, education, service, lifestyle, and jobs. In a previous work (Khosravi 2008: 104–5) I showed how young Iranians link spatial distance to the idea of progress. Going to *kharej* has become synonymous with higher education, progress, and success. Life in Iran is associated with unstructured time, aimless waiting, and "lack." I often heard young people saying, "Inja hichi nist"—there is nothing here. When I asked them what they meant by *nothing*, they referred to jobs, a chance to build a life and a family, or the possibility to "do youthfulness." Another striking and common comment by young people is "There is no future here." There is a widespread feeling that the future is absent in Iran. "Future" is used synonymously with "progress," that is, "the expectations that the future will not be like one's past and that, instead, it will be qualitatively better" (Mains 2007: 665; see also Piot 2010 and Echeverri Zuluaga 2015). Similar to what Mains (2007) shows in his study among young urban men in Ethiopia or Chua (2014) in her book on Indian youth or Piot (2010) in his ethnography on Togo, in young Iranians' narrative, progress can be experienced through spatial movement. Complaints are frequently heard about how "backward" (*aqab mandeh*) Iran is compared with the *kharej* where everything is associated with "progress" (*pish raft*). A frequently heard comment about the time of the Revolution is that "the Revolution took Iran a hundred years back in time." The Persian word for *backward* literally means "staying behind," and the word for *progress* can be translated as "going forward." So spatial mobility or absence of mobility is directly linked to one's experience of time. The idea of progress, not least through education, is based on the expectations of a materially and qualitatively better future than experienced in the past and the present (Mains 2007). For many young Iranians, migration is understood not only as a geographical movement but also as a temporal journey "forward." While Iran is related to boredom and suspension (cf. Echeverri Zuluaga 2015), youth imagine *kharej* as elsewhere with a future. In contrast to Iran where one's capacities have been suppressed, *kharej* is also a place where one gets a chance to develop oneself.

A thirty-two-year-old female architect, unemployed and living with her parents, put it this way: "We want to have a better life, but it is not possible here. Now everyone is thinking about migration." A twenty-six-year-old man, an unemployed economist who also lives at home, stated, "We all are waiting for migration. We are forced to. How can we otherwise reach our aims and desires?" Thus, migration is seen as a way to escape the "absence of a future" in Iran. The spatial movement to *kharej* is believed to be a solution for their temporal immobility, *belataklifi*.

Conclusions

The 60-generation imagines and regards itself as stuck in an aimless "waithood." Unable to start an independent life, this group is trapped between different stages in life, failing to accomplish the transition from youth to adulthood. It has been delayed in the process of becoming an adult or, rather, is stuck in the condition of *not-becoming*. I have used the emic term *belataklifi* to explore the predicament of temporal immobility that youth and young adults face. To cope with *belataklifi*, middle-class youth enter an education game and move from one degree program to another while waiting for a job. Others are underemployed or trapped in the informal labor market. Vast unemployment and underemployment among young educated Iranians results in financial insecurity and, subsequently, the inability to build a family and an independent life, which cause a "collective disillusionment"—a consequence of "the structural mismatch between aspirations and real probabilities"

(Bourdieu 1984: 144). Dependent on their parents even in their late thirties, they suffer from a sense of shame and failure to achieve and follow the norms associated with a successful person. Young people find themselves in a race against time, with a sense of being "left behind" of what is assumed to be the "natural" rhythm of life. The protracted waiting as the condition of *belataklifi* makes young Iranians believe they have no control over their lives. Yet their waiting is collective. The predicament of waithood is what a whole generation is suffering from. It has become a "socially synchronised waiting" (Schubert 2009: 110). Thus, waiting for young Iranians has become a life stage itself. It is now a common social concern. Consequently, young people have created a culture of "timepass" (Jeffrey 2010) or an art of "killing time" (Ralph 2008; Mains 2007). However, young people respond differently to the predicament of *belataklifi*. Their reactions can be either extremely individual, seeking pleasure in the present with no concern about the past or the future, or expressed in a deep estrangement from the present, seeking refuge in a nostalgic past or an expectant future.

Unlike the general idea about how young people live, waithood is not merely a passive act of doing nothing. Waiting is performed. Through performing waithood, young Iranians construct a generational identity, exchange information, build networks, and construct youth cultures. Needless to mention, the performance of waithood varies according to class and gender. However, with the prolonged condition of liminality come precariousness and a sense of social inferiority, the feeling that young people's time and lives are worth less than those of others. The response by the authorities has been to blame the young for their *belataklifi*. Regarded as "unproductive" and a "burden," young people are believed to fail in exercising the role of a responsible, self-sufficient citizen; rather, they embody the "cultural invasion" orchestrated by the Western states as part of the "soft war." *Javan-harasi*, the fear of youth (ephebiphobia) characterizes the state's approach to Iranian youth, as will be shown ethnographically in the next chapter.

CHAPTER 3

EPHEBIPHOBIA, THE FEAR OF YOUTH

In June 2013, a graffiti painting in Ekbatan, a neighborhood in western Tehran with modern apartment buildings, caught my eyes: *Ma mojerm nistim!* (We are not criminals). The graffiti was written in black on a wall behind a school. A few months later when I went back to take photographs of the graffiti, I saw that two letters, written in red, had been added and changed the sentence to *Ma mojrem hastim!* (We are criminals). I had frequently heard young people saying, "Youth is a crime in Iran." *Javan* is the Persian word for "young," and *javani* means "youth" and "youthfulness." The approach to youth in Iranian society is ambiguous. One the one hand, *javani* is praised and hailed as the fruitful, dynamic, and innocent period in life, described with glorifying phrases such as season of beauties, time of opportunities. Nevertheless, youthfulness is at the same time perceived as a period of one's life characterized by carelessness and ignorance, when one is most vulnerable and exposed to immorality and vice. *Javani* is also often used synonymously to *khami* (rawness), referring to lack of experience. *Javani kardan* (literally, doing youth) is a popular expression in Persian and means being thoughtless and making mistakes. Like women, young people are seen to be more oriented toward passion (*nafs*) than intellect (*aql*). In Islam the self is thought of as conflicted between reason and passion. The former directs one toward God and a harmonious life, while the latter represents satanic forces. Although all individuals possess both, the capacity to develop reason is seen as stronger in adult men, while the impulse toward passion is held to be stronger in women and young people. Youth are all about passion; therefore, they have an inclination to commit crime (Khosravi 2008).

This reasoning has led to the criminalization of much of the youth culture, under the label *jorm-e farhangi* (literally, cultural crime). Since the 1970

Revolution young people have been seen stereotypically as law breakers unless proved otherwise. "Cultural crimes" are always reported in the media with images of young people, "improperly" veiled women, or "improperly" dressed men. As sin and crime became synonymous, the law penetrated the very core of young people's lives: how they dressed, whether they danced, with whom they slept, whom they looked at, and so forth. Young people are regarded as more vulnerable to *alodegi farhangi* or "cultural pollution," and since youth are driven by passion rather than reason, they are also thought to be the main target of *tahajom-e farhangi* (cultural invasion) by Western states. Consequently, sin is not only defined and codified in the law, but it has also taken on a political meaning. Expressions of youthfulness and parts of a youthful lifestyle are considered parts of the "soft war" orchestrated by the West. Although cultural crime is not exactly defined in the law, it constitutes any act deemed to be against "public chastity" and the country's Islamic principles. This lack of precision means that the application of the law regarding "cultural crimes" is left to the discretion of the police on the streets.

The result is that any act and performance of youthfulness can be seen as a crime/sin. Trivial acts such as street strolling are thought of as a "source of vice" and the "beginning of criminal behavior.[1] *Ab bazi* (playing with water) is another activity that has been criminalized. On 2 September 2011, a group of young Tehranis organized a water fight via Facebook in Ab va atash Park in northern Tehran. Almost one thousand young men and women gathered and started splashing water on each other with water guns and bottles. The police arrested several young people and charged them with violating Islamic principles, values and "social norms." Two years later, on 5 July 2013, more than five hundred young women and men gathered to throw water at each other in the Iranzamin Park in Karaj, a small town close to Tehran. The police detained fifty of the revelers. Accordingly, the majority of young Iranians are potential criminals. The number of what, in the judicial system, is defined as "crime" is now up to 1,740, and almost all carry a mandatory prison sentence.[2] Almost five million new cases enter the judicial system every year.[3] In some parts of the country, the number of cases has reached critical levels. For instance, according to juridical sources in Kerman province (with a total population of three million), 1,200,000 individuals are involved in various judicial processes—more than one third of the population.[4] In mid-June 2012, I read a newspaper report to a group of my interlocutors. Based on data from the Ministry of Justice, the report claimed that there were ten million pending cases in the judicial system.[5] A young man, an unemployed civil engineer, said,

With a population of seventy-five million, it means almost 15 percent have a case. Every one of them has on average ten people around himself/herself like brothers, sisters, wives, children, and parents. It means that all Iranians are involved or at least are affected by a judicial case.

Everyone laughed and started joking about how they had been subjected to the law. Two had been flogged for attending a mixed-sex party where they drank vodka. Another was once detained for being with his girlfriend, just driving around. Almost all women in the group had been repeatedly stopped, warned, fined, or even detained for improper veiling. A young woman who was a student of architecture told me:

> Every day I think about the crimes I commit. When I go out, I am per definition a criminal because everything I do is unlawful. My veil is not proper. I meet my boyfriend in a coffee shop. I have a Facebook page and in my car I play illicit music. I am a criminal from top to toe.

A young man put his experiences this way:

> Every time I go out the first thing I think about is what crime I am going to commit today: having sex with my girlfriend or watching a forbidden TV channel or meeting and drinking coffee with a girl. I am always ready to find some explanations and excuses in case I am arrested. I have to lie both to the police and to my parents.

Asb heyvan-e najibi ast (Absolutely Tame is a Horse), a black comedy made by Abdolreza Kahani in 2011, clearly shows young Iranians' feelings of being criminals. The film follows a group of friends on the streets of Tehran during one night. The main character is a thief dressed as a police officer who misuses the legal blurriness of "cultural crimes" by taking money from young people for deeds that may or may not be unlawful. He easily makes young people believe they have committed a crime such as playing loud music at a birthday party, having a tattoo, or throwing water at each other. The scenes of the comical situations when young people "confess/negotiate" their "crimes" with the "police" illustrate young Iranians' radical insecurity before the "abstractness" of the law.

The criminalization of the youth culture has become central to the policy of "governing through crime." Governing through the criminalization of youth has been going on since the early 1980s. It creates criminals to be able to punish them. Redefining a social issue as a crime, as well as categorizing an affected group as criminals, is a political strategy to legitimize further intervention into matters not previously regarded as criminal (Simon 2007). It makes crime and punishment the institutional context whereby a criminal population (for example, illegal immigrants, homosexuals, prostitutes, or just young people) is constructed and excluded (see also Rose 1999: 259).[6] The criminalization of free sexuality exemplifies how the youth have been subjected to the govern-through-crime policy. While short-term temporary marriage (for one hour or one day) is accepted and encouraged by the state and the police turn a blind eye to street prostitution, young unmarried couples can be punished for holding each other's hands. Prostitution has become more visible on Tehran's streets than previously. In addition, there are semi-official "dating" sites and firms that facilitate temporary marriages. Yet young people's erotic life outside marriage is harshly controlled and illegalized. The law targets youth rather than the "crime" itself (extramarital sex). Mojdeh, a young woman in her early twenties, said:

> The police do not arrest prostitute women but us. Our veil is much more proper than theirs. The way they dress and wear makeup is extreme but the police detain us if we talk to a male friend.

In the eyes of Foucault, the "production of criminality" is a way to create "the norm." The "illegalization" of youthfulness creates the ideal image of an "Iranian Muslim youth." Criminalizing undesirable aspects of young people's behavior is preeminently a way to constitute an ideal model of citizenship. Unidentified and therefore unmanageable masses of youngsters are contrasted to the ideal young Muslim/citizen. "Failed" citizens are those who are "unable or unwilling to enterprise their lives or manage their own risk, incapable of exercising responsible self-government, attached either to no moral community or to a community of anti-morality" (Rose 1999: 259). The technologies of citizenship constitute a moralizing and "responsibilizing" project, which aims to turn citizens into productive, responsible and ethical subjects, as opposed to irresponsible and unethical ones. In contrast to the ideal citizen, there is the *anti-citizen*: an individual who is believed to exist outside the ordinary regulatory system, one who violates established norms and may constitute a risk to the safety and quality of life of "normal" citizens.

"Unproductive" youth, seen as "burdens" on their families and on the society, are thought to have a negative effect on the welfare and economy of the state and their families. An anti-citizen is portrayed as a criminal, as lacking an identity, and as being irrational, irresponsible, and immoral (Inda 2006: 177). As anti-citizens, young Iranians, like illegalized immigrants in Sweden (see Khosravi 2010), are presumed to violate not only the "ethical values" and "morals" of the citizens but also the aesthetic ones. Since the Revolution, the image of young people as "immoral," "deceitful," "untrustworthy," and "irresponsible" has been reproduced. The 60-generation is usually represented not only by the authorities but also by older generations in terms of "lacking" something. Some of the most common terms are *bi dard* (literally, without pain, careless), *bi arman* (devoid of ideology), *bi hoviyat* (without identity), *bi rishe* (without roots), *bi hadaf* (without goals), *bi khial* (careless), *bi farhang* (without culture, unrefined), *bi band o bar* (without bonds and belonging). All these terms carry the prefix *bi* (literally, without; suffix, less) to signify the young generation's lack of a "quality." Youth are thus unqualified to be included. In the rest of the chapter, I present two cases of "unqualification" processes: one of middle-class singles (*mojarads*) and another of young working-class men (*arazel owbash*). While the former is exposed to a systematic bullying, the latter has been victim of abuse by the police.

The War on Singles

A symptom of licentiousness is believed to be the expansion of the single (*mojaradi*) lifestyle.[7] *Mojaradi* is the adjective of the word *mojarad*, which generally means single, unmarried. During the 2000s, the number of those who live single lives doubled.[8] The National Youth Organization announced in September 2010 that 30 percent of young people in the six largest cities in Iran are single, not including widows or divorced persons.[9] The desire for control over one's own space and time is the core attraction of the single lifestyle. Independency, "independence of mind," and "individualism" were recurrently mentioned by my interlocutors as the main reasons for striving for the single lifestyle.[10] They long to have control over their own mobility, over what they can do at home, and to be able to organize their daily schedule without parental interference. The single lifestyle, characterized by the desire for residential and mobile independence, indicates a growing taste for autonomy among young people.

Leaving one's parental home and starting a single life put young people in confrontation with both their parents and the state. Education and work are two main factors in the negotiation between children and parents on moving out. Young people use work and education to legitimize their *mojaradi* lifestyle to the authorities. The Islamic Free University has certainly played a crucial role in increasing *mojaradi* houses. This school is more accessible to young people because of its less competitive requirements and its geographical dispersal. Founded in 1982, it has an enrollment of 1.5 million students in its four hundred campuses throughout the country. It has mushroomed in big and small cities throughout the country and has intensified the mobility of young Iranians. Hundreds of thousands of young men and women have migrated to other cities for education and started a single life. The mobility of these young people and its consequences concerns the authorities, who, in order to control and limit this mobility, have launched the official strategy of "enrollment of local students." The longing for mobility, a single life, and youthfulness is illustrated in the auto-ethnographic documentary *Nakhandeh dar Tehran* (Unwelcome to Tehran, 2011). The director, Mina Keshavarz, a twenty-eight-year-old woman from Shiraz (a large city in southern Iran) made the film about herself and a handful other young women who moved to Tehran to start a single life, free from their parents' surveillance and control. The women in the film, who had gotten married to liberate themselves from the restrictions at their parental homes, now fight to get divorced and move to Tehran. The sense of movement, from a parental home, from a husband, from a hometown, is central to the film. As my studies in the field of migration show, the right to mobility is the basis for realization of other rights, such as the rights to life, work, and safety (Khosravi 2010). Some key scenes in the film are shot on board trains and long-distance buses or in terminals. Keshavarz states that the desire for an independent life is the reason she seeks divorce and migration to Tehran. The film illustrates single women's continual struggle to cope with the obstacles in their daily lives. We see them in constant negotiation with their parents and other "gatekeepers" (for example, a real-estate broker) to justify their choice of a *mojaradi* lifestyle.

The sense of autonomy and freedom the young experience during their *mojaradi* lives while studying in another city will be lost when returning to their parental house. Behzad, a twenty-six-year-old man, after four years in Tehran as a student had to move back to his parents' house in Shiraz due to financial difficulties. He put his experiences this way:

> It is so hard to live with my parents again. For four years, I lived as I wished. My relationships were arranged and defined by myself. Now it

is my parents who will do it. I have to explain everything to them now, why I do this, why I do that. Who is this girl and what kind of relationship we have. You are always under their gaze.

For Shadi, a twenty-four-year-old woman with a degree in urban planning, a *mojaradi* life means liberation:

We do not want to marry. Our generation is afraid of marriage, of commitment. Why should we have children at all? To make them miserable too? Just like ourselves? For our generation, individuality is important. *Mojaradi* for us means freedom, independence, to perform youthfulness.

Pari, a twenty-eight-year-old unemployed architect, still lives with her parents:

Marriage and starting a family do not fit our style. We want to keep our freedom even after marriage. We do not want the former generation's form of marriage.... *Mojaradi* means independence.... It means experiencing life in its real sense ... experiencing love and sexuality.

A single lifestyle is outside the range of the oppressive surveillance of parents and the state and, therefore, a threat to the well-being and safety of the society. Not surprisingly, the particular concern is about women's sexuality. According to an "expert," "women make up a larger part of the [*mojarad*] group, which is sad and shocking."[11] Six million divorced women in the country, who mainly live alone, have caused moral panic among the politicians who see a direct link between divorce and "social harms" such as prostitution and drug abuse.[12] Furthermore, the single lifestyle is believed to obstruct marriage and delay the transition from youth to adulthood.

Mojaradi is also threatening family authority, glorified and underscored in affectionate terms such as *khan-e pedari* (father's house) or *aghosh-e khanevadeh* (embrace of the family). The "father's house" is a concept referring to safety, comfort, and well-being, but it also connotes parental control and guidance. The harsh patriarchal attitude in Iranian society glorifies the father and his superiority over the children. Similarly, "embrace of the family" is another metaphor for the sheltering and healing aspects of the family. The police job is to identify and collect street children and runaway young women and reunite them with their families, from which many of them had escaped because of various forms of abuse. According to the patriarchal moralism, lacking family (*bi-khanevadeh*) or being "without a father and a mother" (*bi pedar va madar*) is sign of immorality and vulgarity.

In this family-centered paradigm, outside the parental home there is wilderness. In opposition to *khanevadeh* is *khiyaban*, "the street," which is associated with the wild, sexual anomie, and social harms. Iranian parents' main concern is to protect their children from the street and its people, who are stereotypically constructed as divergent: "women of the streets" (*zanha-ye khiyabani*), thugs (*alvat*), charlatans, pedophiles (*bache baz*), or rapists. The stereotype of the street and its people is class based. According to the bourgeois moral geography, the streets of southern Tehran are more "wild and uncivilized" than the streets of northern Tehran. The issue of *arazel owbash* (thugs and ruffians) is an explicit class discriminatory view of the streets of lower-income parts of Tehran. Parents see "street friendships" (*dostiha-ye khiyabani*) as evil. Usually in the news reports on crimes, particularly on rapes and murder by young people, "street friendship" is referred to as the primary cause of the delinquency. The conflation of the patriarch's duty and the government mission is best demonstrated in the eagerness of the state to protect female virtue. Demonization of street is preeminently a way to solidify family authority and domination. The panic about working-class masculinity stigmatized as *arazel owbash* is a way for parents and the authorities to reinforce family dominion as the only locus of safety by staging the streets as insecure and unsafe for young men and women. As would be expected, the family-centered normativity does not tolerate young people's choice of independence from family and being unmarried.

Punishing Young Singles

Single persons have been exposed to harsh stigmatization by the authorities, mass media, and the official popular culture, for example, in television series (see Dadvar 2012) that reproduce stereotypes of singles as careless and disrespectful individualists. In a social order based on familism, the single person is the Other. The 60-generation started criticizing the institution of family in the early 2000s. During the student movements in late autumn 2002, a student monthly called *Rah-e Nou* (New Way) began to publish a series of essays targeting familism. One of the essays was titled "Being a Bachelor: This Is the

Crime" ("Mojarad Bodan: Jorm in Ast"): "In Iranian society the individual is legitimated only as married. The single must be segregated from 'normal' people. She or he is seen as a creature possessing bestial instincts and uncontrollable hedonism."[13]

Represented as polluted and polluting bodies, singles are believed to threaten the purity of the family. In *Purity and Danger* (1966), Mary Douglas explored how distinguishing purity from impurity is a mechanism for preserving social structure and determining what is morally acceptable. In the official discourse, the "impurity" of singles is frequently underscored and regretted. For instance, acknowledging the existence of a large number of single people in the society is regarded as "unpleasant." On a radio program, Majid Omidi, director of the National Organization of Youth, talking about the problem of singles, apologized for giving the "disturbing" information that they comprised almost 30 percent of the whole young population.[14]

Stigma of pollution is explicitly expressed in the sexist term *torshide* (literally, grown sour, used for expired food, a spinster) referring to middle-aged unmarried women. *Mojarad* is presented as the "anti-citizen" (see Inda 2006), an individual who violates established norms and who may constitute a risk to the quality of life of "normal" citizens. In this family-centered social order, which is, on the one hand, a moralizing and, on the other hand, a "responsibilizing" project, singles are contrasted to accountable and decent citizens. The stigmatization and criminalization of singles have severe consequences for these young people who pay a high price for their independence: isolation by parents, social stigma, and financial pressures. The authorities' aim to limit singles' mobility in public places and even exclude them from some parts of public spaces and places. Single men, perceived as troublemakers, delinquent, and molesters, are supposed to be distant, unattached, and isolated from families (cf. Menoret 2014: 54). Indeed, a single man is called *azab*, an Arabic word that means "bachelor" but also "to be distant." Single men are excluded from many public places assigned as *makhsous-e khanevadeh*, "family spaces." The mayor of Shiraz, Alireza Pakfetrat, announced on 18 October 2012 that singles were not allowed to enter three main parks in the city.[15] Single women's public life and mobilities are particularly restricted and monitored. For instance, a single woman cannot rent a hotel room by herself. To restrict single women's mobility, the government presented a controversial bill in 2012 to restrict the right of single women under forty to travel abroad, stating that they needed permission from their parents or legal guardian to leave the country. But the most controversial state intervention was a bill presented at the Majlis in the summer of 2013, and passed in October 2015, that put marriage as a condition for employment as university professor or school teacher, for obtaining a passport, and for getting grants for Ph.D. programs abroad. The bill, named "A Plan for Increasing the Population and Enhancement of the Family," aims:

- To prioritize the employment of married men with children, then married men without children, then married women with children, and then married women without children. To employ single persons should not be any problem as long as there are not any married applicants.
- To forbid the employment of single persons in the scientific boards of public and private universities, research centers, or as teachers at all levels in the education system, . . . exceptions could be made for genius singles.[16]

The bill has been harshly criticized as targeting young, single persons, particularly single women. Feminist groups state that the plan forces unemployed single women to have no choice but "to die, to prostitute, or to become a temporary wife."[17] A lack of resources and legal discrimination against entering the regular labor and housing market force singles toward informal employment and the informal rental market. Subsequently, they find themselves in precarious conditions and short-term contracts. Short-term employment and rental contracts allow employers to renegotiate terms and delay payment and landlords to increase rent frequently. Young singles have difficulties finding housing to rent. Sale and rental brokerage firms do not usually provide services to singles. Often real estate agents put a written announcement on the window: "We do not have housing for singles. Don't ask!" Furthermore, in 2011, the police ordered the Association of Real Estate Brokers and Agents to use harsher measures against single house seekers. Many brokers require more money from singles, particularly male ones, to find a place for them. Abbas, a young man in his mid-twenties, moved from Ahvaz to Tehran to study at Tehran University in 2005. When he could not find a place to rent by himself, his mother came to Tehran, pretending she would live with him, and they rented a small apartment. After two months the landlord, who lived in the same building, knocked on the door and said that Abbas had to move out because he was a *mojarad*, and the landlord could not tolerate such licentiousness (*biband o bari*). Then he threatened to call the police and say Abbas brought prostitutes home. The women he called "prostitutes" were in fact, Abbas's friends from the university. The whole problem was solved when Abbas agreed to pay double for the rent.

The proliferation of the *mojaradi* lifestyle is seen by an "expert" as damage (*aseeyb*), a consequence of the "modern" lifestyle of the young, which conflicts with "traditional" family life. According to the "expert," the list of social damages coming from the *mojaradi* lifestyle is long: "drug addiction, involvement in corrupting groups such as Satan worshipers, disassociation from family, weakening of religious belief, 'identitylessness,' just to name a few."[18] The main focus is on the *khane mojaradi* (literally, house of singles). This "concept" has been circulating in public debates and refers to the moral panic among the authorities and the parental generation, assuming that an increasing number of singles will stimulate sin/crime. "House of singles" does not refer to a house where only a single person (for example, an elderly widow) lives but where the unmarried young (mainly men) live alone. In a "house of singles," several young people may live together. "House of singles" is believed to offer young people an opportunity to do what is illicit, like dating, taking drugs, drinking, having mixed-sex parties, watching pornographic films, or buying sex from a prostitute. It is believed to damage the family because it facilitates infidelity and free sexual relationships. It is a stigmatized space, a locus of "vice and immoralities."[19]

The security approach to single people becomes explicit when *mojaradi* houses are compared with "team houses" (*khanehay-e teami*). Team houses were locations where resistance militia, such as Cherikha-ye Fedaian-e Khalq, hid and planned their operations against the Islamic Republic in the early years after the Revolution. Team houses were referred to as sources of terror and fear. A member of the Majlis discussing *mojaradi* houses stated, "If there are such a places as team houses where organized activities are carried out against social security, it is the state's obligation to intervene."[20] Majid Dostali, deputy minister of labor and social welfare, said, "The growth of *mojaradi* houses is one of the enemy's threats."[21] Accordingly, the police launched an operation in April 2010 in Tehran to "identify and crack down on single houses."[22] A joke among the youth says:

> A police officer knocks on a door.
> A young man's voice: "Who is it?"
> The police officer: "It is me. Your mother."
> The young man: "Don't lie. She is in our hometown."
> The police office to other policemen: "He is a *mojarad*. Break down the door and arrest him."

Mojaradi houses are presented as "crime-promoting places". While criminals are identified as such due to their actions, young singles are seen as a delinquent and immoral simply due to their age and lifestyle. Farshid is a twenty-four-year-old man. A student, he still lives with his parents:

> Being a single man means misfortune. As *mojarad* you are condemned all the time. Being *mojarad* means being suspected by the law. You are like a fugitive. For example if a *mojarad* man gets into an argument with a married woman on the street he is the guilty one no matter what. . . . Even in job ads it is mentioned that married applicants are preferred.

The vulnerability of young *mojarads* exposes them to bullying, extortion, and abuses. Defenseless against violations by others, they are denied the right to security and protection from exploitation and violence. There are countless examples of how single young men, but even more women, have been abused sexually and non-sexually by their landlords, employers, or professors at universities.

When Police Won't Help: An Example

Paria, twenty-six, is from a small city in northern Iran and moved to Tehran to study at a university:

> I did not want to return to my hometown under any circumstances. Returning home to the family meant forced marriage which would ruin my life. . . . I found a job and with two other girls rented a place. As single girls we did not find a better place than an apartment on the third floor in an almost ruined old house. Every day something didn't work, but the landlord did not repair it. One day my boyfriend painted the kitchen. Afterward he was tired and fell asleep. I lay down next to him. I was tired too and fell asleep quickly. Suddenly I was awakened by a kick. . . . It was my landlord who had come inside with his key. He had taken a cell phone photo of us asleep. . . . Another man who lived in the house threatened to call the police, and we knew that there would be a disaster. This man had not missed a chance to sexually harass me since I had moved in. The landlord started to dial my

father's number. It was my father who had signed the rental contract. I begged him to stop. My father would kill me. The landlord did not call [my father] but called me whatever he wanted, "whore," "street woman." My boyfriend and I fled that day. The landlord called me later and asked me to take my things out. When I went there, he talked kindly to me and said if I did not sleep with him he would show the pictures of me and my boyfriend to my father. When I refused he took out his cell phone and started dialing. I told him not. . . . Afterward I felt horrible for several months. I hated my body and could not look at myself naked.[23]

Awareness of their vulnerability makes young women's lives distressing and anxious. One young woman said that she would never let people know she was single at her workplace: "Knowing you are *mojarad*, men think that they can do and say what they want to you."

Every time I asked single women suffering from bullying why they do not seek help from the police, I got the same answer, "The police? It is a ridiculous idea! They bully us more than others."

Being deprived of their citizenship rights and being rejected as political bodies make *mojarads* resemble *homo sacer*, a term from Roman law Georgio Agamben (1998) uses to describe an existence and condition he calls "naked life." The *homo sacer* has been stripped of membership in society and thereby of rights. According to Roman law, *homines sacri* could be killed without it being considered murder. The *homo sacer* is reduced from a complete political being to a simple biological or natural body, stripped of all rights. Agamben believes that the system of nation-states differentiates between naked (depoliticized) life (*zoé*) and a political form of life (*bios*). The *homo sacer* is a completely depoliticized body different from the politicized forms of life embodied in the citizen. In their capacity as *homines sacri*, young singles are left vulnerable not only to state violence (through regulations, political arrangements, laws, priorities, and the police) but also to the violence of ordinary citizens, without being able to protect or defend themselves.

Since 2012, there have been a few attempts to challenge the official demonizing discourse against single youth. In a photo series called *Mojaradha* (2012), the young artist Najaf Shokri shows a different image of young single men in Tehran. The photos are all taken indoors and show young men whose only connection to the outside world is through their laptops or mobile phones. There is no trace of the official "othering" stereotypes of *mojaradi* lifestyle, no party, mixed-sex mingling, or other "sinful/criminal" activities. Black and white photos of half-naked young men in a claustrophobic space of their bare apartments show motionless bodies, as if they were cavemen taking refuge from the wilderness outside. As outcasts, the men in the photos are visibly in an existential "stuckedness" (Hage 2009), waiting for something to happen, to save them from their caves. Another example is *The Noise* (by Pooya Razi, 2015) a seventeen-minute animated film that shows the systematic bullying of a young single man by his neighbors in an apartment building. His life is invaded by public norms, accusing him for his "immoral" lifestyle. Using actual audio footage, the film explores the precarity sensed and lived by single youth. The dark and gloomy indoor scenes illustrate the extreme isolation and loneliness of a single man surrounded by a hostile society. Single women are the focus of a work by the photographer Negar Yaghmaian. In her book *The Blind* (2015), she documents private moments of twelve single women in Tehran. In more than a hundred photos taken in indoor spaces, she illustrates the single lifestyle of women, showing them in their beds, sofas, bathrooms, or corridors. Uncertainties and waithood frame the pictures. What do these women wait for? What is going to happen soon? As in *The Noise*, the composition of colors and lights in *The Blind* expresses a claustrophobic mood. Is the isolation a punishment by the larger society or a choice for self-protection?

In June 2012, the leading reformist daily newspaper *Shargh* published a series of articles in which the condemnation and rejection of singles is replaced with an attempt to understand this lifestyle. The articles were published in a weekly attachment with the title "We Should Respect the New Lifestyle."[24] For the first time in the public debate, single youth were discussed and represented without prejudices and demonization. One interesting article was an interview with Mohamad Said Zukai, a professor at Alameh University in Tehran, who saw the proliferation of the *mojaradi* lifestyle as an indicator of the emergence of the idea of an "autonomous citizen" among some young Iranians. Part of this autonomy is the freedom in choosing a family constellation.[25] Here is a short excerpt from the newspaper:

The End of the Epoch of Marriage

Sociological research shows that new realities are taking place in our country, or at least in Tehran, that change the previous system. The growing new form of life among young people, which is called *mojaradi* life, is in fact challenging the idea among Iranians that independence from the parental family should be only through marriage. It seems that today's young Iranians reassess some notions and social norms and fundamentally criticize the bases of the traditional life. Interviews with young people indicate that they do not see marriage as the only way to be independent from their parents. . . . [For them] marriage is now only an option. Contrary to what repeatedly is said, the delayed age of marriage is neither because of economic difficulties nor the spread of Western culture. What is fact is that marriage is not any more the only form of relationship [between sexes] in the society.[26]

The state's emphasis on sustaining family values and traditional relationships within the family confronts new forms of relations and new family constellations. The family culture is increasingly challenged by young people who choose a *mojaradi* life, divorce, cohabit (known as *ejdevaje sefid*, "white marriage"), and decide not to have children. In post-revolutionary Iranian society, links to the family institution shrunk, and individuals failed in building their own independent families. Iranian sociologist Fatemeh Sadeghi believes that the transformations of Iranian families are consequences of modernization expressed in more autonomous marriages based on love. She states that the younger generation, in contrast to their parental generation, value more individuality (*fardiyat*) within families in terms of respect for individual wishes and desires.[27] Socioeconomic transformations together with ideational changes are likely to shape family patterns for years to come. Social and ideational influences on family behaviors are resulting in changes in gender roles, demography, and sexualities. While anxiety concerning the social collapse prevails among officials and "experts," scholars such as Fatemeh Sadeghi and Yousuf Abazari see the family crisis as an inevitable consequence of modernity and use the term "pain of birth" about the new generation, aware of their parents' weaknesses, knowing that they should take their destiny into their own hands (Abazari 1381/2002: 41).[28]

Punishing Poor Men

The most recent disparaging terms used for some young men are *arazel va owbash* (in everyday language, *arazel owbash*), which literally means "thugs and ruffians." Since 2007, the "govern-through-crime" tactics not only target middle-class "westernized" youth, but increasingly focus on young men from low-income groups. It was first in the summer of 2007 that the words *arazel owbash* appeared in public debates and official discourse to target this specific group. It should be mentioned that the notion of *arazel owbash* is constructed in opposition to the romanticized image of *louti*, a heroic masculine character with moral authority, who is responsible and has control over his violent behavior (see Naficy 2011: 277). Unlike the gallant *loutis*, the stereotype of the villainous *arazel owbash* depicts irresponsible and unreliable materialistic men who use violence only for personal pleasure. Ghannam (2013), in her study of urban Egyptian masculinity, observes a similar dichotomy between the decent and noble masculinity of *gada* and the wicked *baltagi*. The stigmatization and oppression of so-called *arazel owbash* are based on the intersection of gender, class, and, to some extent, ethnicity (since low-income groups in Tehran mainly have an immigrant background from ethnic minority groups). Targeting only working-class young men makes *arazel owbash* a class stigma.

Narratives in the official media on *arazel owbash* and their "crimes" have escalated drastically in the past years, resulting in public fear and moral panic. Moral panic, as Stanley Cohen defines it, occurs when "a condition, episode, person or group of persons emerges to become defined as a threat to societal values and interests" (1987: 9). The characteristics of moral panic are demonization of and disproportionate reaction to the group. Images of beefy men with scars ("evidence" of their violent character) and tattoos (signs of immorality and criminal behavior and belonging to the lower class), along with reports on increased drug and alcohol consumption, violent robberies, thuggish behavior, and rapes, are used in official public discourse to justify and legitimize the brutal zero-tolerance policy against underprivileged young men. Cases of violent robbery (*zorgiri*) and gang rapes receive vast attention in both social and official media, which results in public demands for forceful action. For instance, a police report declared that, in 1390/2011, up to 4,000 cases of stabbings (*chaghu keshi*), 14,000 robberies, and 50,000 arrests took place in Tehran. According to the report, the majority of the crimes were committed by men under eighteen. By using fear of numbers, the official public discourse constructs a threatening image of working-class young men: "These statistics show the presence of tens of thousands *arazel owbash* who freely move in Tehran . . . any mercy and any mildness toward them and their crimes can lead to collapse of public security."[29]

In December 2012, *arazel owbash* became a national concern. A short video clip captured by a surveillance camera mounted on a building was uploaded on YouTube on December 1 and became top news throughout the country. The clip showed four young men threatening people with daggers and robbing a man in the middle of the day on a crowded street in Tehran. The men managed to steal 70,000 toman (then about US$25). The police identified and arrested the men shortly afterward. The whole arrest operation was documented and broadcast on state-run television and by all the major news agencies. To reassure the nation, Sadegh Larijani, head of the judiciary, announced that armed robbery is classified as *moharebeh* (enmity against God), a capital crime punished by death. He stated that the judiciary "chose the death punishment based on the need to act assertively and to increase the cost of committing thuggery." The prosecutor declared that "all four suspects in this case are young, come from broken homes, have prior records, and were unemployed."[30] On December 30, less than a month after the robbery, the four men, all younger than twenty-five, were put on trial. Here are excerpts from the report of the trial:[31]

> The four young men were crying. The main accused man was twenty-three years old. He does not have stable employment. Since he had lost his father, at the age of twelve, he worked to help his mother and younger sister. His mother is sick and can no longer work.
>
> The judge: You are charged with "*enmity against God*" and with "*sowing corruption on earth*" for armed robbery and terrorizing the public with a cold weapon and hurting the victim. Defend yourself!
>
> The twenty-three-year-old man: My mother is sick. I need four million toman [then about US$1,300] for her operation. We have a hard life. My father is dead and my mother works as a maid but now she cannot work any more. I told her she did not need to be worried and I would fix the money for the operation. I did this because of poverty.
>
> The judge: You have a criminal record.
>
> The twenty-three-year old man: No. I have only been arrested twice. Once for a fight and another time for harassment.
>
> The judge: What about the case of bag snatching?
>
> The twenty-three-year-old man: I was acquitted.
>
> The judge repeats the charges and asks the twenty-three-year-old man to give a message to other young persons who are willing to commit similar crimes.
>
> The twenty-three-year-old man: You young people, sinful money is not worth it. If you love your family, do not do these things.

The cases of three other young men were similar: young men from broken families, who had been working hard since their early teens to take care of their younger brothers and sisters. Shortly after the trial, the twenty-three-year-old man and another young man were sentenced to death, and the remaining two were sentenced to ten years in prison, five years in exile, and seventy-four lashes each. In the early morning of 20 January 2013, the two young men were executed by hanging in Park-e Honarmandan (Artists' Park, close to Khan-e Honarmandan, a famous art institution) in central Tehran. Less than fifty days after the robbery, two young working-class bodies were hanging in the air from a crane truck in a park where middle-class Tehranis come for a walk, dates, and to relax. A crowd had gathered to watch the hanging. The most common complaint by people against the execution, which was broadcast by the official media, centered on the choice of location. They argued that the hanging would disturb the artists and people who came to the park for a walk. In January 2016 I brought up this issue with Jinoos Taghizadeh, a Tehran-based artist, while walking in the same park. She said that even artists objected to the choice of location, not the hanging itself. Generally the reaction by the wider community and human rights organizations (which usually have immediate reactions against mistreatment of political activists) to the unjust and excessive punishment of two so-called *arazel owbash* was weak and insignificant. The two working-class young men were condemned not only by the law but by the bourgeois moralism of middle-class Iranians as well.

After the trial, General Ahmad-Reza Radan, deputy commander of the Iranian police, declared that the police "rejoiced" on hearing the head of the judiciary's verdict to charge *arazel owbash* with capital punishment. Soon thereafter, the police launched a new round of confrontation against *arazel owbash*.[32] Within a few days in January 2013, more than 230 men, mostly younger than twenty-five, accused of being *arazel owbash*, were arrested in Tehran. The plan of battle against *arazel owbash*, part of a larger program known as the "public security plan," had already started in April 2007. It was a strategy to calm public anger over the increase of crime. Between April 2010 and March 2013, the police force conducted twelve major operations throughout Tehran to cleanse the city from *arazel owbash*. In March 2013 and at the ceremony of the end of the twelfth operation, Tehran police chief Hossein Sajedinia announced that, during the year 1391 (2012) alone, more than 1,600 *arazel owbash* had been arrested.

The pattern of arrests followed age, gender, and class. Operations against *arazel owbash* targeted almost entirely young men. According to police statistics, 95 percent of the arrested *arazel owbash* were younger than twenty-five.[33] The problem of *arazel owbash* was linked to the male *mojaradi* lifestyle and *mojardai* houses. The term *arazel owbash* has rarely been used to describe women. Only a few times have there been notices about female *arazel owbash* in the news. A rare example is this odd phrase that appeared in some news agencies: "*Arazel owbash* of the soft sex."[34] In April 2011 five women, called *arazel owbash*, were arrested, but, unlike the case of male *arazel owbash*, the women were never publicly shown and their "crimes" never mentioned.

The scapegoating and criminalizing of *arazel owbash* are punishing and disciplining young poor. *Arazel owbash* are always from the south of the city. Social inequalities in Tehran have historically been represented spatially in a dichotomy between the rich north of the city (*shomal-e shahr*), also called "the upper city" (*bala-ye shahr*), and the poor south (*jonob-e shahr*), also called "the lower city" (*paeen-e shahr*). Following the news, we can see that the arrested young men were from the low-income neighborhoods in the southern and eastern parts of Tehran, such as Khani Abad, Khazaneh, Chaharah Nezamabad, Shahr Rey, Eslam Shahr, and Tehran Nou. In the anti-*arazal owbash* campaign, these neighborhoods are referred to as "neighborhoods with a high crime rate." Only one of the twelve operations was conducted in northern parts of Tehran, where middle-class Tehranis live. Compared to the 1,600 people arrested in the low-income neighborhoods in southern Tehran, only forty-five were arrested in the better-off neighborhoods. On television newscasts, the image of *arazel owbash* as lower-income groups is reinforced both in pictures of poor neighborhoods, with their ragged houses, and in the words of reporters who repeatedly refer to *jonob-e shahr*.

By manipulating citizens' fears, the authorities justify the inhumane methods that violate citizens' rights. By producing a "circuit of paranoia," the police receive support from parts of society, particularly from the middle class, for the brutal methods against so-called *arazel owbash*. I once brought up this issue with a group of middle-aged parents. They did not hesitate to show their support for police brutality toward *arazel owbash* and said that it was necessary to bring security back to the society. Their arguments exactly matched the official narrative. The public perception of *arazel owbash* is the result of inaccurate and manipulated information produced by the police and state-run media. The "circuit of paranoia" presenting *arazel owbash* as the main source of social harms and insecurity has now reached a hegemonic consensus. Sirus, a fifty-two-year-old, well-to-do man, put it this way: "If two of them would come to your neighborhood, you would understand what we mean."

Having discussed this problem for a while with my interlocutors, I found out that none of them had ever seen or met a so-called *arazel owbash* or been affected by their "crime." When I asked them whom exactly they referred to as *arazel owbash*, one parent said, "Those types on the street." Thus, the criminal profile of *arazel owbash* is shaped by moral geography and class prejudices. Stereotyping *arazel owbash* is a spatial othering of lower-class men by representing them as deviant from the household-centered family idea. The remark "those types on the street" indicates the dichotomization of family as a civilized space and the street as a space of wilderness. And, of course, the north/south and upper/lower divisions are the basis for this moral geography; farther south, the streets become more "uncivilized" and "dangerous." Targeting *arazel owbash* does not intend to keep young working-class men out of upper-class areas but rather to keep them *in their places* in terms of class hierarchy. This was expressed by Farideh, a middle-aged woman, who said, "They are from low classes and want to get rich quickly overnight." What she meant was that these poor young men do not wait for their turn. Generally, those who cannot "persist in waiting for their turn" (if their turn would ever come) are from the lower classes, since people with privileges do not need to wait at all for "their turn." *Sabori*, waiting out and endurance crises, becomes a form of governmentality. A good citizen is one who can endure; those who cannot are failed citizens. As the quote above shows, it is often the "lower" classes who do not endure and, therefore, become stigmatized as uncivilized and uncultured.

The Right to Look

If a single scene were to capture the brutality young working-class men are exposed to, it is the image of naked, injured bodies—broadcast by the state-run media—of these men displayed for public "appreciation." The first wave of media images of *arazel owbash* was broadcast by the official media in 2007. A series of pictures showing the police breaking into a house and severely beating a young man with batons before detaining him was broadcast by the national mass media. Showing police brutality was shocking at first, but it became usual soon. Images of beaten and humiliated bodies of *arazel owbash* have regularly been shown on television or in public places since then. Along with media misrepresentation, the oppression of *arazel owbash* has often been orchestrated in form of public "mobbing," spectacular shows performed in public places, similar to medieval public displays. Different from bullying singles, mobbing of *arazel owbash* is organized by a huge apparatus involving the police, the media, and the public. Half-naked, injured, and brutally beaten, the "criminals" are put on display in the main squares. Journalists from the state-run media are invited to cover the events. The scene is arranged carefully. To increase their degradation, the young men are forced to perform a physical parody related to their "crime." They are "decorated" with different objects such as plastic or wooden swords or *aftabeh* (a watering can found in toilets to clean oneself instead of using toilet paper) hanging around their necks. Some men are forced to wear "funny," brightly colored ("girlish" colors), puffy, loose pants. Others are dressed in a veil. This method is used on political dissidents too. Majid Tavakoli, a student activist, was arrested after a political speech at Amir Kabir University in December 2009. A few hours following his arrest, the state-run media published his picture; Majid was covered in a veil in an attempt to "degrade" him. According to the phallus-centered authority, a way to break down men's self-control and "respect" is to undermine their "male honor" by feminizing them. In the images and video clips, we see the men with down-averted gazes. Sometimes black strips are put on their eyes in the press. While the public look at them, the young men are not allowed to look back.

The control over gaze is a domination technique. Visuality and the right to look are powerful means to label, categorize, and define groups of people and reproduce social hierarchy (Mirzoeff 2011). The judgmental and prejudicial gaze of the mob, media, and police produces a "circuit of paranoia" among the middle class. This biased mode of seeing evokes feelings of the "dangerous" working-class young men and the "purity" of the family-centered middle class. The hypermasculine bodies are covered in tattoos and knife scars, tattooing being a sign of immorality and unlawfulness. *Khalkoobi*, or tattoo, in praise of masculinity, parents, and friendship has become a sign of criminality and working-class masculinity.[35] Photos appear in the media showing police officers pointing to the tattoos of scorpions, women, Chinese characters, tigers, or flowers found on young men's bodies as evidence of their involvement in crime.[36] One striking tattoo that caught my eyes was on a young man's arm and featured the following words (written in bad English): "I am not crazi [sic]. Only God can judge me."

The vulnerability of the young *arazel owbash* is best demonstrated by their "animalization," being dehumanized and treated like animals. In the media coverage, the young men are called by "their nicknames" with which they are known among their friends. These names are mainly mixed with names of animals: Said Soske (Said the cockroach), Farshid Babaie (Farshid the lamb), Morteza Gorbeh (Morteza the cat), Peyman Kharchang (Peyman the crab), Said lashkhor (Said the buzzard) or Mosh Sia (black mouse), to name a few. Using animal nicknames to address men is not the only form of animalization. After the public show, the young men are usually transported in cage-like vans. The term for these shows used by the media and the authorities is *jam-avari*, a degrading term, resembling rag picking. It is no coincidence that Kahrizak, the detention camp assigned to keep *arazel owbash* in custody, was later used to "detain" confiscated dogs when owning a dog became illegal. Dehumanizing the young men is best demonstrated in a short video clip uploaded on YouTube in the spring of 2014, which shows four detained young men in a police truck driving around Isfahan. The clip, which was recorded by the police, shows four handcuffed young men standing in the back of the truck. Two masked policemen on each side beat them ruthlessly on their necks and heads. Then, after a few minutes in the video, the policemen force the young men to eat leaves and to make animal noise.[37]

Dehumanization of so-called *arazel owbash* takes the form of both seeing them as "human animality" and hearing their voices as animal noises. Interestingly, a recurrent accusation of *arazel owbash* in police reports is their yelling, "*Arbade keshi.*" Young working-class men are merely heard as noisy animals, and their speech is understood as noise. Rancière (2010) shows how the power, that is, the police, functions through an order of the visible and the sayable, making distinctions between what is visible or invisible and between a speech understood as discourse and another speech as animal noise. So, it is not a coincidence that the young men in the police vehicle are forced to sound like animals. Subjugation occurs through erasing the distance between the human and the animal. As Hannah Arendt in her analysis of the mechanisms of totalitarianism shows, one "can be fully dominated only when he becomes a specimen of the animal-species man" (Arendt 1994 [1951]: 457). Animalization of *arazel owbash* does not mean that it makes them nonhuman; rather, it reduces their humanity to what Grégoire Chamayou (2012) calls "human animality," men who are forced to eat a leaf, are put in cages, are called by animal names, and make animal noise.

In mid-July 2012, more than 130 *arazel owbash* were "displayed" on a flatbed truck trailer in Chahrrah-e Amirabad in central Tehran. Handcuffed, they sat in a row so that people could see them from both sides of the truck. A month later, another forty-four young men were "displayed" on a similar truck trailer in the Khaniabad and Yaftabad neighborhoods in southern

Tehran. This has become a recurrent scene in Tehran and other large cities. Young men are often displayed and shamed in their own neighborhoods to maximize the humiliation. Naked, in front of the public, the humiliation is even more intensified. The display of *arazel owbash* is broadcast widely by the state-run media. Television reports broadcast by the IRIB (Islamic Republic of Iran Broadcasting) show the audience, usually middle-aged men and women, who praise the police and demand harsher punishments for the young men. This police method has systematically become a spectacular media show to impress the public. The public mobbing of *arazel owbash* is justified as a way to "increase a sense of security" in the city.

The images of the working-class young men's bodies (beefy, covered in knife scars and tattoos) that circulate around the nation turn the bodies into public objects, exposed to the public's observation and judgment. At the same time, the men are deprived of the right to look back. They are ordered to look down, their eyes are covered, or blurred in the press. The body, decorated with tattoos and knife scars, is indeed the only means the deprived young men have left to earn respect as macho and threatening. We can also hear their voices in the video clips as they confess their "wrongdoings." Their "typical south Tehrani" (*jonob-e shahri*) jargon and "talking like a thug," their body movements—in Bourdieu's terms, their *bodily hexis* (1992: 93)—is represented in a way to reproduce the young men's social "inferiority." Profiling of *arazel owbash* is based on visual discernment and verbal understanding of class, gender, and age.

The juxtaposition of the images of masculine bodies, their "lumpen jargon," and the fright-inducing images of knives and other weapons (claimed to be confiscated from the *arazel owbash*) associate young working-class men with a threat to ethical as well as aesthetic norms. As would be expected, the target of the anti-*arazel owbash* campaigns is the very body of the working-class male. Their bodies are observed, registered, exhibited, mobbed, and judged. In line with this thinking, the usual punishment for *arazel owbash* is corporal, flogging in public.

The police attack on working-class male bodies is at the same time a visual representation of public fear. In almost all visual reports of "public shame," a mob of "normal" citizens watches the spectacle. The public is encouraged to participate in the mobbing, to perform "mob justice," for example, by throwing tomatoes (delivered by the police) at the young men in handcuffs or chanting slogans in support of the police actions. Middle-aged women and men usually make up the audience, watching the "sources of terror." The camera focuses on the fearful faces of the spectators, who also comment on the issue of *arazel owbash*. On a television newscast from December 2012, one middle-aged man speaks straight into the camera: "Look they do these things to their own bodies [knife scars], so what could they not do with others?" In the background, a male voice screams, "These parasites!"

These spectacles of public shame usually end with the audience thanking the police for the efforts to increase public security. The clips show people, again, mostly middle-aged men, chanting, "*Niroye entezami tashakor, tashakor*" (The police, thank you! Thank you!). Afterward, the police officer in command usually announces on the loudspeakers, "Thank you, the people *hamish-e dar sahne* [literally, always on the scene, always prepared to act]. This is only a small part of what the police do for your safety. Please leave now."

By generating a culture of terror in which the *arazel owbash* play the main villains, the people increasingly turn to the police for refuge. The fear of *arazel owbash* on the streets legitimizes the police's violent operations against young working-class men. Claiming that the people not only support but even "like" and "enjoy" the power imposed on them is part of a deployment of a form of "pastoral power" that operates through a discourse of "caring" and "saving," emphasizing the concern for the public's well-being and salvation. Furthermore, generating a circuit of paranoia makes the "families" believe that the real threat against their well-being is young working-class men, classified as criminals, and not the widespread unemployment, political oppression, institutionalized corruption, financial insecurities, or even the alarming air pollution. In a similar way, the police often announce that parents "thank the police" when they break into their houses to confiscate their satellite dishes. The parents thank the police for "saving" their children from watching illicit television channels that tempt them to commit sin/crime.[38] I often heard comments that police brutality against *arazel owbash*, as a necessary force to bring "security" back to society, may be a tactic to make people forget the memories of the police brutality used against middle-class young people in the post-election protests in 2009.

The term *arazel owbash* has no legal definition, and it is not clear on what legal and judicial charges the men are detained. The treatment and detention of young men as *arazel owbash* violate the Penal Code of the Islamic Republic (Article 2).[39] In police statements, an *arazel owbash* is described as a person who is accused of

> disrupting public order through creating fear and intimidation, vandalism, unethical behaviors, drug consumption, robbery, violent behaviors, sexual harassments of people's *namous* [here, people's women], selling

pornographic films, drinking alcoholic beverages, disturbing the public safety by yelling.

Thus, in the absence of a clear legal definition, anyone can be *arazel owbash*. Moreover, the police encourage people to report *arazel owbash* in their neighborhoods. Being defined and seen as criminals simply by their gender, class, and bodily hexis leaves young working-class men without legal rights to security and protection and renders them vulnerable and defenseless not only to the violence of the state but also to the violence of their fellow citizens. When a neighbor calls the police and complains about young men causing a disturbance in the neighborhood, the police are convinced that the young men are the "suspects." In the case of *arazel owbash*, the legal procedures surrounding their arrests, detentions, and subsequent sentences have systematically lacked accurate investigations.[40]

Being listed as *arazel owbash* means being in an extrajudicial prison. Poor young men are detained without trial. Many of those displayed in the public shame shows have not been through a proper trial. They are usually still in detention waiting for their trial when they are put on display in front of the mobbing public. Some of them have already served their sentences but are still picked up by the police for a public mobbing. The police "collect," more or less arbitrarily, a group of poor young men, recognizable as *arazel owbash* through their body hexis, "just to show off their authority."[41] A television report from a "public shaming" in December 2012 shows the journalist asking the young handcuffed men on the flatbed truck trailer what they were arrested for.[42] The men, while looking down, answer. Their words testify to the vagueness and legal uncertainty of the term *arazel owbash*:

> I was in a fight and served two years for that. I was released fifty days ago after serving my sentence. And now they picked me up from my home and brought me here.

Another man states:

> Someone else [in my neighborhood] caused a fight, but the police took me here because they did not find him.

Some of the young men clearly had a drug addiction and suffer from psychological problems. In the same televised report, we hear a twenty-four-year-old man with several tattoos on his neck, shoulders, and arms being asked by the journalist about a deep knife scar on his left arm.

The young man: I did it myself.
The journalist: Why?
The man: For getting exempt from military service due to having a mental disorder.

In this footage, we see many young men with what could be self-inflicted cuts. That the number and pattern of the cuts are focused on a specific part of the arm indicates that they could be self-injuries. There is no information as to how many victims of police brutality against so-called *arazel owbash* suffer from a "mental disorder."[43] However, it is clear that many of them suffer from drug addiction, long-term unemployment, broken families, and generally from a harsh life.

Arazel owbash face harsh punishments for burglary, vandalism, or petty thefts such as breaking into vehicles or purse snatching. The police reaction is disproportional to juvenile delinquency. It is not known how many have been convicted and executed on the ambiguous charge of being *arazel owbash*. In mid-December 2012, many newspapers reported on the arrest of a "notorious" *arazel owbash*. The news reported how the police "professionally" and "according to the gun law" shot the unarmed man to death. The police announcement says that the man was one of the most "dangerous" *arazel owbash* in western Tehran. However, his crime record showed that the crimes the "dangerous and notorious" *arazel owbash* had committed were drunken behavior, causing public disorder, terrorizing the public, and selling drugs.[44] Similarly, in a tragic incident on 20 July 2012, a sixteen-year-old boy, called *arazel owbash* in police reports and media coverage, was shot in the face by a police officer in a working-class neighborhood in southern Tehran. There have been different official narratives of the incident. In one report, a boy was suspected of being drunk, sitting on his motorcycle, when the unprovoked police officer shot him at close range (20 cm.). In another report, a young man was vandalizing some cars. The boy had no criminal record.[45] In the case of young working-class men, the focus is on the image of the criminals, rather than any actual crime. The disproportion of punitive reaction to the "crime" committed by *arazel owbash* help us understand better the bourgeois moralism dominating Iranian society. Drawing on Émile Durkheim, I argue that, instead of focusing on the "crime," we should examine the *opposition*, the punishment:

It is thus the opposition which, far from deriving from the crime, constitutes the crime. In other words, we should not say that an act offends the common consciousness because it is criminal, but that it is criminal because it offends that consciousness. We do not condemn it because it is a crime, but it is a crime because we condemn it. (Durkheim 2014 [1933]: 64)

The term *arazel owbash* has also entered the political discourse, referring to political dissidents. Mohammad Khatami, the reformist president (1997–2005), was perhaps one of the first high-ranking politicians to use the term. On the eve of 8 July 1999, a couple of hundred students gathered at a campus in central Tehran to protest against the new press law and the closure of the reform-oriented newspaper *Salam*. There was a brutal crackdown on the protest. Khatami called the young men and women who started the protest *arazel owbash*. Ten years later, President Ahmadinejad, in his victory speech, called young protestors to the election fraud *khas o khashak*, "riff-raff." The post-election protestors who vandalized banks and stores have recurrently been labeled *arazel owbash*. On 6 October 2012, a crowd spontaneously gathered in central Tehran protesting against the financial instability. The police attacked the crowd, and the official news agencies called the protestors vandalizing banks for *arazel owbash*. Human rights organizations have warned that political dissidents have been executed for being *arazel owbash*. In December 2012, a right-wing politician accused reformist politicians of having paid money to *arazel owbash* to join the post-election protests in June 2009. Not surprisingly, the young people arrested in the post-election protests in June and July 2009 were sent to Kamp-e Kahrizak (Kahrizak Camp), the detention center built in 2007 in southern Tehran specifically to hold *arazel owbash*, where they were exposed to same pattern of torture and harassment *arazel owbash* had been going through.

Kamp-e Kahrizak is a *camp* in its true meaning. As I have written elsewhere (Khosravi 2010), a camp is a place separate from society where stigmatized identities and undesirable groups are placed. Camps function to protect the virtue of the nation. In case of the Nazi camps, the juridical foundation of internment was *schuzhaft* (literally, protective custody). Camps are for the *exceptions* to the nation-state system (refugees, stateless people, *azarl owbash*, or political dissidents), those who violate the norms of society and are deemed impossible to integrate into the prevailing legal system. Kamp-e Kahrizak earned the nickname "Iran's Guantanamo" and, similar to America's Guantanamo, it is where norms end and exceptions begin.[46] The camp fell outside the national jurisdiction and soon became the most atrocious detention center in the country.[47] It was, however, only after the 2009 election protests, when "non-*arazel owbash*" young people were detained here and several of them died due to brutal torture, that Kahrizak became a national issue. When middle-class youth were treated just like working-class men, public awareness about the fearful detention center was raised, and protests against Kamp-e Kahrizak increased. Prior to 2009, the camp regime targeted only working-class young people, so it was not *news* for journalist or a *case* for human rights activists.

Because of the absence of a legal definition and because the distinction between what constitutes a sin, a crime, and political dissent is blurred, anyone can be *arazel owbash*. Any young person who thinks and behaves contrary to official ethical codes and social norms faces the risk of being regarded as *arazel owbash*. Many activities associated with youthfulness, such as dating, drinking, going to parties, are for young Iranians seen as something *arazel owbash* do. A young blogger wrote after watching the "display" of *arazel owbash* on television how he was arrested one day just for walking on the street, taken for being *arazel owbash*. He was released only after he gave a signed pledge that he would never be seen outside again after 8 p.m.[48] Another young man, a university art student, told me that he was detained for several days, just because he "looked like *arazel owbash*."

The Rage of the Poor

One consequence of the representation of *arazel owbash* in the media has been that values and views on this group in everyday discourse have been depoliticized. Those labeled and demonized as *arazel owbash* are mostly marginalized and unprivileged young men who, because they lack the "right" cultural capital, education, and, even more significant, social capital, are stuck in their marginal position. Like the case of the Puerto Rican youth in East Harlem in Philippe Bourgois's ethnography (2002), oppressed by the state and their financial situation, the only remaining way to gain "respect" for many so-called *arazel owbash* is violence. *Arazel owbash*, as Tehran's urban outcasts, express their class rage, similar to young people with immigrant background in the suburbs of Paris, London, or Stockholm, by vandalizing cars and official buildings. On 11 June 2012, a group of young men labeled *arazel owbash* "attacked citizens" and vandalized cars in *park-e Taleghani* in northern Teh-ran.[49] On 5 September 2012, more than twenty cars were vandalized by *arazel owbash* in Gholhak, a wealthy neighborhood in northern Tehran.[50] The com-mon act is to vandalize cars in the affluent parts of northern Tehran, but there was also a case of the plunder of a Shahrvand supermarket in the summer of 2007. The Shahrvand chain belongs to the municipality of Tehran. In state and public discourse, the term *arazel owbash* is the opposite of the term for citi-zens. In the official discourse, the victims of actions of *arazel owbash* are re-ferred to as citizens (*shahrvandan*). Making a clear distinction between *arazel owbash* and citizens robs the former off their citizenship rights. For instance, in the summer of 2012, the police promised to "purify" public places, such as parks, from *arazel owbash* so that citizens could be safe. The "govern-through-crime" policy has constructed *arazel owbash* as a category of people charac-terized by being *anti-citizens*, threatening the well-being of the social body. As anti-citizens, "irresponsible," "unproductive" young men have to be regulated, administered, and disciplined.

Generally in official representations, the behavior of so-called *arazel ow-bash* is depoliticized and decontextualized. Their class rage is represented as insanity and pure violence. Yet official violence feeds street violence. An ex-ample showing the conjunction of state violence and the violence of margin-alized youth is the fact that the state has attempted to incorporate some so-called *arazel owbash* as "the actors of oppression." Some young men col-laborated with the police to crash the protests in 2009 on the promises of conditional release or payment or the threat of heavy sentences.[51] The inter-weaving of two forms of violence erases the boundary between the legitimate civilized violence of the law and the illegitimate savage violence of so-called *arazel owbash*. Following Frantz Fanon (1963), Michael Taussig's (1986) anal-ysis of forms of violence practiced in Putumayo in Latin America shows that the violence among the people is logically an extension of the colonial vio-lence they have been exposed to. Similarly, Fanon understood the violence among Algerians as a reflection of the violence they experienced under French colonialism. Drawing on Taussig's approach, *arazel owbash* violence can be understood as mimesis of the systematic violence they have been exposed to.

The whole issue of *arazel owbash* is an issue of class oppression, a recent feature of the post-revolutionary neoliberal state. Mobbing of young men from poor backgrounds should be seen in line with bullying street vendors and terrorizing homeless people, street kids, and residents of informal settle-ments (see Chapter 7). In October 2013, huge billboards displaying the message that beggars were criminals could be seen all over Tehran. The number of minors and young women who beg for money or sell flowers or chewing gum at almost every major intersection in Tehran has soared in the past decade. State policy toward them has been punitive and harsh. There have been plans to collect and deport street beggars from Tehran. On 30 October 2015, a mob attacked homeless people who used to sleep in Haghani Park in the Harandi neighborhood. The mob beat homeless men and women and burned their tents and belongings while the police watched. In an announcement, the police supported the attack and defended the "citizens' right to self-defense."[52] Nevertheless, the absence of accurate policies undermined the plans, and beggars and vendors were soon back on the streets. A culture of disbelief directed against young beggars is produced by middle-class Tehranis who blame the young and poor for their situation. Structural criminalization of beggars attempts to represent them as organized criminal gangs who are not really in need. In May 2010, the Tehran municipality announced that beggars in Tehran made "the equivalent of $ 1,500 a month—five times the official minimum wage."[53] The images and words on the billboards in Tehran in October 2013 also depicted beggars as charlatans and members of mafia-like organizations. Like the attack on street beggars, the attack on working-class young men stigmatized as *arazel owbash* demonstrates a fundamental change in Iran's state ideology. The revolutionary ideals to support the oppressed poor (*mostaz´afin*) are being gradually replaced with a harsh neoliberal attitude toward the unprivileged.

Conclusion

The young generation is caught between the only two existing institutions: the family and the state. As Omid Mehregan, a leading young post-revolutionary intellectual, puts it as regards his own generation: "between the family and the state there is only a bare wasteland" (1388/2009: 16). In the absence of a functioning civil society, young people are sent back and forth between these two institutions, and any form of life outside them is ineligible and rejected. This chapter shows how these unauthorized forms of life are punished through the bullying of young singles and mobbing of poor youth. Spaces outside the control of the family and the state are stigmatized, controlled, and regulated, such as "houses of singles" and the streets. The presence and mobility through urban space and the youth's new urban practices have become an arena for political and generational contestations (as the following chapter will discuss). Drawing on Taussig (1986), I see the state's terror against young people as a result of its own fear of the imagined wilderness and violence of the youth.

The construction, criminalization, and punishment of so-called *arazel ow-bash* demonstrate the conundrum of Iranian neoliberalism and young people's lives. Lowering the age of "criminal" responsibility points to the absence of a juvenile justice system. As shown above, some behaviors by males as young as sixteen are classified as criminal acts. The neoliberals' war on undesirable youth as potential criminals (*mojarads*, unmarried women, *arazel ow-bash*, the homeless, and street beggars) attempts to discipline and turn individuals into governable, family-based subjects. Stuck in a radical insecurity "rather than being at risk in a society marked by deep economic and social inequalities, youth have become the risk" (Giroux 2002: 35).

The post-revolutionary neoliberal turn constructs the youth category as a subject of lack (*bi*), for example, "without identity" (*bi-hoviyat*), "irresponsible" (*bi-masooliyat*), or "indolent" (*bi-aar*). The prefix *bi* (without) signifies a lack of quality and youth's failure to "reproduce" the life they are expected to reproduce. While singles are punished because they do not produce the next generation, *arazel owbash* are punished because they are failed entrepreneurial subjects. Young people incapable of self-management and self-development or unable to reproduce the life they are supposed to reproduce are either *thing-like*, considered "burdens on the family" (in the case of singles), or turned into *human-animality* (in the case of *arazel owbash*). By painting a picture of violent, hypermasculine working-class young men, the whole issue of social inequality, structural discrimination, and exclusion of these young men from society is suppressed and neglected. However, the public spectacles of mobbing working-class men make visible the various forms of inequalities determined by class, age, and gender. Sporadic riot-like protests and vandalism of cars and public buildings in middle-class and upper-class neighborhoods by so-called *arazel owbash* indicate clearly the class dimension of Iran's generational conflict.

CHAPTER 4

STREETS

To walk is to lack a place.
—Michel de Certeau (1984: 103)

Loitering in street is the last enjoyment left for our generation.
—A young woman in Isfahan

Where can we go to if not to the street?
—A young man in Tehran

On Saturday 20 June 2009, a protest demonstration was planned to take place at 5 p.m. at the Meydan Enqelab (Revolution Square). The government did its best to break down all means of communication. Cell phone and Internet communication was interrupted. However, calls summoning people to join the demonstration were flowing through "small" media: face-to-face communication in taxis, in shops, and on the streets. One could repeatedly hear, "Do not forget. Five o'clock at Meydan Enqelab." In the morning of that day, I went to Cheshmeh, a popular bookstore among young people. I started a conversation with a young woman, in her late teens, about a novel she had in her hands. When I was leaving, she reminded me about the demonstration later the same day: "For God's sake, come." In her gloomy voice there were glimpses of hope and fear. "There will be blood," I wrote in my notebook before I left home at 4 p.m. to join the protest demonstration. The city was under siege. I had never seen Tehran like this. Paramilitary forces occupied every main square and all road intersections. There were middle-aged men holding batons in their hands.

The cabdriver stopped his car next to the Eskan Towers on Valiasr Avenue, a few hundred meters north of Vank Square. He was anxious and said that he would not go any farther: "It is too dangerous." I got out of the cab and headed south toward Vank Square to see what was going on. Vank Square, a huge square with six main streets, is a commercial center in the northern part of the city. While passing the Eskan Towers, I noticed a young woman around twenty years old walking just a few meters in front of me, heading in the same direction as I. I walked just behind her for several minutes. Dressed in a bright blue short coat, a colorful shawl on her head—covering just a little of her black hair—blue jeans, and wedge heel shoes she was definitely in the wrong place at the wrong time. Getting closer to the square, there were more middle-aged paramilitary men with batons in their hands. These men wore khaki pants, plain shirts hanging over the tops of their pants, and boots. Some wore a Palestinian shawl, and were unshaven with a two-day stubble. The generational difference between the middle-aged men with batons in their hands and the young people chanting "Where is my vote?" was striking. I panicked on the young woman's behalf. Not only was she "improperly veiled," but she also wore a green wristband—the color of the opposition, the Green Movement. Considering how she looked, she would definitely not pass through the square unharmed. I expected her to take off her wristband at the last moment. I hoped so. For a moment, I walked faster to catch up to her to ask her not to go farther or at least to take off the band. But I did not. I could not. It was *her* day, *her* protest. Probably this was the moment she had waited for so long, after years of being bullied day after day by the police for expressing her youthfulness, her way of life, of being subject to gender inequalities in the education and labor markets, of sexual segregation in the public spheres. So she walked on, with confident steps, toward the middle-aged men with batons in their hands. And I followed behind her. Nearer to the square, we came closer to the middle-aged men with their batons. I could now see how they waved the batons in the air, before landing them on the young bodies.

Everywhere I looked around me, historical scenes were unfolding. I remembered a day in the fall of 1978 in Isfahan. I was thirteen. We had been sent home early from school that day. The principal announced over the loudspeaker that the authorities had ordered the closure of all schools for a long period of time. On my way home from school, together with other kids, I joined a protest march on Ferdowsi Street and chanted slogans against the shah. Suddenly, the police forces attacked. They arrived in plain clothes in unmarked cars and started beating protesters with batons. The pain on my back and shoulders, but even more the fear of state violence against teenagers' fragile bodies, robbed me of sleep for a long time to come. "Has nothing changed since then?" I thought. Historical images unfold a continuity of protest, the repetition and replication of street politics. This is the method of hope. The young woman with the green wristband, who was heading straight toward the waving batons in 2009, was a successor of my own experiences of batons in 1978. What has not changed is young people's hope for change.

Arriving at the square, I lost sight of the young woman, as there was a sudden tumult. All streets and roads to the center of Tehran where the protest was going on were blocked. My search around the square to see a trace of her was in vain. She was gone. How and where to? The level of violence the state used against the peaceful protesters was unexpected. The number of casualties is still unknown. Human rights groups say that hundreds of men and women disappeared, were killed, or were arrested. That day went down in history with the tragic death of Neda Agha-Soltan, a young woman murdered by a gunshot to her chest. The moment when Neda was shot and blood came trickling from her mouth, nose, and eyes, covering her face, was caught by several cell phone cameras. Pictures and video clips of her death were broadcast over the Internet within a few hours after the incident. Her death, described as "probably the most widely witnessed death in human history,"[1] radicalized the revolt, and Neda Agha-Soltan became the symbol for the Iranian youth protest.

Another iconic martyr of the youth protest movement, though less known internationally, was Sohrab Arabi, nineteen years old. He had already disappeared a few days earlier, during the huge demonstration of 15 June. His body was found on the outskirts of Tehran, killed by gunshot wounds to his heart. The symbolism of names in the political context of Iran is conspicuous. Neda, which in Persian means "voice" and "calling message," metaphorically became a voice for the gender aspect of the political conflict between the younger generation and the state. Groups, actions, and websites have been named after her, for example, Neda-ye Sabz (Green Voice) and Neda-ye Azadi (Voice of Freedom). Neda Agha-Soltan became the icon of the youth movement. Iranians in exile hold her pictures in front of their own faces during protests. In the case of Sohrab, it is a striking coincidence that his name is that of a well-known Persian legend that symbolizes a generational conflict. Prominent among the myths in the *Book of Kings* (*Shahnameh* by Abolgham Ferdowsi from the 1000s) is the epic story of Sohrab. It is a story of the brief life and tragic death of a young hero, Sohrab, who dies in his father Rostam's arms (see Clinton 1987). Sohrab had never met his father, Iran's greatest warrior. Raised in a foreign land, he too became a great warrior and decided to go to Iran to overthrow the shah Kay Kavus. Being an enemy of the shah makes Sohrab an enemy both of Iran and of God. His rebellion against the authorities puts him at war with Rostam, his own father and the only one in Iran who stands a chance to defeat Sohrab. Unaware of each other's identities, they fight, and Rostam kills Sohrab. The legend, in Mostafa Rahimi's words, depicts a "son-killing complex" in Iranian society. In his analysis, the son stands for a new order, whereas the father protects the ancien régime (Rahimi 1369/1990: 245). "Sohrab revolts not only against the political and social system but also against the family system" (243) and the father has to kill him to save the power. Rather than being a son, Sohrab was regarded as an enemy from a "foreign land." In a similar way, the post-electoral young protesters have been accused of being pawns of a "soft war" orchestrated by foreign states. Myth and reality are intertwined.

In the following months, more names of young people who disappeared, were killed, or were arrested were publicized. Several young women and men were raped and beaten to death in the Kahrizak detention center. Most victims of state brutality during the post-election protests belonged to the 60-generation. The young woman with the green wristband compellingly walked toward the square to make her voice heard. She was in the street, where she was not supposed to be that day. Lacking any other medium, she used the street to talk to the state. And she did. Like many others of her generation, the 60-generation, she found the street the only outlet to "make their voices heard." Common expressions that I heard from young Iranians, complaining about nonexistent state accountability, contained words of voice (*seda*), not hearing (*nashenidan*), and ear (*goosh*), for instance, "there is no ear to hear" (*goosh-e shenava nist*) or "to whose ear should we bring our voice?" (*sedamon ra be goosh-e kee beresonim?*). The street offers audibility and visibility to those who are not supposed to be heard and seen. This chapter is about *khiyaban*, the Iranian street, and what Jacques Rancière has coined "the distribution of the sensible," that regulates and arranges "the divisions between what is visible and invisible, sayable and unsayable, audible and inaudible." Drawing on Rancière's ideas, the street is where "the police" (the everyday order) is challenged by "politics," when "those who have no right to be counted as speaking beings make themselves of some account" (Rancière 1999: 27). Politics exists at the moment when one speaks when she or he is not to speak and when one partakes in what she or he has no part in (27).

The Iranian Street

Khiyaban is the Persian word for street. In the Revolution of 1979 and the Green Movement of 2009, both urban revolts, Iranians took to the streets. Since 1979, the street has been a major pillar of Iranian politics, an arena both for the official manifestations of state ideology and for oppositional protests. During the past three decades, the presence of people in the streets, not to consume or go to work but to claim their rights to the city and to demonstrate their protest, has transformed the political landscape entirely. The street is accordingly turned into a site for a series of contradictions and confrontations, such as conflicting lifestyles, political contestation, parodies of conventions, new forms of religiosity, interventions of the state in daily life, performances of youthfulness, and generational conflicts. This is how the street became the stage on which Iranian modernity is materialized in everyday life. Modernity as an experience and anticipation of constant transformation takes place in the urban landscape, characterized by the hypermobility of people, ideas, images, signs, and commodities through cables, highways, streets, squares, digital media, schools, universities, and public transportation. A setting for collisions of individualities, the streets are where creativity extends and modern urban identities are composed.

This is exactly what Marshall Berman argues that modern streets are about: the experience of constant disintegration. A street in Tehran, like those in New York, in Berman's words, "is a paradoxical unity, a unity of disunity: it pours us all into a maelstrom of perpetual disintegration and renewal, of struggle and contradiction, of ambiguity and anguish" (1982: 15). On the streets of Tehran, struggles, inconsistencies, paradoxes, and inequalities (of class, gender, age) are explicitly disclosed. They offer an opportunity for presence, youthfulness, adventure, political contestation, and transformation. As Berman put it, the street is where "everything we have, everything we know, everything we are" is challenged, threatened, and destroyed. On the street, "all that is solid melts into air" (15). This is the subversive power of the street: it is the space between the family and the state—the only space left beyond the control of both—and thus, a threatening place for both. The perceived threat of the street and of youth's "nonproductive" and "aimless" mobility is reflected in the negative connotations of terms such as "strolling along the streets" (*khiyaban gardi*), "going around in circles" (*dor zadan*), loafing (*allafi*), and loitering (*velgardi*) used to disparage young people. However, "going around in circles," without no other intention than just to move around is not a passive act of "killing time." It rather, in Walter Benjamin's view, expresses a protest against the spatial order and the division of labor:

> There was the pedestrian who wedged himself into the crowd, but there was also the flâneur who demanded elbow room and was unwilling to forego the life of the gentleman of leisure. His leisurely appearance as a personality is his protest against the division of labour which makes people into specialists. It was also his protest against their industriousness. (Benjamim 1983: 53)

For Benjamin, the "heroic flâneur" observes the expressions of modernity in the streets, that is, the constant disintegration, contestations, conflicts, and struggles. The flâneur turns into, in Benjamin's words, an "unwilling detective" who observes, investigates, and documents city life and its political and social crises. Therefore, the flâneur is seen as a "suspicious person," who like Georg Simmel's stranger, escapes social norms and whose "view contains dangerous possibilities" (Frisby 1994: 91). By this act of citizenship, the flâneur closes the gap between the state and the citizen (Shields 1994). Strolling thus becomes a politically charged activity (Frisby 1994), and the simple act of walking is linked to political action. In the Iranian context, the word *rahpeymai* means both a walk and a political march. As public figures, feeling at home in the streets, Iranian flâneurs are rejected by both state and society. They embody, as Benjamin says about flâneurs in Paris's arcades, an alienation from the metropolitan modernity, that is, consumerism, productivity, time effectiveness, and a rational mode of mobility through the city. Young Iranians' *rahpeymai*, in both meanings of the word, triggers an urban subjectivity through the actions of politics, challenging the everyday order that the police maintain. Furthermore, an interesting feature of the youth's street politics is that their urban practices trigger a disruption of the public/private dichotomy. As the ethnographic snapshots in this chapter show, young Iranians bring the private sphere more and more into the public sphere. Paraphrasing Benjamin, young Iranians turn coffee shops into living rooms, walls into notebooks (graffiti), and cars into balconies (a private space with a view over the public).

Street Politics

I arrived in Tehran a few days before the eleventh presidential election in 2013. On the night of Saturday 15 June, one day after the election, thousands of young people occupied the streets and squares in Iran's larger cities to celebrate Hassan Rohani's victory in the election, or rather to rejoice the end of Mahmoud Ahmadinejad's presidency. Three nights later, on 18 June, young Iranians again flooded the streets to celebrate Iran's victory over South Korea in a football match that qualified Iran for the 2014 World Cup finals. These nights were rare moments when bodies were liberated in the streets. When the police forces were more or less absent, there were scenes of a remarkable fusion of nationalist sentiments, anti-regime chanting, and youthful carnivalesque. During these nights, central streets in Tehran and other large cities were seized by young people. The main streets were blocked by cars, and loudspeakers blasted illicit music. Some women took off their veils. Men and women danced openly. People switched car lights on and off and honked car horns. Other people simply used anything at hand to make noise. Sound and noise are key elements of carnivals. The carnivalesque entails both visibility and audibility (Dragićević-Šešić 2011). To make noise is subversive. The phrase *saro seda kardan* means both "to make noise" and also "to protest." To make noise is to disrupt the everyday order, the police. Raising one's voice and making noise make oneself audible, part of what Rancière means by the term politics. *Saro seda kardan* is an attempt to find "a receptive ear" (*goosh-e shenava*), to make oneself heard. Considering the subversive force of *saro seda kardan*, it is not surprising that making noise is criminalized, labeled as sound pollution (*alodegi souti*). The police stop and penalize young people and even impound their cars when they play music or make noise. What happened during these nights was the "carnivalization" of society, a sort of youth movement to reclaim their rights to the city and their youthfulness. Young Iranians wait for opportunities, on any pretext, to catch the short-lived and elusive moment to occupy the streets and make the urban spaces something of their own. During both nights, I heard people chanting "Ya Hossein, Mir Hossein," praising Mir Hossien Mousavi, the leader of the Green Movement, and thereby generating historical links to the post-election protests in 2009. These two nights in June 2013 recalled the days and nights four years earlier, before and after the previous presidential election.

June 2009

I was in Tehran to follow the tenth presidential election in 2009. The week before election day, the streets of Tehran and other large cities were transformed into an arena for a collective fiesta and a space for public political engagement. The streets were occupied by young people dressed in green T-shirts and green wristbands, headbands, and banners. The rallies were nonviolent and cheerful. Afterward, young people talked about the nights before the election as an unforgettable time when freedom was felt bodily. My interlocutors told me that women had removed their veils. Young men and women danced to music from car stereos, a scene otherwise unthinkable in the Islamic Republic. The rallies were called "nightly parties" in the official discourse to depoliticize the presence of the young people in the streets. However, the nightly rallies had a carnivalesque character. The carnivalesque, as Mikhail Bakhtin (1984) puts it, contains political potentialities. The nights of the election offered young people a celebration of chaos, disorder, and anarchy, the inversion of social norms and codes, a pause from the seriousness of everyday life. The carnivalesque has taken on a more political significance in Iran since collective joy has been suppressed since the Revolution of 1979. Generally, any collective gathering and action, other than official ones, has been banned. As Arendt (1994 [1951]) states, the heart of totalitarian regimes is the experience of deep loneliness. The use of isolation—disabling people from doing collective actions or being in direct contact with each other in public—has been a salient characteristic of oppressive regimes. Totalitarian rule destroys the space between individuals, a space in which people can act spontaneously and as free subjects and citizens. In this context, the carnivalesque ambience of the nights before the election offered a moment of what Durkheim (1965) calls "collective effervescence." Durkheim sees such emotional collective experiences as an essential aspect of religious rites and rituals, forging a collective identity over subdivisions.

Hardly twenty-four hours after the polls closed, the official news agency announced that Ahmadinejad had won with 62 percent of the votes. Most people I talked with used the word "shock" to describe their feelings at that moment. The shock soon turned into resentment, and angry young people took to the streets to launch a large, dynamic, and vigorous social movement under the slogan "Where is my vote?" The streets of Tehran and other large cities became the stage for huge demonstrations and protests on a scale not seen since the Revolution of 1979. Clashes broke out between police and groups of young protesters. Three days after the election in June, the twelve million people in Tehran took to the streets for a historic demonstration. It was in the streets that the contestation between the police and the young protesters unfolded. In addition to political clashes, the protesters displayed the authority's weakness by parodying the conventional.

The carnivalization of society involves irony and sarcasm, ridiculing and playing with official slogans. A remarkable example was when young people displayed carnivalesque responses to the official event of the 2009 Quds Day. Since 1979, the last Friday of Ramadan has been assigned to the International Quds Day, a day for the Iranian state to orchestrate annual ceremonies to denounce Israel. The annual ceremony has been significant for the Iranian state to remind Iranian and non-Iranian people of its state ideology. In 2009, Quds Day was on 18 September, a few months after the contested presidential election. Since all public manifestations by the opposition were banned, the official ceremony of Quds Day was a good opportunity for young protesters to demonstrate the limitations of the hegemonic order and turn Quds Day into a counterdemonstration. Traditionally during this celebration, march slogans are chanted first by government agents over loudspeakers, to which the crowd responds. On Quds Day in 2009, the crowd responded differently. Instead of the slogans "*Esteqlal, azadi, jomhuriye eslami*" (Independence, Freedom, Islamic Republic), young people shouted "*Esteqlal, azadi, jomhuriye irani*" (Independence, Freedom, Iranian Republic); instead of "*In khon ke dar rag-e mast hediye be rahbar-e mast*" (The blood running in our vessels is a gift to our leader), they shouted "The blood running in our vessels is a gift to our nation"; instead of "Death to America! Death to Israel," they shouted "Death to China! Death to Russia" (two states believed to support Ahmadinejad). Young Iranians also chanted "*Felestin ro raha kon, fekri be hal-e ma kon*" (Forget Palestine! Do something for us) or "*Na Gaza, na Lobnan, jaanam fadaa-ye Iran*" (No to Gaza, no to Lebanon, my life for Iran) in response to the Iranian authorities' support for Palestinians in Gaza and Hezbollah in Lebanon.

The tactics (de Certeau 1984) used by young protesters—parody, sarcasm, and distortion—disclosed the limitations and ineffectiveness of the hegemonized order (Kelly and Kaplan 1990: 137). This Quds Day showed how young Iranians refused to "satisfy the authorities' narrative demand." Here I refer to Homi Bhabha's notion of "sly civility" (1994). Bhabha uses the term to explore the colonized subject's civil disobedience and rejection of the colonizer's domination. Like the colonizers, the Iranian authorities demand feedback. The young people do not respond, and when they do give feedback, it is for purposes other than those intended by the authorities. On 17 July 2009, Iranian protesters used the same "sly civility" strategy when they participated in the Friday prayer (usually the conservative forces' weekly manifestation) to display their power. It became a controversial Friday prayer. Young people were pushed back by the police and forced not to take part. Disrespecting the strict gender segregation for religious rituals, young men and women, side by side, prayed in the streets. In a similar way, my interlocutors told me that, in schools and universities during morning prayer ceremonies, students had chanted back altered Quran verses or slogans. Another salient example of sly civility was a parodied version of Ashura (the tenth of Moharram, the day of martyrdom of Imam Hossein in the year 680). The ritual is a complex arrangement of collective, public, ritualized mourning. Sarcastically called a "Hossein Party," it is a symbolic parody of the convention, an altered performance of one of the most holy ceremonies for Shia Muslims (see Khosravi 2008). As Bakhtin puts it, "Parody . . . is especially well suited to the needs of oppositional culture, precisely because it deploys the force of the dominant discourse against itself" (as quoted in Stam 1992: 173).

Another outstanding example of sly civility happened when Majid Tavakoli, a student leader, was arrested in December 2009 on National Student Day. Several hours after his arrest, official news agencies published pictures of Tavakoli dressed in women's clothing or the hijab. In the authorities' sexist ideology, the pictures would "discredit" and "humiliate" him by "reducing" him to a woman. Iranians' response was quick and spectacular. Hundreds of Iranian men posted pictures of themselves in veil on websites, Facebook pages, and blogs, as well as in other forms. For many of them, this was also a gesture of solidarity with Iranian women for whom it has been compulsory to wear the hijab for the past three decades. In these examples, young people deployed the force of the dominant discourse against itself. Bhabha (1994) asserts that sly civility generates a sense of paranoia for the colonizer who does not see the meaning of his colonial project. Similarly, young Iranians' refusal to satisfy the authorities' demand has generated paranoia among the authorities, which, in turn, has triggered a series of conspiracy theories. Young people's various forms of refusals are all categorized as parts of "cultural invasion" or "the soft war," a plot believed to be designed and financed by hostile foreign states.

Streets and Sidewalks

Since the 1980s, the street has been monopolized by the state for well-orchestrated rituals by bringing "the people on the scene" (*ummat-e hamishe dar sahneh*). People have come to the street, by force or by promise of rewards, for designed and planned anniversary rallies or official ceremonies. However, any other forms of political use of the street is not tolerated and, therefore, forcefully oppressed. During the Green Movement, the state used violence to protect and preserve its monopolized "right" to streets. The use of public places by people is tolerated only when *passively* used, for instance, for walking, for shopping, or for going to work. The state considers itself the sole authority that manages and controls public spaces (Bayat 2010). Any activities in the street is controlled and regulated by the state through traffic laws and the police force. To separate the sidewalks from the streets is, for instance, a technique used to regulate citizens' movements; the sidewalk (*piadero*) is for the people, but the street is for the state. As the blogger and freelance journalist Mehdi Jami writes,

> The idea of people on sidewalks is exactly the meaning of politics in Iran. The people should be in the margin and not in the center. They are only used as decoration. When the state wishes they can be on the streets but then they are sent back to the margin.[2]

Sidewalks in Tehran, particularly those on smaller streets, are in a state of disrepair, making pedestrians' use of sidewalks difficult. Abundant cracks and broken concrete make the ground uneven. Usually, Tehranis park their cars in front of their houses, thus occupying parts of the sidewalks. Moreover, due to the absence of standards or rather because of institutionalized corruption (among municipality employees), new constructions have invaded the sidewalks. All these hinder pedestrians, make walking difficult, and sidewalks become inaccessible for people using wheelchairs or parents with baby strollers. The violent removal of street vendors by municipality agents is also part of the state's attack on sidewalks and pedestrians. While the poor vendors are brutally removed from the pedestrians in order to "alleviate mobility," private companies use the sidewalks as their location of business. Construction companies use the sidewalks to store construction materials, car dealers place cars on sidewalks to exhibit their goods, and rich people park their expensive imported cars on sidewalks to protect them from damage by other cars.

The street-sidewalk border is best visible in the most politicized parts of Tehran. In specific places in central Tehran, railings have been put up to keep pedestrians off the streets. For instance, in Haft-e Tir Square, and around Chahrah Valiasr (the intersection of the Enqelab and Valiasr streets), the sidewalk is separated from the street by 1.5-meter metal railings. The municipality and the police argue that the railings have been put there for traffic safety reasons and "to save lives." People are directed to use footbridges or underground walkways to cross to the other side of the street. The construction of the Valiasr underpass in 2014 has been a harsh attack on pedestrians. A complex underground walkway is built to "alleviate mobility of cars." Blocking the sidewalks from the streets with railings and directing people to use an underpass is a way to regulate and control the movement of walkers. The underpass is open only between 6 a.m. and 12 p.m. and is equipped with surveillance cameras. This is an example of the "securitization of the urban spaces" in Tehran and vacating the streets (Tehrani 1394/2015). The intersection is no longer a space for intersecting and connecting but only for passing through. Controlling the movement of people is much easier now. In January 2016, at each entrance to the underpass, there was a policeman with a gun in his hand. Now four armed policemen could monitor the movement of people across the whole intersection. Meanwhile, in the underground tunnel, the municipality had put large cartoons on the walls with messages against vendors in the metro. Similarly, railings in the middle of Enqelab Street block, delay, and restrain the movement of pedestrians.

Interestingly, all three spots mentioned here were crucial loci for urban uprisings during the Revolution of 1979 and the Green Movement in 2009. Chahrah Valiasr is located in the middle of several large and important universities, for example, Tehran University and Amirkabir University of Technology, and next to Park-e Daneshjoo (Student Park) and Teatr-e Shahr (the City Theater). Since the Revolution of 1979, this intersection has been the center for political manifestations in Tehran. Historically, the most dynamic and vigorous student movements have emerged from this place, in the middle of two important universities. Haft-e Tir Square is also a place with many coffee shops, bookstores, and newspaper offices. Tehran University is located on one side of Enqelab Street and numerous bookstores and coffee shops on the other. Along several main streets, such as Enqelab Street (which ironically means "Revolution Street"), there are two rows of railings in the middle of the street that designate the middle lane to the Bus Rapid Transit. It is not difficult to see how the installation of railings, blocking pedestrians' access to the streets, is part of a new urban design to avoid urban revolts.

The restriction of safe and easy crossings makes pedestrians' ability to occupy squares, intersections, and streets difficult. The "failure" of the post-electoral protests in 2009 showed that Tehran is designed to prevent urban uprisings. The protesters were unable to keep together, move fast, and hold places, whereas the police could move fast and efficiently using the freeways and Bus Rapid Transit corridors. The opposite could be said, for example, of the Tahrir Square in Cairo, inspired by Baron Haussmann's model for the re-construction of Paris. Its huge size with several streets converging into the square facilitated the movement of the protesters while the police found it difficult to get a good overview of the whole square. Such features of urban design allowed for the congregation and occupation of the square by several hundreds thousand of protesters (see Weizman 2015).

However, while spatial relations contribute to the creation of "docile sub-jects," space can also provide opportunities to contest power. The spatial has both an element of order and an element of chaos (Massy 1993: 156). One form of defiance is the carnivalization of society (cf. Jackson 1988). While the "carni-valization of society" in a political context is criticized as depolitization and demoralization of politics, for instance, in the United States (see Braun and Langman 2011), the carnivalization of the streets by Iranian youth is a form of collective action by people who feel isolated from each other and lack any means to mobilize themselves or to network. Carnivalesque manifestations have been condemned by the authorities as street festivities, as middle-class youth's leisure seeking. Indeed, these carnivalesque occasions were valuable moments of the conjunction of politics and everyday life. It is from the carnivalization of the streets that new political battles emerge—young people's claim for their votes, the right to the city, and their youthfulness. The street is preeminently an arena for politics. The street, for those who structurally lack any institutional setting to express discontent, is the only locus of collective protest. The street offers a channel for "instantaneous communication among atomized individuals, which is established by the tacit recognition of their common identity and is mediated through space" (Bayat 1997: 16). The street is the medium through which peo-ple can address the state. This is what Bayat calls "street politics":

A set of conflicts and the attendant implications between a collective populace and the authorities, shaped and expressed episodically in the

physical and social space of the streets—from the alleyways to the
more visible sidewalks, public parks, or sport places. (1997: 15)

Individuals' active use of the street (their presence on the streets, civic engagement, political mobilization (Jacobs 1961), and "stranger-sociability" (Warner
2002: 56) lead to "public sentiments" (Barker 2009: 157). Thus, the street
serves as a medium through which strangers establish communication and
recognize mutual interest and shared sentiments (Bayat 2010: 12). Through
this medium, isolated individuals can become active citizens claiming citizenship rights and demanding state accountability.

A recent example of an act of citizenship in the streets is the witnessing
(observation, documentation, and spread) of police brutality. For instance,
the violence against "improperly veiled" women has for long been unnoticed.
Today, such violence often leads to interventions by people who have witnessed an incident. It is not uncommon that the intervention leads to clashes
between the people and the police. Police violence is increasingly recorded on
cell phones and, within a short period of time, is broadcast via social media
or YouTube. The brutal oppression of post-election protests was recorded and
documented, almost entirely by ordinary people on the streets. So-called citizen journalism, as an alternative way of spreading news and information,
raises awareness of social injustice and civil rights. Citizen journalism is an
aspect of street politics and is, thus, a result of and shaped by a combination
of events unfolding on the streets. Rather than a "tweeter revolution" (as it has
been called by foreign journalists and media scholars), the Green Movement
emerged from street politics, either in the form of the nightly carnivalesque
presence of young people on the streets or in the form of protest demonstrations afterward. The election in 2009 became an event that for the 60-
generation turned the streets into an arena for political actions. The persistent
presence of young Iranians has produced political spaces (de Certeau 1984)
out of places that otherwise were used passively for transportation or shopping. Interestingly, during the post-election protests, a tactic used by young
people to elude police violence was to *depoliticize* their presence on the street
by pretending to be there for shopping or waiting for buses. This illustrates the
double function of the street: open for shopping or passing through but closed
for politics. This dialectical function of the street is a characteristic of
modernity.

Since the commencement of the Green Movement, *the street* became a
predominant and central concept in the debates among the 60-generation's

intellectuals and activists. This younger generation is influenced by modern philosophers such as Jacques Rancière, Alain Badiou, and Slavoj Žižek, who believe that political change is possible only through a politics of the public body. Intellectuals, writers, and translators such as Omid Mehregan or Amin Bozorgian (1391/2012), just to name a few, emphasize the necessity of street politics for real change. This generation of activists/intellectuals believes that, without street politics or the politicization of the street, any movement is bound to fail. In their view, for real political changes to take place, street clashes between those who lack any kind of institutional power and the authorities are inevitable. "To live politics," that is, to bring politics into the streets and make it part of everyday life, is characteristic of modernity. Compared to the Arab Spring, Iranian activists/intellectuals argue that the main weakness of the Green Movement was leaving the streets at night. The experiences from the Revolution of 1979 and the Green Movement in 2009 show that only politics of/on the streets can turn isolated individuals into citizens in Iran.[3]

Civility

The political is materialized on the street since the street functions as a medium connecting the self to the collective, reconciling individual interests with the interests of the collective. In turn, it can result in the configuration of a certain kind of civic self that assumes responsibilities toward others. Street politics, or acts of citizenship, is also linked to civility. A society requires a shared and communicated civility among its members. Streets are arenas for communication and performing (political) civility. The youth movement, manifesting itself in the Green Movement, is perhaps the first social movement in modern Iran that goes beyond political ideologies to concentrate on citizenship rights. The absence of ideologies increases the chance for diversity, tolerance, and pluralism. A comparison of the slogans of the Revolution of 1979 with the slogans of the Green Movement shows a change in Iranians' political behavior. In the former, wishing death on enemies (for example, "Death to the Shah" or "Death to America") dominated, whereas, in the latter, "death slogans" were rarely heard. "Silent demonstrations," civil slogans (for example, "Where is my vote?"), or even slogans such as "Long live my enemy" characterized the 2009 protests. Furthermore, following the mass arrest of protesters, a new political behavior has occurred: the open expression of love and affections for the imprisoned by their partners outside. *Del-neveshteha* (heart writings) on blogs or other media linked the individual experience of politics to the experiences of the collective. Publicizing private emotions interweaved the personal with the collective political civility. This opened a space for sharing not only love and affections but also experiences of other emotions. For example, Young men and women's testimonies of rape in detention shocked the nation. Their individual accounts of rape generated also a wave of former prisoners' personal stories of rape from the early 1980s.

Nostalgic narratives about the display of solidarity and civility during the post-electoral protests, and even during the Revolution of 1979 are often shared and remembered. These narratives testify to the politeness, tolerance, and generosity that people showed each other on the streets during the political tumults. It is said that drivers, who otherwise would never respect traffic rules, gave space to others; people shared cars, opened their houses to protect people fleeing police brutality, or shared sweets and drinks with protesters on the streets. These narratives of civility convey the link between the street and civility. Civility is experienced when street politics is most intense. Ideas of tolerance and pluralism were also spread via social media. If only one image could visualize the political civility by youth in the post-electoral protests, it would undoubtedly be a picture depicting a young female protester stretching out her arms trying to protect several policemen from the angry crowd. The photo is from a few days after the election, at the most intensive time of the protest. In the photo, a handful of anti-riot policemen are crammed in the corner of a street surrounded by a crowd of protesters. A young woman is standing between the crowd and the policemen, stretching out her arms. Behind her we see an injured policeman with blood running from his forehead. A few months later this picture was published on personal blogs and Facebook walls next to an image of *The Intervention of the Sabine Women*. Painted by the French artist Jacques-Louis David in 1799, it illustrates the Roman legend of Hersilia who rushes between her husband and her father to prevent bloodshed. The juxtaposition of these two images explains two characteristics of the youth movement. First, it recognizes and emphasizes the woman's role for social changes. Second, historical awareness historicizes the nonviolent philosophy (for example, with references to Iranian history, Zarathustra, and Cyrus the Great).

Ideas of tolerance in Iranian history (coupled with nationalist sentiments) have inspired political civility among the young generation. A quote from Zarathustra appeared everywhere, on city walls as graffiti and on people's

Facebook pages: "My war is only with darkness. To fight darkness, I don't draw a sword, but light a lantern." Another historical reference was to Cyrus the Great, the founder of the Achaemenid Empire. It is believed that he was the founder of the first charter of human rights and that the persecution of the Jews ended in Babylon under his reign. In a time of intolerance, extensive corruption, and political violence, young Iranians built an idea of political civility based on their own imagined or real history of tolerance and the recognition of the Other. As I will show in the next chapter, a new wave of graffiti signals images and words of peace and tolerance and brings attention to social injustices.

The Moral Geography of the Streets

For the parental generation, young people's street life is also subversive. Youth's persistent presence on the streets violates the norms and the moral geography that strictly separate the family sphere from the street. The official moral geography in Iran is organized so that it segregates the family (read: women) from the public (read: *namahram*, unrelated men) assumed to be a potential threat to the moral order of sexual purity that is upheld and protected by the omnipresence of the patriarch. How the patriarchal father pays attention to the female virtues (*namous*) of his family resembles how the state manages public spaces. The youth use the streets as a means for emancipation from the family. The street is the opposite of the home and the school. On the streets, young people experience liberation from their parents and the state. The street also functions as a medium for the transition into adulthood. A feeling of independence arises once teenagers get permission to spend time alone on the street. This permission is interpreted as the acceptance of his or her maturity (Sadr 1392/2013). Needless to mention, this struggle for the street differs for men and women. Boys are granted permission to stay on the streets on their own much more easily and at a younger age than their sisters.

Bourgeois moralism distinguishes *khane* (literally, home, the civilized family sphere) from *khiyaban*, which is perceived as a space of immorality and vulgarity. "Civilized" bodies are those that have been socialized in the private family sphere (*tou khan-e bozorg shodan*, literally, growing up within the family), while "uncivilized" bodies have grown up on the street or in society (*tou jamme-e*). Family belonging (*khanevade-dar bodan*), being a family-possessed (*khanevadeh-dar*) person connotes morality, civility, or virtue. As mentioned in Chapter 3, according to this family-centered paradigm, outside the home and the family there is wilderness. In opposition to *khanevadeh* is *khiyaban*, the street, which is associated with the wild, anomie, and sexual harm. *Koche* (the alley) is an interstitial space between the private and the public, under the control of patriarchal gaze of parents and neighbors. The alley is part of the quarter, a protected and monitored space. The streets, in contrast, are spaces outside the family sphere, where there are serious moral dangers that threaten the physical and mental hygiene of young persons (see Rejali 1994: 86–89). As the urban sociologist AbdouMaliq Simone argues, the street is imagined as "something outside normative social life. . . . Outside an over-coded regime of civility" (Simone 2010: 223).

The spatial imagination of the binary opposition of *khane/khiyaban* is based on class. The street is the fate for those whose lack of education, re-sources, and connections makes them marginal everywhere else (Simone 2010: 222). That the street could be one's fate is what parents say to warn their children: "If you don't succeed in school or work, you will finally end up on the street." The street, thus, is place of "failed people." The further south of the city (*jonoob-e shahr*) and in less privileged neighborhoods, *khiyaban* is per-ceived as even more "uncivilized"—a fear embodied in the hyper-masculinity of working-class men, labeled *arazel owbash*, as previously discussed. Work-ing-class men who hang around on the streets are animalized. "The streets are full of wolves," parents usually tell their children. Interestingly, the term *vel-gard*, "loafer," is used both for human beings and dogs. The term commonly used for dogs is *sag-e velgard* (stray dog). The bodies on the streets, whose movements are regarded as meaningless, are thought of as stray dogs.

In October 2013, accompanied by an interlocutor, I went to Cinema Azadi to see *Hees, Hees, Dokhtarha Faryad Nemiznand* (Shush! Girls, Don't Scream, by Pooran Derakhshandeh, 2013), a film about pedophilia and how a combi-nation of a sexist legal system and traditional values of family honor (*aberou*) leaves the victims unprotected, alone, and even blamed and punished. The film received a lot of attention and won the audience award at the Fajr Film Festival in 2014. It was an early afternoon on a weekday. The people who watched the film with us were young, probably students. Cinema Azadi is a several-story modern theater located in the northern part of central Tehran, where tickets cost more than in theaters farther south in Tehran. Cinema Azadi, in my interlocutor's words, has a cultural atmosphere (*fazay-e far-hangi*) and is patronized by middle-class people. My interlocutor, a twenty-six-year-old woman who worked as graphic designer, believed working-class people usually go to the theaters in the central and southern parts of Tehran, such as the Cinema Pars at Enqelab Square. In her words, these theaters have "a male and working-class atmosphere" that makes visiting "unsafe" and "uncomfortable" for young women. *Hees, Hees, Dokhtarha Faryad Nemiznand* discusses a problem barely discussed in Iran. Nevertheless, it misses the mark since it is based on class prejudices and patriarchal moralism. The two pedophiles in the movie are working-class men from an unknown background, without family, without home. One of them is a young worker, originally from a village along the coast of the Caspian Sea, who has migrated to Tehran for work. He lives in what resembles a shed more than a house. The other man is a concierge in a high-rise building, seemingly living in a room in the basement. In contrast to these two single (non-Tehrani, at least one of them) working-class men, presented as without home/family (*khane/khanevadeh*), the victims' families are middle-class, successful business people, living in homey places. Moreover, the film implicitly blames the mothers, whose absence from home (one runs a bridal shop, and the other is not taking her "motherly duty" seriously) makes the children easy prey for the offenders. My interlocutor and I watched the bourgeois family-centered film in a "middle-class" theater far from those who were presented in the film as dangerous, immoral offenders, those from the south of the city or migrant workers from the provinces, those without home and family, and thereby imagined as evil, unreliable, and dangerous. My interlocutor's fear of working-class men in the theaters in southern parts of Tehran fits the same imagined moral geography the film reproduced. When I challenged her, she admitted that verbal and even physical sexual harassment is also very common at middle-class parties and gatherings. In contrast to what the praised movie illustrates, statistics show that rape and pedophilia are more common among married men than among singles.[4] The piety of "home/family" and the demonization of the street are also a recurrent and central theme in several television serials. The dichotomy between the family sphere and the street is, however, preeminently gendered and sexualized. I do not play down the gravity of physical and verbal sexual harassment that women and even young men (60 percent of all victims of registered rape in 1390/2011 were young men) are exposed to on the streets (see Abazari et al. 1387/2008). However, I argue that the demonization of the street is preeminently a way to reproduce class-based patriarchal family authority and domination.

Strolling Around

Deprecation of loafing and loitering is reflected in the Persian language. As mentioned above, *velgard*, the one whose mobility has no meaning or value, refers both to a human being and to a dog. The terms used for loitering such as *velgardi, khiyaban gardi, parse zadan*, and *dor zadan* connote irresponsibility and immorality. Young people's loitering is provocative. An expert warns that young Iranians hold the "world record" in loitering:

> Not having a planned and organized life young people spend a lot of their time in the streets. . . . This has become a social habit and an entertainment for them. . . . The streets are full of polluted elements. . . . In the streets these young people are beyond control of the family and the society and therefore exposed to social damages.[5]

Loitering is also seen as damaging the family since young people spend more time in the streets than at home with their families (Hoshangi 1391/2012). Conservative forces in Qom (a holy city south of Tehran) criticized youngsters loitering in streets and argued that their loitering was an act of disrespect to the martyrs.[6] Article 712 of the current penal law classifies loitering as a crime and imposes a prison sentence for up to three months. This article originates in the first modern legislation. Article 273 of the 1925 penal code identifies a loiterer as "a person older than fifteen years old who has no specific accommodation or livelihood." In 1321/1942, the article was modified, identifying a loiterer as one "who due to indolence and thoughtlessness does not work." The penal code obligates the state to put loiterers to work by force; if they refuse, they can be sentenced to jail. Unchanged since 1925, the penal code still deprives *velgards* of their citizenship rights. For instance, their testimony is not valid in courts, and they are not entitled to hold a passport.[7]

In a series of books published by the Social and Cultural Studies Office of Tehran, young people's mobility and visibility in public places are presented as social harms. One of the books on youth's life in the city focuses on young Tehranis' loitering. It is a short book (seventy-six pages) based on interviews with young people about the causes and incentives for loitering. It shows some of the problems pushing young people from their homes and explains why the streets attract them. In conclusion, however, the author identifies a long list of social damages that street loitering causes the family and society: "family conflicts, a generational gap, emotional damages, criminalities, public violence, unlimited freedom, escape from the family, increase of social anomies, indifference, and unlawfulness" (Sadr 1392/2013: 60; see also Hoshangi 1391/2012). The mobility and visibility of young men and women in the streets challenge the patriarchal state and the parental generation. In this context, walking can easily be turned into a defined form of defiance and protest. It is in this context that the Persian word *rahpeymayi* means both to walk and to demonstrate. The conjunction of loitering and street politics can also be seen in other societies. A recent youth movement in São Paulo, Brazil, is called *rolezinhos* (literally, a little stroll). The term refers to the gathering in shopping malls of hundreds, and in some occasions up to a thousand, young people from *favelas* (slums). *Rolezinho* is often just a leisurely activity for the working-class young to pass time in luxury malls. These gatherings have, however, sometimes turned into protests. On one occasion in January 2014, when up to three thousand young people participated in the *rolezinhos*, the police used rubber bullets and tear gas to disperse the crowd.[8] The police and shopkeepers believe that *rolezinhos* scare away their middle-class customers. Anthropologist Rosana Pinheiro-Machado sees *rolezinhos* as something more than just a search for fun: they express the tension regarding visibility and citizenship rights.[9]

The sociopolitical aspect of young people's, and particularly women's, mobility and visibility in public places is a recurrent theme in independent cinema and visual art. For instance, Dariush Gharahzad captures the youthfulness and changing urban youth culture, patterns of mobility, and countercultures in his paintings. Another young artist is Saghar Daeeri. Her series of paintings *Passazhha* (Shopping Malls) portray young Tehrani women in shopping malls. They convey perfectly the tension between the aesthetics of modesty imposed by the state on the young women and their self-assertion of individual will, desire, and eroticism. *Passazh gardi* has become a main urban practice for young Iranians (Khosravi 2008; see also Kazemi 1392/2013). *Flânerie* in shopping malls is not only about leisure. It is also a struggle for subjectivity. "Strolling in malls" is a subversive form of mobility and visibility of bodies not supposed to be mobile and visible. As I showed in my ethnography of the Golestan Shopping Mall in northwestern Tehran (Khosravi 2008), malls for young Iranians are sites of pleasure and agency. A majority of young people cannot afford the commodities on sale in these modern shopping malls. Like *rolezinhos* for the youth from the favelas in São Paulo, "strolling in malls" for young Tehranis is to be visible, as citizens, as members of society. They stroll around looking at commodities, imagining, and talking about consumption. The mall is a place for imagining what it would be like to be part of a world beyond their own, a scene for performing and consuming youthfulness. It functions as a center of communication, vision, and imagination for young people. The repetitive, innovative, and collective performance of loafing at malls leads to a collective imagination of youthfulness. This is what turns the malls into a space of agency and defiance. Daeeri's grotesque paintings in strong colors of figures, expressive faces, and incisive gazes illustrate a carnivalesque, subversive, and seditious young generation of Iranian women. The young women in her paintings are provocative and grotesquely covered in heavy makeup, making extreme gestures. Their behavior illustrates the will and yearning of young Iranians to perform their youthfulness in public. The carnivalesque figures and their "exaggerated" behavior express the 60-generation's reaction to the restrictions they face in their daily lives. They perform sly civility. The fact that the young women in Daeeri's paintings "incite a sense of anxiety" in some viewers (Saghafi 2009: 38) stems from the sly civility performed by the figures in the paintings who refuse to satisfy the demands of their parents' generation and society.

The Private in the Street

Patriarchal moralism is based on a rigid dichotomy between the private and the public. After the Revolution, Iranian society experienced two different, even contradictory, transformations of the public/private spheres. On the one hand, the private/public dichotomy has deepened. On the other hand, there has been a pattern of penetration of the public into the private and of the private into the public. Private issues have become national concerns and thereby issues for the public. This is perhaps best illustrated by looking at the vanishing distinction between the illegal, the immoral, and the sinful, and the fact that crime, vice, and sin have become synonymous. The streets have become arenas for the government's "engineering of goodness," underpinned by the Quranic rule of *amr-e be m'arouf va nahi az monkar* (literally, the need for what is beneficial and the rejection of what is reprehensible). Performed by a huge governmental apparatus, *amr-e be m'arouf va nahi az monkar* has publicly targeted citizens' private issues (see Khosravi 2008). In a hyperpoliticized society like Iran, every detail of everyday life is politicized and thus becomes the public concerns. Bahram, a twenty-three-year-old man, put it very well:

What we do in private, like how we have sex or if we drink alcoholic beverages is their [the state's] business but not what happens with us when it comes to public issues such as jobs, housing or education.

State intervention into the private sphere is well documented by Iranian artists. For instance, the art photographer Shadi Ghadirian's *Nil Nil* series is one example. In her photographs, she juxtaposes military equipment with ordinary, everyday household things: bullets in a makeup bag, military boots standing next to a pair of red stilettos in the living room, a hand grenade in a fruit bowl, and another one in a bed. Military equipment, symbols of state violence, encroaching upon every corner of the home illustrates how the arms of the state reach into Iranians' most private spheres. Perhaps not surprisingly, most artists who reveal the public intervention into the private are women. Contrary to the conservatives' aim to keep the private distinct from the public, there has been an increasing diffusion, overlap, and penetration of what is considered private or public. As shown in the previous chapters, the private sphere of the home is now a place where a significant part of education, elder care, and (informal) business goes on. Pushed back from the public places, young people take refuge at home. Since the street is also a site where state brutality against young people is performed, parents have learned to have a more liberal attitude toward their children in order to protect them. They willingly or reluctantly tolerate their children's new lifestyle and allow them to perform activities that are illegal. The private space of the home has thus become a space for "cultural crimes." Basements have been turned into music studios and sites for mixed-sex parties. Living rooms have become a place for dating. Even activities such as art performances, seminars, fashion shows, and illicit music concerts are arranged at home in semi-private forms (only trusted people are invited). Furthermore, more and more middle-class homes have become a space for private education for preparing students for university entrance exams. These public activities in private spaces have blurred the private/public distinction.

During the post-election protests of 2009, one political behavior enacted was the nightly chant of *Allahu Akbar* (God is Great) from the rooftops. Every night at 10 p.m., people climbed up onto the roofs of their houses to express their discontent and make their voices heard publicly. The rooftops of private houses were turned into platforms for acts of citizenship, with people demanding answers from the state: "Where is my vote?" Or, as I will show in the next chapter, walls are used by young Iranians to express their love and passion. These are some examples of how young Iranians challenge the private/public dichotomy.

The active presence of women in the Revolution of 1979 and the Green Movement resulted in the "breach of the public/private binary" (Sadeghi 2012). Actions and mediations initiated by women during and after the Green Movement blurred the boundaries between the private and the public even more. Women published their love letters to their imprisoned husbands online and organized the public manifestation of the "Mourning Mothers" (2012: 125). In general, there has been a tendency to present Muslim societies in terms of a strict dichotomy between the public (outside, political, male) and the private (indoor, domestic, female) spaces. This chapter attempts to draw attention to changes in the urban setting and show how new urban practices have transformed the gendered spatial order. The ethnography of the everyday life of young Iranians and their visibilities in Tehran and other large cities questions this dichotomy. What has been regarded as domestic and private has been politicized and thereby made public. All these transformations of the function and the use of the private and the public spheres and young people's new urban practices have unsettled and blurred the Orientalist distinction drawn, usually, between the private and the public life in Middle Eastern societies.

Coffee and Conflicts in Isfahan

Kafeneshini is one example of where the boundary between the public and the private is blurred. *Neshini* means "sitting" in Persian, and the term *kafeneshini* (literally, sitting in a café) refers to another form of youth visibility and a new urban practice: spending time in coffee shops. Youth *kafeneshini* is a new practice of visibility that began in the early 2000s when modern coffee shops in larger cities mushroomed. The increasing popularity of coffee consumption and coffee shops among young Iranians is clearly seen in terms of their numbers. Between 2006 and 2011, importation of coffee increased fivefold. And the number of coffee shops in Tehran has now reached three thousand. These coffee shops are presented as *modern* spaces. The whole concept—the interior, menu, and ambiance—displays a modern lifestyle. Coffee shops are associated with a youth culture. Above all, the coffee shop is a modern space, where urban modernity, in Berman's meaning, that is, constant disintegration, struggles, and contradictions take place and are performed.

The coffee shop, known in Iran by its English term, is different from the traditional coffee houses called *qahveh khane*. Historically the latter have been a hangout for Muslim middle-aged men and more or less closed to women. *Qahvaeh khane* are places frequented by neither young people nor religious minorities. They function as a hub for working-class men, migrant workers, newcomers in town to network, people searching for jobs or housing. They are also a space for performing and constructing urban masculinity. *Qahveh khane* have been geographically and symbolically linked to *zorkhane* (literally, house of strength, a traditional body-building club). Symbols and images of champions (*pahlevanan*) hang on the walls. Moreover, the performance of *naqali*, telling epic and mythical stories, turned *qaveh khane* into a masculine space for male homosociality. Unlike *qahveh khane*, modern coffee shops are more gender democratic and more accessible to religious minorities and young people. Like *kafi shobs* in Cairo, "feminized coffee shops" provide new spaces for leisure for women (Peterson 2011). Not surprisingly, the coffee shop boom started during the reform era when Iranian society experienced more political and cultural openness.

Ethnography in this section was collected in the Julfa neighborhood, an Armenian quarter in Isfahan. In the first decade of the seventeenth century, hundreds of thousands of Armenians were moved from the Julfa region (today in the Republic of Azerbaijan) to Isfahan, the capital of the Safavid Dynasty. Known as skilled artisans, Armenians moved as labor migrants to establish industries and workshops in the capital. The Julfa quarter has since then been one of the most dynamic parts of Isfahan. Industries, trade, art, and architecture have flourished in this ethnic enclave throughout the centuries. Julfa is located in the southern part of the city, which is divided by a river, the Zayandeh roud. The city is divided both geographically and metaphorically. The river (which in recent years has been dry for most of the year due to severe draught) is a "symbolic boundary," dividing the city into different stereotypical "states of mind" and "lifestyles." The northern part, where the older quarters and historical places are, is imagined as more religious and culturally conservative. The southern part, with modern urban planning, is associated with more liberal attitudes and is represented as "Westernized" and modern. It is important to underline that this is how the city is imagined and represented, not as it actually is. As I have been told, the "liberal" attitude found in the southern part of the city attracts young people from the other side as a place where they can dress and behave in ways that would be impossible in their own neighborhoods.

Until the turn of the millennium, it was the beautiful churches in Julfa that made the neighborhood an urban attraction, particularly the Vank Cathedral (built in 1664) and a museum of Armenian history. In the early 2000s, Julfa became a leisure spot for young people who come there from all over Isfahan to kill time ("timepass") in the coffee shops, or to stroll around "window shopping" in malls and numerous boutiques. The center for these activities in Julfa stretches from the Tohid-Nazar intersection in the east to the middle of Khaqani Street in the west, with the streets around the Vank Cathedral in the middle. Mehrdad Street, a block south of Julfa Square, is packed with fast-food restaurants; about five hundred meters north of the square is the Farshchian Cultural Center, where exhibitions and concerts are held and movies shown. Like Shahrak-e Gharb in Tehran (see Khosravi 2008), the "relative freedom" young people experience in Julfa is the main attraction. Here, young Isfahanis can perform what they cannot perform in their own neighborhoods, where their look, performance, and behavior are scrutinized and regulated by family members and neighbors. Thanks to a feeling of anonymity, young Isfahanis can escape the strict moral mores imposed on them in their own neighborhood. A combination of capital and leisure has turned Julfa into a "tolerant zone" for "immoral activities." As shown in my work on the Golestan Mall in Tehran (Khosravi 2008), there is a correlation between "relative tolerance toward immoralities" and a concentration of capital in commercial spaces. Another example of a similar zone is Kish Island in the Persian Gulf. This free-trade zone has also become a "free cultural zone" where tolerance for "immoral behaviors" is higher than in the rest of the country. Together with Julfa, Mardaveej Street, in an affluent neighborhood in southern Isfahan, has also become a leisure area for young Isfahanis thanks to its many coffee shops. Mardaveej Street is also where young people come driving their cars for *dor dor zadan* on Thursday evenings (see below).

In the late 1990s the area around Vank Cathedral was put on UNESCOS's World Heritage list, and the municipality started a huge restoration of the neighborhood to attract domestic and foreign tourists. At the same time, the neighborhood has been commercialized. Land prices have soared, and the main streets in Julfa have attracted lucrative businesses targeting young consumers. Non-Armenian businessmen and women began to invest in properties and entrepreneurship in Julfa. Shopping malls, boutiques, fast-food restaurants, and coffee shops mushroomed in the blocks around the cathedral. Khaqani Street, on the west side of Julfa, became Isfahan's fashion district. Boutiques are crammed with imported commodities, mostly clothes and accessories.

The most recent and chic trends from abroad can all be found here. The colorful neon signs and fanciful decorations of the boutiques have turned the street into a window on the "global" consumer culture and youth lifestyle. The Julfa neighborhood clearly shows the link between strolling, consumption, and coffee shops. Needless to mention, the pleasure of the neighborhood is class-based. In the summer of 2015, the price of a shirt in a boutique in Julfa could easily reach almost half a worker's monthly wage (according to the official minimum wage for workers in 2014). A meal in the Khan Gostar restaurant cost around 10 percent of a worker's salary. The price of a sandwich in Arabou Fast Food was three times that in other places in Isfahan. The prices in Julfa are even beyond reach of many young people classified as middle class, usually unemployed or underemployed, although well-educated, whose salaries are slightly higher than unskilled workers' salaries.

In the streets around the cathedral, there are about twenty-three coffee shops, all opened during the past decade. About a hundred meters east of the cathedral lies Julfa Square: 1,300 square meters, and rectangular. Until the early 2000s, the square with its groceries, small stores, and local craft shops was a place elderly Armenians frequented for a large part of the day, sitting outside the stores chatting. However, the square, like the rest of Julfa, has gone through a restoration project organized by the municipality and the Iranian Cultural Heritage and Tourism Organization. The square is now closed to traffic. The buildings have been renovated, and the square has been transformed from a local market to a place for young people from all over the city to hang out. The local stores and workshops have been replaced by coffee shops. Around the square, there are five coffee shops. In the evenings, the square is full of young Isfahanis. While those who can afford to buy food occupy the coffee shops, others sit on the stone benches around the square. Going to coffee shops in Julfa is preeminently class-based because it is too expensive for most young people. Going to coffee shops also requires a "cultural capital" that not all young people possess. The names on the menu are foreign, unfamiliar, and hard to pronounce, though written both in English and Persian.

The class conflict among the young in Julfa Square is palpable. It is not only put in terms of class difference but also in terms of "cultural differences" between those who have the "right" cultural capital and those who lack it. Pejman is a twenty-six-year-old man, with a university degree, who is unemployed and lives with his parents in a gated neighborhood in a better-off part of south Isfahan. His father is a successful architect. Pejman and his family

regularly travel abroad. For him, the presence of lower-class youth is
disturbing:

> We hang out in coffee shops because of *allafi* [unemployment, idle-
> ness]. We come here almost every day. Here I can meet my friends and
> new people. Before it was better . . . now all sorts of people come here
> from the lower classes. . . . From all over Isfahan. From Zeynabiyeh [a
> poor neighborhood in the northern outskirts of Isfahan]. They are
> different, not only economically but also culturally. Some others are
> nouveau riche. They have money but no culture. They make trouble,
> fight in public, physically harass others. Their women, too. They are
> *arazel owbash*. They don't have the culture of going to coffee shops, so
> they gather in the square. . . . They don't come in because they can't
> even say what they want. They would say "Al Pacino" instead of "cap-
> puccino." Their presence disturbs us. Julfa is not like before. In the
> evenings the police round them up and force them to leave. But people
> who sit in coffee shops are different.

Setare is a twenty-five-year-old woman with a university degree in economics. She is unemployed and lives with her parents in another part of the
city. Like Pejman, she is a regular visitor to the coffee shops in Julfa Square:

> In the coffee shops I have control over my relations with my boy-
> friend and other friends. I cannot do that in other places. Julfa is like
> a home for us. We care about it. But in the evenings it gets ugly.
> *Biklass* [literally, classless, meaning without taste, without etiquette]
> people come. Young women in high heels come and after them come
> young men. They do not have the same culture as us. Julfa Square
> belongs to us. I care about this place. Sometimes I walk around pick-
> ing up garbage.

By sitting inside the coffee shops avoiding "biklass" women in the square,
middle-class women demonstrate their own class position and feminine decency. *Biklass* indicates bad taste, in terms not only of how people consume
(commodities as well as leisure activities) but also of how people behave in
public places. Good taste means "appropriate behavior," which distinguishes
"decent" women from "shameless and vulgar" women. The distance, the gap,
between the women sitting inside the coffee shops and those in the square

indicates not only a class distinction but also the idea of being decent. Women in the square are repeatedly described by women sitting inside the coffee shops as "vulgar," "uncultured," or even "kharab" (literally, destroyed, here meaning a prostitute). The expensive menu and the right cultural capital render passing time in coffee shops a privilege of class (cf. Peterson 2011). Free WiFi, books, and magazines (usually about art, philosophy, and literature), and digital devices on the tables connect the youth to international networks, accentuating the social inequalities between the young people inside and outside the coffee shops. Through regular visits, middle-class youth personalize the coffee shops and cultivate a relationship with the place and the staff. The class differences are also palpable in the young people's mobility patterns. Expensive imported cars owned by the visitors to the coffee shops are parked in the outdoor parking lot next to the square. A majority of the young people coming from the fringes of the city uses public transport, motorcycles, or shared taxis to reach Julfa.

The competition over the right to the square is multifaceted. It is a political competition between the police and the young people, as well as a class and gender competition among the young themselves. The conjunction of political, class, and gender oppression is manifested daily when the police patrols appear in the square. Young people who cannot afford the coffee shops are more exposed to police violence. Sitting outside in the square is not seen as a plausible reason for their presence. Every evening, the police drive them out not only from the square but from the neighborhood. Middle-class young people remain in the coffee shops, watching the spectacle, feeling protected from police violence by their act of consuming. Their presence is legitimated by consumption. The young men and women in the square do not consume, are not "good for business," and are thereby removable. We can find similar processes of exclusion of the poor from commercial spaces. Young working-class Tehranis, labeled *javad*, are exposed to more discrimination when their presence in shopping malls is rejected and questioned, even seen as suspect in comparison with their middle-class peers (see Khosravi 2008). In a similar way, *favela* young people who come to the shopping malls in São Paulo, Brazil, to practice *rolezinhos*, are stigmatized as "favelado nigger," criminalized, and thereby subject to removal. Likewise, shopping malls in Cairo filter their visitors based on class signifiers (Abaza 2006).

Café Ebi, opened in 1999 by a young Armenian man, is the first hot spot for young people in Julfa. Café Ebi has become my daily hangout during my regular visits to Isfahan since the early 2000s. Every time I visit this city, I spend a couple of hours in the morning reading newspapers, writing field notes, and chatting with other regular visitors. From early evening until midnight (when all restaurants and coffee shops should close according to law), the café is crammed with young men and women. Café Ebi is not large. It has six small round tables and around twenty wooden chairs. The simple menu offers cold and hot drinks and sometimes chocolate cake. However, its espresso is the best in the whole of Julfa. It has a dim interior. For several years, painted portraits of Kafka and Nietzsche have decorated the walls. A little farther inside the café, opposite the portrait of Kafka, is a small printed announcement on the wall reading "Women are forbidden to smoke!" Another reads, "We don't give service to improperly veiled women." All shops, restaurants, and coffee shops are ordered by the police to display these kinds of warnings. All fruitless. I have never seen a woman there who was "properly veiled" according to the official model of veiling. Daniel, the owner of Café Ebi, a handsome thirty-year-old Armenian man, emphasized several times in our conversations the role of coffee shops for the emergence of a modern lifestyle. He believes strongly that more public life would lead to more interaction and thereby to a culture of tolerance. One afternoon in the summer of 2014, he told me:

> For many years after the Revolution, there were no coffee shops in Isfahan. People had to go to a hotel to drink coffee. There was no culture of the coffee shop. We got the idea from Tehran. Armenians always have new ideas. Our coffee shop is the first modern coffee shop in Isfahan. Today there are hundreds of similar coffee shops in Isfahan. . . . A coffee shop is a cultural place. In coffee shops you learn to have tolerance. It is a public place. People come out from their homes. In Europe people spend a large part of their lives on the streets. Today in Iran young people live with their parents until the age of 40. They come here to meet their peers and to make connections. . . . This is exactly why the police do not like us. They have closed down our coffee shop more than ten times for different reasons, like women being improperly veiled or women seen smoking.

The youth's attraction to coffee shops has attracted constant criticism from the conservative forces, and coffee shops are constantly targeted by police raids. Many have temporarily or permanently closed down, accused of encouraging sin and immorality. Some are under more pressure than others. The police can order popular coffee shops to install surveillance cameras and hand over the recorded material to the authorities. Café Prague, on Keshavarz Boulevard in central Tehran and close to Tehran University, was the most popular among students and young artists. It was closed down in 2012 when the owner refused to install surveillance cameras. The last day it remained open turned into a collective mourning ritual. The regular visitors crammed into the coffee shop, even sitting on the floor, playing music, singing, and crying along with the staff.

Coffee shops offer an alternative space to socialize beyond sex segregation and general restrictions imposed on youth by the authorities and the parental generation. Similar to the case of Beirut in Deeb and Harb's study (2013) and Cairo in Peterson's research (2011), coffee shops in Iran provide new spaces for leisure that promote a sense of flexibility in moral norms. Like the state, parents do not like their children's attraction to coffee shops, complaining about the costs and about young people doing nothing but killing time there. However, the main reason, although implicitly stated, is that they do not know what their children do and whom they socialize with in coffee shops. In the eyes of the parental generation, going to coffee shops is loafing and "wasting time." Going to coffee shops is usually considered a sign of *belataklifi*, "time-pass," passivity, and a lack of agency. But the young hanging out around Julfa Square and in the coffee shops can also be seen as an act of creativity. Spending time at coffee shops and in the square is, in fact, an act of active waiting. When listening to middle-class young people in the coffee shops or working-class youth in the square, I always found them engaged in intense discussions about education, job opportunities, migration, the cinema, music, politics, social injustices, sexuality, and life in general. Young people's *belataklifi* allow them to obtain new imaginative resources; subsequently, a youth culture is being generated. Their action has nothing to do with passivity. Rather it forms part of a strategy by the young to improve their situation.

This performance is highly gendered. In Julfa Square, like the rest of the city, women's mobility is more restricted than men's. The normative modesty imposed by both the state and the family regulates and limits women's mobility in public places, both spatially and temporally. The normative modesty requires that a "respectful" woman does not run or jump in public. Neither is she supposed to be in male-dominated places. Her mobility is also restricted in terms of time, that is, how frequently she is allowed to be outside the home and until how late at night. A recurrent and common subject young men and women talk about during the time they sit and "do nothing" is sex and relationships with the opposite sex. Watching, teasing, verbal sexual harassments of young women are mentioned by young men as part of what they do when they allow time to pass. As Pejman puts it:

> Julfa is like going to the cinema. Here you can see good things [referring to the objectified female body]. We sit here and watch women.

The coffee shop offers a "relatively free" space because of its liminal position, its in-between-ness, between the family and the state, between the private and the public. It is a public place, yet it offers a space for private issues. The coffee shop is a space for young people to socialize beyond any gendered expectations and obligations imposed on them by their parents and the state. Julfa offers an opportunity for escaping suburbia, isolation, parental oppression, and a free room for imagination. Like the Parisian arcades in Benjamin's work, the coffee shop is today a place for dreams, for daydreaming. For the Marxist philosopher Ernst Bloch (1996 [1959]), daydreaming generates hope. In contrast to night dreams, daydreams are subversively oriented forward into the new, a "not-yet" world. For Bloch, daydreams signify a lack and a will to change toward a better life:

> The daydream projects its images into the future. . . . The content of the night-dream is concealed and disguised, the content of the day-fantasy is open, fabulously inventive, anticipating, and its latency lies ahead. . . . The daytime wishful dream requires no excavation and interpretation, but rectification and, in so far as it is capable of it, concretion. (Bloch 1996 [1959]: 99)

Going to coffee shops offers an opportunity to be less "invisiblized," less second sex, less second citizen. In my field studies on undocumented migrants in Sweden, I found that the coffee shop has, in similar ways, become a space in which the marginalized can take part in city life. For those who are "invisiblized" or supposed to be invisible, whether they are young women in Iran or young immigrants in Stockholm, coffee shops offer an opportunity to participate in a form of social life that is otherwise inaccessible. The young artist Amirali Ghasemi's photo series *Coffee Shop Ladies* (2006) shows young women in cafes. Their faces are blanked out in white, as if they are cut from the pictures. They represent "invisiblized" citizens, included in society without being recognized as members.

It is not surprising that coffee shops are usually opened by people living on the margins of society: immigrants or minorities. The very first café in Paris was opened by an Armenian in 1671. Another Armenian opened the first coffee house in Vienna in 1685. A British immigrant founded New York's first café in 1696. In Stockholm, it is now almost impossible to find a coffee shop that is not run by immigrants. Visiting a coffee shop is a unique type of socialization; you are anonymous yet in public. It is an exercise in the rhythm of urban life. It is more than just the act of drinking coffee. *Kafeneshini* means you are in a public place but at the same time in a private sphere. It gives a sense of belonging to the community, to be doing the same as others. Coffee shops allow those who are supposed to be invisible to see and be seen. The persistent presence of young people in Julfa Square and the various groups contending over the right to the city—on the one hand between authorities and youth and on the other hand between middle-class and lower-income young people—disclose social inequalities and injustices. In the daily contest for the right to the square, young people construct urban subjectivity. The repetition and replication of presence and hanging around in the square signify the hope and will of the youth. Julfa is a scene for performing/consuming/learning youthfulness, a site where the knowledge of how performing youthfulness is communicated. It is also a center for information, vision, and imagination for youths on the periphery. Julfa has been a node in the Armenian diasporic world, connected transnationally to other Armenian communities. Therefore, as a non-Muslim neighborhood, Julfa has been regarded as a venue for infiltration of "foreign" values, styles, and tastes. In the eyes of the conservative forces, a "cultural invasion" has materialized in Julfa.

Mapping Morality

The Julfa quarter is a contested urban space, morally and therefore also politically. This was clearly seen at the intersection of Tohid and Nazar Streets, 150 meters east of Julfa Square. On one corner of the intersection, there is a police kiosk. *Gasht-e ershad* (literally, guidance patrols, the moral police) are usually standing around the kiosk. At the other corner, there was a large Hosseiniyeh, a Shiite institution used as a congregation hall for religious rituals and ceremonies, particularly of Moharram, the annual commemorative ritual of the martyrdom of Imam Hossein and his family. The massacre took place in the month of Moharram 61 A.H. (October 680 CE), on the plain of Karbala, in today's Iraq. The Moharram ritual is a collective mourning through public recitation, chanting of elegies, and weeping. The name of the Hosseiniye was Beitul Abbas (literally, home of Abbas, named after the brother of Imam Hossein, who was also killed with his brother). Beitul Abbas, a simple, large, covered yard, was founded in 2000. For a decade and half during my fieldwork, it was a center for religious activities. It claimed on its website that it was a "non-governmental independent organization funded by private individuals."[10] However, because it was located on one of the most expensive streets in the city and hosted frequent and generous free activities, including free dinner events, many believed it was funded by the state.

Throughout 1392 (March 2013–March 2014), more than fifty different activities were organized in Beitul Abbas. The main activities were related to Moharram and Ramedan rituals, such as seminars and exhibitions, mass prayer, Ashura rituals (mourning), family consultations, Quran classes, and welfare assistance to underprivileged families. The aesthetics created by Beitul Abbas was spectacular. During the ten nights between Moharram the first and tenth, the ritualized mourning with its songs, *ta'ziyeh* (a theatrical representation of the tragedy), the Moharram procession (*dasteh*), and rhythmic breast beating (*sin-e zani*) were all spectacular performances to create an "aesthetics of modesty and self-abasement" (see Khosravi 2008). During these ten nights of the ritual, free dinners were served. Likewise during Ramadan, free *iftar* (the evening meal with which Muslims break the fast) was served. Usually large numbers of pious Isfahanis participate in the rituals, and during these nights the intersection is turned into a scene of pious performances. Rather than being merely a religious institution, Beitul Abbas was a "space of morality," in opposition to the "immoral" leisure area of Julfa. Beitul Abbas was located almost in front of the historical Beitul Lahm Church (Bethlehem Church). However, rather than standing in opposition to Christianity, Beitul Abbas opposed the "immoral leisure" in the Julfa area. The directors of Beitul Abbas explicitly expressed the significance of its location on the website: "the aim of this great movement in this *sensitive* [*hasas*] area . . . is introducing young people to Quran culture" (emphasis added). What made the Julfa area "sensitive" was the performance of youthfulness and leisure that Beitul Abbas aimed to fight against by arranging religious and cultural activities targeting young people. The spatial contestation, based on what was conceived and presented as (im)moral practices, took place along the boundary between the pious milieu of Beitul Abbas and Julfa. Julfa, as an urban space, is conceived and lived through constant contestation about what is moral and immoral. However, Beitul Abbas represented the failure of the state in its oppression of

leisure and youthfulness over the past three decades. Beitul Abbas materialized what I have heard frequently: "The authorities have lost control over the
youth." In my previous fieldwork, I saw the youth's leisure activities and claim
for youthfulness as acts of defiance. Today, I see Beitul Abbas as an attempt to
resist the pervasive and forceful youth movement.

I ended *Young and Defiant in Tehran* with an answer to the question, "Can
a political situation be changed by a carnival?" I wrote: "Perhaps not, but
imaginations of young people may yet act as a site for social change in the
future" (2008: 174). Several years after I wrote those words, I can see how
young Iranians' urban practices and visibilities have transformed the urban
landscape. By spatial navigation through a maze of moralities and social
order, young Iranians have further pushed back the boundaries of what is
morally and politically accepted, and they have forced the authorities to recognize their presence and rights to the city. In the summer of 2015, Beitul
Abbas was closed down. I see this closing as a victory for the youth's urban
practices and visibilities over official policies. As Deeb and Harb (2013: 222)
define it in the context of Beirut, urban citizenship refers to mutual tolerance
and recognition of the city's various forms of life. Simple acts of spatial practices such as loitering, passing time in coffee shops, riding around in cars, and
scrawling graffiti (Chapter 5) may lead to new forms of urban citizenship.

Automobility, Tehrani Style

Another form of a new urban practice of visibility, performed by the young to
challenge the public/private dichotomy, gender segregation, and "invisiblizing
policy," is automobility. *Automobility*, as Urry uses it, is an assemblage of specific
human activities, machines, roads, buildings, signs, and cultures of mobility:
"Automobility can be conceptualized as a self-organizing autopoietic, nonlinear
system that spreads worldwide, and includes cars, car-drivers, roads, petroleum
supplies and many novel objects, technologies and signs" (Urry 2004: 27). Automobility in the context of this field refers to the use of cars, not only as a
means of transportation but also as a means to entertain, pass time, date, make
friends, create a semiprivate space in public, and navigate through the moral
geography of the city. Through automobility, young Iranians turn the streets
into an interior setting. With a complex maze of freeways, tunnels (some several
kilometers long), and two-level highways, Tehran is an auto-city, designed to
facilitate and encourage private automobility. Mass automobility is a crucial part

of Tehranis' urban life. Almost 30 percent of all vehicles (more than 15 million in 2012), that is, 4.5 million, are used in Tehran (Tehrani 1394/2015: 7). Thousands of new vehicles enter Iranian streets every month. With an annual production of above one million automobiles, Iran is among the twenty largest automaking countries in the world and the largest in the Middle East (7).

Social inequalities generate stratified mobility, and immobility reproduces social inequalities. So a car became a signifier of class. From the first decade after the Revolution until the mid-1990s, the cars seen on the streets were almost all Iranian made or foreign cars imported before the Revolution. Similar to socialist countries, domestic-made cars, such as the Peykan, were only a "means of transportation" and thus not signifiers of class distinction (cf. Gatejel 2011). After the war and due to the liberalization of the market, new foreign cars were imported, and class distinction in the streets became more visible. Today, cars signify status, class, and masculinity (see Menoret 2014). The class aspect of mobility among young people is palpable. How one gets around in the city signifies class and social position. While middle-class youth move around in their private cars, lower-income young people use public transport, packed in overcrowded buses, or are squeezed into shared taxis. While some enjoy mobility rights (by having access to means of mobility), many others' mobility is restricted. For instance, *Tarh-e traffic* (limited traffic zone, congestion charges) in Tehran, a relatively successful attempt to reduce traffic in central parts of the city, have hit low-income groups hard. Between 6.30 a.m. and 5 p.m. on weekdays, all vehicles must have a permit to enter the downtown. In the winter of 2013, a day pass cost 18,000 toman (US$ 6). Thus, the congestion charges affect the automobility of low-income Tehranis.

Young Iranians, however, show a strong longing for cars and for driving. According to one site, 4,600 new driving licences are issued daily.[11] Cars and automobility are not only signs of a modern lifestyle and class but also of independence and entertainment. Driving around in cars, car skidding, drifting, and car races are young Tehranis' entertainment (Hoshangi 1391/2012: 179). *Nafas-e amigh* (Deep Breath, by Parviz Shahbazi, 2003) is a noir film about two young men from different classes in Tehran. The film is centered on the young men driving around Tehran in a nihilistic ambiance. The car is their last shelter in an antagonistic city. Another film, *Asb heyvan-e najibi ast* (Absolutely Tame Is a Horse, by Abdolreza Kahani, 2011), is a black comedy about a few young people searching for money while driving through Tehran's streets during a long night. In the film, like many other movies about youth, where homes are sites of insecurity and conflict, spaces easily exposed to police interventions, the car, when roaming around the city, becomes a safe space where the young can find peace. Between the family and the state, there is the street, and cars offer an intermezzo between private and public spaces. Automobility empowers young Iranians to escape parental as well as state control. Automobility is a pause from the home, and a means of self-assertion and self-expression. Omid Vaghefi, a commentator and a young man who belongs to the 60-generation, sees automobility as a subversive act:

> Cars in Iran are a space between home and the city. . . . Iranian cars are mobile private spaces. [A car is] a home on wheels which swerves from the father's orders and the state's rules. . . . The private space of the car protects us from the state. Inside the car we are sheltered from the eyes of the guards. . . . The cars take us to the city to find others, friends. In the car, we let our hair come out from the veil, we listen to illicit music, we exchange telephone numbers [with the opposite sex], we put on our high-heeled shoes and sometimes even have sex.[12]

However, the police have a different opinion about the car as a private space. The chief of Iran's National Police Forces, Esmail Ahmadi-Moghadam, declared in April 2012 that the police would deal with "cultural crimes" committed in cars. Subsequently, to obstruct "cultural crimes" in cars, the police forbade tinted car windows.[13] According to the police statistics, in the first eight months of 1394 (April–November 2015), more than forty thousand cars were impounded in Tehran alone for different crimes/sins.[14] Cars, however, are turned into spaces of "cultural crimes." Bahram, a twenty-three-year-old man who lives with his parents, says:

> I can't take my girlfriend home. Her parents don't like to see me at their place, either. So what can we do? Where can we have privacy? We drive around. Stop in empty and dark spots. Kiss and touch and then after twenty or thirty minutes drive to somewhere else. If we stay in one place for a long time, a patrolling police car may see us.

Afsoon, a twenty-four-year-old student, with a dark blue Peugeot 206, told me:

> In my car I don't care what I have on me. I can smoke my cigarette and listen to music. . . . The car is the only entertainment left for us. What can we do without it?

Mobility is related to class and gender. A woman at the wheel has been a usual sight in Iranian cities for decades. Nowadays, there are even a sizeable number of female taxi drivers, driving instructors, and, in fewer numbers, bus drivers. Women who can afford a car or have access to one enjoy a form of mobility and access to the city they would not otherwise have. Many believe that the public transport system is not safe for women. Verbal and even physical sexual harassments are daily experiences for Iranian women in large cities. Public transport, particularly shared taxis, is where many women are exposed to groping and molesting. Accordingly, women's mobility is restricted, and many parents regard driving a personal car as the only safe form of mobility in the city (Hoshangi 1391/2012: 145; see also Banakar 2016). Cars and the ability to move away fast from unpleasant situations, such as sexual harassment or police surveillance, give women a sense of safety. In a society characterized by radical insecurity, personal vehicles offer a sense of protection. Automobility for women, however, also offers them extended social relationships. Cars are mobile spaces for socializing. For instance, the term "mobile female parties" (Hoshangi 1391/2012: 121) refers to women gathering in cars to drive around. The photographer Shirin Aliabadi's *Girls in Cars* (2005) documents the new visibility of young Tehrani women and their automobility. In her series of photographs, Aliabadi shows young women cruising in their cars on the streets of Tehran, wearing makeup, improperly veiled, and laughing into the camera. Nevertheless, sometimes not even the private space of a car can shelter women from harassment and discrimination. Homa is a thirty-two-year-old woman who moves around Tehran in her silver Samand:

> Once I was driving along Keshavarz Boulevard. It was early evening. I lit a cigarette. Two young men on a motorcycle started to verbally harass me. I think that the fact that I smoked provoked them. I ignored them and rolled up the window. But they got very close and one of them broke the rear mirror on my side with his leg. I got mad and turned left to stop them. When we stopped, a crowd gathered, and soon a police car showed up. What did the police officer do first? He looked at me to check my veil. Automatically, I pulled my scarf forward and pushed some strands of hair under it. I threw away my cigarette too.

That the first act of the police was to scrutinize Homa's veil turned her into a suspect. Her automobility, smoking, and improper veiling provoked the patriarchal spatial order and turned her into a potential offender of the law, rather than a victim of harassment. Presenting women and female sexuality as the causes of traffic problems is not unusual in public debates and in daily life. I frequently heard men saying that female drivers are a danger to others since they do not drive properly. The prejudice against female drivers is that they are "cowards," "clumsy," not "risk-takers," and "turtle drivers," and thus that they disturb the traffic (Hoshangi 1391/2012: 21). Not only women's automobility, but also their presence in streets is believed to "incite" traffic chaos. On an early Thursday evening in June 2013, I was in a taxi heading to Julfa to have coffee with two young Isfahani interlocutors. Approaching Julfa on Tohid Avenue, we got stuck in a traffic jam. Tohid Street, a wide boulevard, with new office buildings, shops, and restaurants, has become a main shopping street targeting younger consumers. At the intersection with Mehrdad Street, known for its fast food restaurants, in a long queue behind cars and traffic lights, the taxi driver said:

> You see, this traffic here is because of pizza. Here around Julfa, there are a lot of pizzerias where young women hang out. Then young men come in their cars to date women. All this traffic is related to sex. This is a street of sex. Men drive back and forth to find a woman to pick up.

That young men clog traffic to ask for a telephone number or persuade a woman (usually waiting for a cab) to enter their cars is blamed on women, even in the official discourse. Women's improper veiling is believed to incite sin and provoke men to commit cultural crimes. Youth's automobility, generally, is represented to be inherently linked to delinquency (Hoshangi 1391/2012).

Driving Around in Circles

One form of "cultural crime" related to automobility is known as *dor dor zadan* (literally, going around in circles). The term refers to a recent urban practice. Young men and women drive back and forth along a street to occupy the urban space they are not supposed to occupy. On Thursday evenings, innumerable cars from different parts of Tehran gather on Jordan Street in northern Tehran or Iranzamin Street in Shahrak-e Gharb in western Tehran.

In Isfahan the place for *dor dor zadan* is Mardaveej Street. The cars, packed with young men and women, drive back and forth for several hours and sometimes until late into the night. Illicit music is played at high volume, and women are "improperly veiled." Long lines of cars, with their drivers stopping in the middle of the streets to exchange telephone numbers, and police interventions cause irrepressible traffic chaos. Many other young people stand along the streets enjoying the scene. *Dor dor zadan* is a way of dating, but perhaps it is rather a moment exemplifying the carnivalization of the society. As has been explained previously, carnivalesque offers youth a celebration of chaos, disorder, and anarchy, the inversion of social norms and codes, a pause from *belataklifi* and the dullness of everyday life. In a carnivalesque situation, the aspects of youthfulness that are suppressed by the official ideology are in focus: bodies, laughter, dance, and sexuality. In the early evenings, the police set up barricades to control the situation and block U-turns, but all in vain. Police officers sitting in their cars address the young over megaphones and give orders to move. Usually, the officers first call out the brand and the color of the car and then say, "Don't stay! Move on!" Rather than the mystical/religious power of Althusserian interpellation, Rancière believes that state intervention is in breaking up, removal, and keeping people in circulation: " 'Move along! There's nothing to see here!' The police is that which says that here, on this street, there's nothing to see and so nothing to do but move along" (Rancière 2010: 37).

The persistent presence of the young's automobility, as well as their refusal to obey police orders, transforms the politics and space of circulation into a space for the emergence of a subject, the citizen. Another practice by young men is car drifting on Tehran's highways. Late at night, Hemat, Yadegar Emam, or Niyaysh highways turn into sites for drifting or joyriding. The young men drive fast and aggressively on the highways, close to other cars. Car drifting is an entertainment for middle- and upper-class youth. This fatal fun leads to many young people's deaths. In one young man's words, "highway therapy" is an act of the "release of youth energy." As in al-Qtaibi and Menoret's study of young Saudis (2010), *dor dor zadan* and car skidding for young Tehranis is a furious reaction to the social vacuum, *belataklifi*, and boredom (see also Menoret 2014). Usually the police only warn and threaten these young drivers and direct them away from there. Many, however, are arrested and accused of various "cultural crimes," of making "trouble" for citizens and the local businessmen, and have their cars impounded. Youth's automobility, "mobile female parties" in cars, and *dor dor zadan* are means to reclaim urban spaces and turn them into spaces of defiance—though short lived. In the words of Omid Vaghefi, a young social critic,

> The movement of cars is our longing for social movements, which we are deprived of. A car in Iran is not a vehicle for getting to a destination. It is a way to regain spaces which have been stolen from us. The space that belonged to us now is captured by others.[15]

However, to restrict young people's automobility, the police have initiated campaigns to criminalize *dor dor zadan* and, in collaboration with the state-run television IRIB, have attempted to generate moral panic about youth's automobility. Police Chief Esmail Ahamdi-Moghadam declared in the winter of 2011 that *dor dor zadan* is against public ethics. It, in his words, also causes related problems such as air pollution, sound pollution, and traffic disruption.[16] In late October 2012, the IRIB produced and broadcast a report in two episodes about young Tehranis' *dor dor zadan*. Called "street disturbances," the episodes were part of a longer television program called *Birahe* (literally, road leading nowhere). *Birahe* included fourteen "documentaries," each focusing on a specific social problem and young Tehranis' "delinquent behavior." The themes of different episodes ranged from young people "watching satellite TV channels," their "automobility," "desire for emigration," and "online friendship" to thuggery, armed robbery, drugs, and homicide. Juxtaposing the practices of youthfulness alongside major crimes such as murder and burglary is part of the repertoire of the criminalization of youth and youthfulness. The two episodes about young Tehranis' automobility begin with the reporter following several young men driving through the streets in search of a date, but also to "harass women." When the young men are pulled over, the reporter asks the drivers to explain their "harmful behaviors." The "interviews" end with the young men confessing their sins/crimes and "regretfully" apologizing and promising not to repeat the "offense." The episode showing young people practicing *dor dor zadan* is accusatory and condemning. Filmed at night, when *dor dor zadan* takes place, the scenes show car lights passing. Using a horror movie-like soundtrack, the scenes, which depict young people stopping their cars in the middle of street causing traffic chaos, are supposed to cause viewers angst and worries. Apart from a "university professor," who comments on and pathologizes the "anomic" behavior of the young drivers, the reporter interviews several middle-aged men who run restaurants and shops on the street where *dor dor zadan* was taking place. No woman is shown or interviewed. Women are presented either as the target or the victim of young men's *dor dor zadan*. In fact, women participate very much as drivers in *dor dor zadan*. In the report, all the businessmen complain that *dor dor zadan* causes trouble and perils for "people's wives and children." Another issue they mention recurrently is the harmful impact of *dor dor zadan* on their businesses. They say that it scares away families and customers. The criminalization of young people's automobility, representing it as a threat for citizens and businessmen, makes the young drivers easy targets for the police. They are stopped, checked, and face various accusations. In the first eight months of 1394/2015, more than forty thousand cars were impounded due to being used for various "cultural crimes." Detecting "crime" potentialities turns any young driver into a suspect. Reza, a twenty-two-year-old man, had this experience:

> I was arrested one night when I was driving to my sister's place. I had some food in the car that my mother had prepared for her. Not so far from our house a police car asked me to stop. I was asked why I was driving around. I told them I was heading to my sister's place. They did not believe me and took me to a police station. It was only after the officer in charge at the station saw the food in the car that they let me go.

Young Iranians' automobility has entered the political realm as well. According to official claims, youthful automobility causes 30 percent of all traffic jams in Tehran.[17] Furthermore, a series of various forms of pollution, from air and sound pollution to social pollution, not to mention the "soft war," are associated with young people's automobility.[18] Young drivers are likewise presented as the main culprits for the high fatality rate in car accidents. With around 800,000 accidents per year, Iran has one of the highest rates of car accidents in the world. Throughout the 2000s, 265,000 people were killed in car accidents in Iran. While the traffic injury/death rate on the global level is three people per 10,000 vehicles, in Iran the rate is thirty-three people per 10,000 vehicles (Moafian et al. 2013). Women and young people's low position make them easy targets when explaining traffic chaos (cf. Monroe 2011). In forty-four educational videos about traffic and road safety broadcast by the IRIB television channels, the main traffic offender character is a young "Westernized" middle-class man who is dressed in Western style and playing illicit music in his car. Another element of danger is said to be female drivers, who are presented as weak and inept, thus constituting an unsafe element in traffic (see Farji and Hamidi 1385/2006). In official discourse, the whole traffic problem is reduced to the individual. It emphasizes the "poor culture of driving," lack of "citizen ethics," or the role of the family in educating young people in citizenship and civility as the main reasons for traffic problems in Iran.[19] The officials are silent about systematic defects in vehicle manufacturing. Iran-made vehicles are known for their poor safety records. The lack of air bags, ABS system, efficient seat belts and poor road standards are mentioned by the people as the main causes for accident fatalities.

Young people's automobility makes the streets in Tehran a social text in which a gender, class, generational, and political contestation is going on. Traffic becomes an arena for the interaction between the youth and the state. I do not mean that youth's automobility is a political act of resistance, but rather it is a politics of fun and a claim of youthfulness (Bayat 2010). Like joyriding for young Saudis, automobility for young Iranians is a way to get along with the city, "to learn the city with its geography, its itineraries, its various social atmospheres, its recourses, and its dangers" (Menoret 2014, 163). In discussion with my interlocutors about automobility and traffic problems, a recurrent issue was the absence of the law and the presence of state corruption. Afsoon, while driving her Peugeot 206, said:

> They are busy arresting the young for dating or taking part in political protest, so they have no time to control and manage the traffic chaos. . . . The police officers are indeed everywhere, but they never do anything else than issuing tickets. Look at them! In one hand they have a pen and in the other the ticket block, ready to issue tickets. This is how they make up the budget for traffic department.

Afsoon is right. Traffic offenders have increased in the past years, and now twenty-five million tickets are issued annually.[20] Between 2010 and 2014, the traffic-fine income for the traffic police increased four times, to reach the sum of US$ 600 million in 2015.[21] This huge sum of money enables police corruption. Young drivers, particularly young women, see themselves as easy targets for police officers who can stop them just to collect bribes. Furthermore, young people associate the high fatality rate in accidents with corruption and the absence of accountability. Babak, a twenty-six-year-old civil engineer, in his mother's Pride (the Iranian version of the subcompact South Korean car), told me,

That so many die in traffic accidents here is not strange. Here nothing is built according to acceptable standards; streets, tunnels, you name it. No one cares. Show me a street in Tehran that you do not find any holes in. They have built several-kilometer tunnels but have installed few air ventilation fans, so many motorcyclists have crashed into other cars because of lack of oxygen. It is about corruption. For example, they import poor quality fans from China because someone makes money from it. No one thinks about the people. The state cheats. The municipality cheats. The contractors cheat. Then all problems are blamed on us. . . . For the state, people's lives are worth nothing. . . . So how can we expect people to follow the rules and respect others' rights when the state constantly violates citizens' rights?

Many believe that, when individuals' dignity is not respected, individuals do not show respect for others.[22] Ghazi Tabatabai and Rezai (1388/2009) argue that young Iranians' "bizarre and dangerous" driving is a natural reaction to a society in which their individual, political, and social rights are not respected. As Monroe (2011) shows in her study of automobility in Beirut, institutionalized corruption and state ineffectiveness have resulted in a broader social disorganization in society. Traffic problems cast a light on the paradoxes of collective contra-individual interests. Young drivers are blamed for thinking only about themselves, and while driving they try to find a way pass other cars, no matter if they violate other's rights or cause danger for others. A middle-aged male taxi driver put it this way:

The young generation are spoilt. They drive crazily and do not care about others. When you ask them why they behave like this in their cars, they just say they want to. I do not dare argue with them. They are spoilt, vulgar, and rude.

In my previous fieldwork, another taxi driver said:

Driving a car means thinking about the lines and about respecting the space of other cars. Iranians cannot see lines and directions. Their minds are chaotic. Traffic should mean collective collaboration, but we want only to do *zerangbazi*, defend our individual advantage. (Khosravi 2008: 163)

Zerangbazi literally means "playing clever" and refers to acts of prioritizing your own advantages at the expense of other people's rights. Monroe observes a similar behavior among drivers in Beirut, identified as *shatreen*, "clever" (2011: 105). That Iranians generally are concerned only with their individual interest is heard in different contexts. The frequently used saying "If the pot is not cooking for me, I don't care if a head of a dog is cooking in it" (*deegi ke baraye man nemipaze mikham sar sag tosh bepaze*) expresses the belief in the absence of a sensitivity for the collective cause among Iranians. Payam is twenty-eight and a well-educated unemployed man:

> On the streets, it is the law of the jungle that governs. I tell you this. Every day you sit behind the wheel, it is like going into a battlefield. You should prepare yourself for fights. Seriously, like back in time, you should wear a military helmet and have a stick under your seat.

Payam is not joking. It is not unusual that people have a stick in their car under the seat. When asking my interlocutors about *zerangbazi* and not respecting other people's interests and rights, they have more or less the same answer: in the current situation of lawlessness (*biqanoni*), you have no other option. "Lawlessness" here means the inaccessibility of citizens to their rights, *the lack of the right to have rights*. In other words, the law is available but not accessible. It is the "inclusive exclusion" mechanism of the law. It excludes young people by depriving them of legal protection, but includes them at the same time by making them objects of the exercise of the law. The double function of the law, invisible as protective and just but visible as a punitive system (targeting weaker groups of the society) is best expressed by a young male vendor: "Where is the law? The law is for the poor." In the view of many young Iranians, the law, embodied in the police officer at the intersections, is present but not to protect them or make the traffic safe for citizens: rather, he is there to punish citizens. The sense of not having access to the law, of being stripped of one's citizenship rights, triggers a sense of insecurity and precarity. The chaotic traffic, poor infrastructure, police corruption, unsafe cars, an inefficient state, gender-based violence, a high rate of fatal accidents, and other's *zerangbazi*, all result in deteriorating social capital and engendering a prevalent sense of loneliness and uncertainty.

Bullying the Urban Poor

Access to the street, the right of mobility to the city, are formed by age and gender but preeminently by class. The way that the mobility and visibility of the urban poor, vendors, street children, homeless people, working-class young men stigmatized as *arazel owbash* are controlled and regulated by the authorities reveals the structural class discrimination in Tehran and other large cities. Systematic bullying by the police and municipality agents has become a widespread tactic to push the urban poor out of public places. The most demonstrative and explicit form of physical and psychological bullying of the poor is the regular spectacle of public mobbing of working-class young men, labeled as *arazel owbash* (see Chapter 3). Bullying in the workplace is also common. Reports on how workers are insulted and bullied by employers appear increasingly in newspapers. In January 2016, more than ten workers were arrested in Asaluyeh in southern Iran when protesting delayed salaries. In the same week, twelve workers were arrested for the same reason in Doroud in Lorestan Province. A recently added form of bullying the poor is flogging sentences as punishment for protesting and striking workers. At the end of March 2015, five mine workers at the Chadormalu Mining and Industrial Company in Yazd Province were sentenced to flogging and prison. They were "accused" by the employer of having organized protests. In the eyes of the employers, flogging would deter similar protests in future. Nor was this the first time protesting workers have been punished by flogging. In September 2014, four workers at the Razi Petrochemical Company in Bandar Emam Khomeini were sentenced to fifty lashes each and imprisonment.[23] In the last days of May 2016, seventeen mine workers in Western Azerbaijan were flogged. Their employer had filed a complaint against them for "preventing people from doing business by disturbing the peace."[24]

The groups most exposed to bullying, however, are people who work and live on the streets: street vendors, homeless people, sex workers, and street children. They are bullied not only by the police but also by municipality agents, by the media, and even by ordinary people. The bullying of street people is legitimized by an official discourse of criminalization of poor. The media spread reports and "worrying statistics" (based on unreliable data) that depict street children as a threat to social well-being: for instance, that HIV prevalence among street children is 40 percent or that the majority of these children are "foreigners" (that is, undocumented Afghan minors born in

Iran).[25] A recent form of mobbing the urban poor is an assault on homeless people by organized local residents in order to remove them from their neighborhoods. In the cold winter of 2015, homeless people in Haghani Park were exposed to an arson attack by local residents. They were severely beaten, and their tents and shelters were burned down while the police watched.[26] Generally, attacks on beggars, homeless people, and vendors are backed by the police. Similarly, bullying of beggars by the municipality has been going on for a long time. In October 2013, the city of Tehran launched a massive campaign of criminalization of the poor. Giant billboards appeared all over the city with messages and images presenting beggars as organized swindlers and not really needy. The Tehran Urban and Suburban Railways Organization (Metro) also organizes regular propaganda campaigns against vendors.

Vendors, another group of street people, are also depicted as being involved in illegal gang activities, such as selling drugs to passengers.[27] In recent years, bullying against street vendors has become more and more brutal. Hassles of various sorts, extortion, plundering, and demands of bribes are daily experiences for street vendors. An ordinary scene on the streets of Tehran is a cat-and-mouse game between poor vendors and municipal agents whose task is to "alleviate the mobility of citizens" through "removal of barriers of crossings." Thanks to cell phones and other recording devices, some of these recent assaults have been recorded and broadcast on social media, covered soon after by national and foreign news agencies (for a few documented cases of brutal bullying of street vendors, see Chapter 7). Bullying of the poor has become institutionalized in conjunction with the growth of harsher social policies. As Molé (2012) shows, bullying and precarious-ization are an entangled pair. Along with the harassment of street vendors, residents of informal settlements are also subjected to systematic bullying by officials. One example is Shahrak-e Niayesh, an informal settlement in the middle of Tehran, labeled as the "Texas of Tehran."

The Texas of Tehran

A few months after I read a report in *Tejarat Farda* magazine (no. 50/2014) about Shahrak-e Niayesh, or as it also called, Islamabad, I headed north to visit this place, represented as so unsafe that it resembles "lawless Texas in Western movies." Of all those I asked, just a few people had heard about the neighborhood, and none of them had been there. No one could give me exact directions and how I could get there by car. I, like many other Tehranis, had passed the neighborhood many times without seeing or noticing it. My search for information about this part of the city resulted in only a handful of short notices in the press and longer interviews with municipal officials about "the problem" of Shahrak-e Niayesh in newspapers. From some taxi drivers I heard prejudiced rumors: "high rate of criminality"; "It is a bad place"; or "Only Afghan people live there." Tehran is a segregated city. While rich and middle-class people live in the northern and central parts of the city, poor Tehranis live in the south and on the peripheries. What makes Shahrak-e Niayesh unique is that, unlike other slums and informal settlements located on the fringe of the city, it is in the middle of a wealthy part of Tehran. Shahrak-e Niayesh is located in District 2 in northwestern Tehran, surrounded by Tehranis with, on average, a higher position in the socioeconomic hierarchy of the city.

The privatization of Tehran's skyline since the mid-1990s led to the mush-rooming of luxurious high-rises. The spatial division between classes in Teh-ran is now not only horizontal between north and south but also vertical. Wealthy Tehranis withdraw upward in high buildings to keep their distance from the poor on the ground level. *High-rise* in Persian is called *borj*, which means "tower" but also recalls a castle. In Shahrak-e Niayesh, which is at riv-erbed level, the high-rises on hills on the west side, located in affluent Shah-rak-e Gharb, seem even higher. Shahrak-e Niayesh is isolated from the rest of Tehran geographically by Chamran Highway on the eastern side and Hemat Highway on the southern side. Though surrounded by two large highways, the neighborhood can be accessed only by a small road from Chamran Highway and is a cul-de-sac. Furthermore, no public transport service links the neigh-borhood to the rest of the city. Highways and freeways not only isolate the neighborhood, but invisiblize it as well. Shahrak-e Niayesh is located along a riverbed, that is, lower than the highways. Construction of highways on the higher levels has concealed the neighborhood from people passing by in cars. Not surprisingly, only a few Tehranis knew about the place. The population is estimated to be between four thousand and six thousand, of whom around 70 percent are migrants from the countryside. People have lived here since the 1960s (known before as Deh-e Vank). In the late 1980s, the city of Tehran declared the neighborhood an informal settlement and planned to remove the residents to turn it into into green space. When the residents refused to move, systematic bullying by the municipality started. Their shanty houses were de-stroyed. Their water and electricity have been cut off time and again. They have no right to repair or rebuild their houses. One resident told me that the municipality controlled the entrance so no construction material would be transported into the neighborhood. To justify their aggression against the poor residents of Shahrak-e Niayesh, the authorities started stigmatizing and demonizing the neighborhood. It has been represented as a nest of illegalities with a "high rate of criminality." Reza Taghipour, a high-ranking official in the Tehran city government, called the neighborhood the "Texas of Tehran."[28] Bitterly laughing at the labeling, a resident told me that the only illegality here is conducted by rich kids who come in their SUVs to smoke drugs.

The residents of Shahrak-e Niayesh have, however, shown powerful resistance. They smuggle construction material into the neighborhood at night to rebuild their houses. They "document" their rights to the place by planting trees. They keep sending petitions to the authorities at all levels, despite repeated disappointments. Their tactics include encroaching and capturing land, prolonging their illegal residence, and tapping electricity from the municipality. In his study of Iranian subaltern groups in Tehran, Asef Bayat coined the notion of "quiet encroachment of the ordinary" to encapsulate the urban poor's

> noncollective but prolonged direct actions to acquire the basic necessities of their lives (land for shelter, urban collective consumption or urban services, informal work, business opportunities, and public space) in a quiet and unassuming illegal fashion. (2010: 45; see also 1997: 7)

Like other urban economically dispossessed groups, such as homeless people, street children, "runaway girls," and street vendors, the residents of Shahrak-e Niayesh use informal and "illegal" tactics to manage their social precarity and to secure their insecure lives. Street people disturb the division of the private sphere from the public sphere, by turning parks into bedrooms, squares into living rooms, and streets into workplaces. Similar to youth's urban practices and visibilities, the urban poor's resistance displays "modes of struggle and expression" (Bayat 1997: 55), not only of a changing urban scene and social relations but also of new modes of civility and civic engagement.

Conclusion

This chapter has dealt with young people's acts of negotiating the city. It has aimed to show how power relations are configured through mobility or lack thereof. Urban citizenship is enjoyed differently by different groups due to access to mobility and public places. The spatial order since the Revolution of 1979 has aimed to "invisiblize" undesirable youth. The street, a space between the family and the state and a public place that is supposed to be used merely for authorized activities, such as shopping or going somewhere, is turned into a site for performing new urban practices. By performing youthfulness in the streets, young people produce a form of urban visibility for themselves. The presence of those who are not supposed to be visible or audible is a political protest over mobility and visibility. Performing youthfulness in the streets is a practice to resist this unequal accessibility to public spaces, making the youth's practices "acts of citizenship" (Isin and Nielsen 2008). I started this chapter with a quote from Michel de Certeau: "to walk is to lack a place," followed by quoting two young interlocutors who expressively showed this lack. Lacking a *place*, either within the family or in the society (a job, house, one's own family, a secure future) makes the street the last way out. In his classic work on urban practices, de Certeau (1984) states that movement creates the city and urban subjectivity. In his chapter on walking in the city, he asserts that pedestrians give meanings to the streets. For de Certeau, walking, as a spatial practice, actualizes the possibilities for the transformation of a regulated and controlled place into a space for defiance. By escaping rules and regulation and instead moving around, people create the city. It is the movement of people (walking, demonstrating, driving) that writes the "urban text" (93) and creates the meaning of their city. Through their practices (scrawling graffiti, hanging out in coffee shops), the ways in which they move around (walking, driving around), and their imagination, young Iranians interrupt the official "urban rhythm" and "grammar," and thereby they re-create the urban space. By these urban practices, youth resist *belataklifi*, a sense of being stuck in time. Their spatial mobility is a response to their temporal immobility.

Reclaiming urban spaces is indeed a struggle over the definition of identity, social relations, and aesthetic values. "The right to the city," as David Harvey puts it, is more than individual access to urban resources; it is, instead, the collective power to reshape the process of urbanization and "to change ourselves by changing the city" (2008: 23). The presence of the "to-be-invisible" groups alters the public space and offers a subversive interpretation of the city. This may explain the Iranian state's intolerance of coffee shops, automobility, and loitering in the streets, for it is precisely in these places and practices that the private enters the public, and, thus, possibilities of spontaneity may emerge. For Arendt (1994 [1951]) spontaneous human action and the capacity to "make a new beginning" are the forceful potential for action and political change—as shown in the ethnography presented in this chapter materialized in the carnivalization of society and unexpected street politics. Therefore, totalitarian regimes, she writes, strive to eliminate any form of spontaneous human relations: "Total power can be achieved and safeguarded only in a world of conditioned reflexes, of marionettes without the slightest trace of spontaneity" (457).

Urban practices reveal the character, rhythm, and political dynamics of the city. Focus on the new visibilities does not mean I want to play down the economic poverty experienced by a majority of young people. Neither do I neglect class divisions within the Iranian younger generation, nor the gender and class spatial segregation in the Iranian urban landscape. Rather, all these features make youth's new urban visibilities more complex and remarkable. New urban practices and visibilities, neither organized nor ideologized, have been developed by means of the art of a collective presence, rather than a collective protest. It is street politics that "assert collective will in spite of all odds, to circumvent constraints, utilizing what is available and discovering new spaces within which to make oneself heard, seen, felt, and realized" (Bayat 2010: 26). Youth's new visibilities are subversive since the visibility of those who are supposed to be invisible draws attention to discrimination, gender segregation, a high unemployment rate among Iranian youth, and systematic bullying and mobbing by the police. A new form of visibility and urban practices of youthfulness in Tehran and some other large cities in Iran is graffiti and street art, which will be the focus of the next chapter.

CHAPTER 5

WALLS

Wherever I am, the wall is mine.
                    —Nafir, Tehrani graffiti artist

In the winter of 1979, I was thirteen and lived with my family in a lively neighborhood in the central part of Isfahan, the second-largest city in Iran. We were
migrants from the Bakhtiari region, and our life oscillated between urban and
tribal life. In early winter of that year, the Revolution had penetrated all segments of society, including the shah's palace. Mohammad Reza Shah Pahlavi
recognized the nation's will, expressed in the famous speech: "I have heard the
message of your revolution." As a last attempt to avoid a total defeat, he asked
one of his critics, moderate liberal Shahpour Bakhtiar (1914–1991), to become prime minister. An opponent to the shah and follower of the iconic
nationalist politician Mohammad Mossadegh, Bakhtiar stood for hope for a
peaceful solution to the dictatorial monarchy. Within just more than a month
in office, Bakhtiar had released political prisoners, ended censorship of the
press, and ordered the shah's notorious intelligence service SAVAK to be dis-
solved. All these reforms, however, took place too late, and could not stop the
revolutionary forces of the Iranian people. As Bakhtiaris, we supported him
(not the monarchy, though), more due to our tribal sentiment than to his
political visions. Many nights I went outdoors and painted over the anti-
Bakhtiar slogans on the walls in our neighborhood, only to see new ones
written on the same walls the following day. I never met the people who wrote
those slogans. However, our political dispute on walls in our alley continued
until Bakhtiar left the country after the victory of the Revolution in February
1979. The Revolution turned the walls into a crucial medium, offering a way

to frame, perceive, and communicate politics in Iran. Walls are also part of street life. As in Cairo (see Schielke and Winegar 2012), in urban Iran whoever has something to say writes his or her message on a wall: job announcements, advertisements, announcements of people's deaths, political disputes, or expressions of personal emotions, such as affection or rage toward someone. Walls are also used by individuals to send messages: "Don't park your car here. Risk of puncture" or "Damn the parents of those who dump trash here."

As part of the street, walls are where people who have no other media to talk to the state can express themselves. As Henri Lefebvre puts it, "the street is a place to talk, given over as much to the exchange of words and signs as it is to the exchange of things. A place where speech becomes writing. A place where speech can become 'savage' and, by escaping rules and institutions, inscribe itself on walls" (Lefebvre 2003: 19). What appears on the walls (written, drawn, in the form of a poster or a sticker) are central, in Rancière's (2010) meaning, to politics since they redistribute the sensible by visibilizing the invisible and making the inaudible audible. This politicizes the walls, no matter if the message is a political slogan, graffiti, or a job notice in the informal sector. Walls hide what is behind them but, at the same time, display the unseen. This chapter focuses on the "aesthetics of politics" or "the politics of aesthetics" as illustrated on walls. Drawing on Immanuel Kant's understanding of aesthetics, as "the science which treats of the conditions of sensuous perception," Rancière uses aesthetics not as the philosophy or the science of art and the beautiful but as a reconfiguration of sensible experience (2010: 15). The official distributor of the sensible (the police) decides over the allocation of acts of seeing, saying, and doing. It determines what/who is visible and what/who is not. Any contestation, challenge, disruption of this order is, in Rancière's meaning, politics: "This is what a relation between sense and sense means: a relation between what people do, what they see, what they hear and what they know. It is what I call a distribution of the sensible: a relation between ways of doing, ways of seeing, ways of speaking, thinking and so on" (17).

Street art includes a broad range of activities, such as graffiti, wall writings, stickers, performances, or posters. Here I will look at what appears on walls as a new practice of urban citizenship. In the Iranian context, the distinction between graffiti and wall writing is blurred, and the terms are therefore used interchangeably here. Graffiti as a form of public marking—either as written words or as images on walls—has a long history in Iran, just as in other places in the world. However, modern graffiti intensified drastically during the 1979 Revolution and became a small but crucial medium for mobilization and

propaganda (see Sreberny-Mohammadi and Mohammadi 1994: 143). Between 1978 and 1979, alongside political slogans written on walls, stenciled
graffiti images of Ayatollah Khomeini and other revolutionary figures covered
walls all over Tehran and other large cities. During the Revolution, walls were
turned into a forum characterized by pluralism. However, when established,
the Islamic Republic monopolized urban walls for its own propaganda murals. Pluralism disappeared, and walls became part of state media. Like the
political murals in Northern Ireland (see Sluka 1992), the enormous murals
in Tehran have become part of the political culture of post-revolutionary Iran.
Huge portraits of martyrs and officials or paintings with religious or political
(often anti-American and anti-Israeli) themes, appeared on walls in central
parts of Iranian cities in the 1980s and early 1990s. Mainly created by the
Foundation of Martyrs (Bonyad-e shahid) or the Foundation of the Oppressed
(Bonyad-e mostazafan), the murals have become the most visible part of the
aesthetics of authority in Iran. These two organizations monopolized public
walls until the late 1990s when the Council of Wall Painting (Shoraye naghashi
divari) took over control and coordination of the murals.

The murals differ in quality. While some of them are painted by profes-
sional artists such as Hannibal Alkhas, others (usually portraits of martyrs) are
made by amateur artists. One of the best-known murals in Tehran is a huge
painting of the Stars and Stripes on the façade of a building on Karim Khan
Avenue. There are skulls instead of stars and falling bombs at the ends of the
stripes. Another one near Tehran University shows portraits of Ayatollahs
Khomeini and Khamenei. Moreover, there are countless portraits of martyrs
of the Iran-Iraq war. The presence of portraits of political leaders, religious
icons, and martyrs gives the impression of a ubiquitous panoptic gaze over the
urbanscapes. Islamic iconography and Quran verses have been used in murals
to disseminate and promote the "aesthetics of modesty," which is explicitly
gendered: chastity for women and self-sacrifice for men. While the murals
target male bodies as symbols of martyrdom, they promote the veiling of female bodies. Some murals depict properly veiled women labeled with famous
slogans, such as "My sister—your veil is more vital than the blood of the martyrs" or "Improper veiling dishonors the blood of the martyrs of Islam." Other
murals depict blood-stained male bodies to illustrate suffering and pain—
hallmarks of dignity and purity (see Khosravi 2008). By focusing on commem-
orating martyrs, the murals aim to generate guilt and desire for martyrdom (cf.
Peteet 1996). Similar to Christian iconography, visualizing suffering intends "to
move and excite, and to instruct and exemplify" (Sontag 2003: 40).

After the end of the Iran-Iraq war in 1988 and during the so-called Reconstruction Era in the early 1990s, the authorities launched a project to "prettify" (*zibasazi*) the walls. The gray urbanscape was replaced with colorful nature murals (*divarnegari-ye giyahi*). Gradually, murals depicting themes such as green lands, blue skies, and waterfalls appeared in Tehran. Scenes of peaceful pre-urban life, rural villages and tropical seasides, set against the harsh urban environment of Tehran with its traffic-clogged highways and polluted and sometimes poisonous air, make a bizarre contrast. Tehran suffers from severe air and soil pollution, threatening the health of Tehranis. In Tehran in 2012, only 5 percent of the year was measured to have clean air. In April 2014, the Health Ministry declared that, on average, every hour two Tehran residents die due to air pollution.[1] Tehran is also threatened by soil pollution and a looming water crisis. It is not only polluted and overpopulated, but also located in an area of high seismic risk. A devastating earthquake, expected in the near future according to experts, will almost obliterate the city. For people who are exposed to dense smog, who spend hours in congested traffic, and who hear experts predict an approaching apocalyptic scenario for Tehran, seeing the walls decorated with green hills, lakes, and blue skies simulates calmness, an attempt to conceal the actual suffering of urban life in Tehran. The nature murals attempt to compensate not only for the lack of green space in Tehran but also for the lack of hope and happiness (Kamrani 1389/2010). The murals with scenes of pure nature promise a utopian and liveable life to Tehranis but at the same time conceal the dystopian reality of a disorganized city. Ideological as political murals, these murals, like the beautification of cities in the Southeast Asia (Lee 2012: 307), are part of the "futurism of state-based nationalist urbanism."

Since the end of the war with Iraq, Iran has experienced aggressive urban expansion, particularly in Tehran. The land area of Tehran expanded dramatically, and the city's population grew at a rate of a hundred thousand people per year in the 1990s (Ehsani 2009). Gholamhossein Karbaschi, mayor of Tehran between 1989 and 1998, launched a huge reconstruction program financed mainly by capital from private people who in exchange were exempted from zoning laws, which resulted in advancing the privatization of the urban skyline. Urbanization became possible through mobilization and control of surplus production (Harvey 2008). By 1997, 64 percent of all building permits issued in Tehran were for buildings over four stories (Ehsani 2009). The privatization of Tehran's skyline, enormous building sector profits, and skyrocketing house prices forced underprivileged groups out of the urban center.

More and more affluent people moved upward in the high-rise buildings (*borjs*) to keep their distance from the poor on the ground level. With private indoor parking, gyms, swimming pools, and other facilities, as well as high security technology (e.g., cameras and alarms) and guards, these high-rise buildings are Tehranis' gated communities.

During the time of Karbaschi and later when Mohamad Ghalibaf was mayor (2005–2016), Tehran's urban character changed forever with the proliferation of freeways, tunnels, interchanges, and private high-rise buildings. The "Reconstruction Era," characterized by neoliberal capitalism, also opened doors to foreign capital and brands. Privatization dominated the five-year plan (1989–1993) that brought another major transformation of public urban space. An aggressive commercialization of the urban space was launched. The number of huge billboards along highways and other outdoor advertisements in parks and squares, all promoting national and international brands, increased. The brutal commercialization of the urban space can perhaps best be exemplified in the gigantic digital billboard advertising SONY along Hemmat Highway, built in 1998. While the size, lighting, and height of the billboard make the brand visible from afar, a couple of undocumented migrant workers, whose job is to take care of this monstrosity, live in the small space of the foundation under the billboard.[2] The promises of consumerism are made visible through making invisible those who lack the means to take even a piece of the promises but are necessary due to their cheap and docile labor.

The altitude differences between the residents of towers (*borjs*) and those who live on the ground can also be seen in the height of their advertising. While overhead huge corporate billboards advertise international and national brands, travel abroad, and luxury condominiums, walls at ground level are used by the urban poor active in the informal economy. Handwritten or typed on stickers, the informal labor force announces its various services: cleaning, repairing refrigerators and coolers, building maintenance, well offloading (*takhliye chah*), cleaning pipes, washing carpets, driving taxis or other transport services. Those among the urban poor who have nothing more to sell use the walls to advertise their organs for sale. Close to several hospitals in Tehran and centers for organ transplantation, the walls are packed with notices mostly "kidneys for sale" (*foroush-e koliye*) but sometimes also livers. These notices are handwritten directly on the walls or on a piece of paper posted on the walls. They contain the donors' blood type, sometimes even the donors' age and phone number. For instance, one notice reads:

Kidney for sale. Urgent! Urgent! 25 years old. Blood type: B+. Tested healthy. Price is negotiable. Telephone: 091. . . .

Almost all organ sellers are under thirty, the 60-generation. Sometimes the notices reveal the reason for the sale: "university fee" or "mother's surgery costs," to mention two. The organ trade displayed on the walls illustrates poor people's struggle to survive in the shadow of unequal distribution of resources and hope. What can be seen on the walls is a bizarre combination of revolutionary anti-capitalist wall paintings alongside billboards encouraging consumerism, murals decorating the polluted metropolis with idyllic images of rural scenes, and the presence of the marginalized informal labor force.

Graffiti

When the second half of the 60-generation came of age in the early 2000s, a new form of graffiti flourished, indicating a change in the public culture and urban scape. Although using walls for political contestations is not new, the 60-generation have used them to produce and circulate a new form of street art, different from previous ones in form, style, and meaning. Tehran is a city of walls, often whitewashed, making it a heaven for graffiti artists. However, graffiti is mostly seen in the middle-class neighborhoods of Tehran, such as Shahrak-e Apadana or Ekbatan, though also in central parts of the city. Ekbatan, a large middle-class neighborhood of apartment buildings in western Tehran, with light gray concrete walls, is considered, as the street artist STONE puts it, the "land of graffiti." These places are also centers for other urban youth practices, such as skateboarding and Parkour training. Iranian graffiti artists use a range of styles, such as tagging, "Throw Up," or scribing. Stencil graffiti is a popular style because it can be done quickly. The artist cuts out shapes from cardboard or similar stiff material, places them on a wall, and sprays over it. The influence of famous graffiti artists like Banksy is obvious in the works of many Iranian graffiti artists, mainly men of middle-class background. There are, however, some female graffiti artists. Salome, perhaps the only well-known female graffiti artist, is also recognized for being the first female rapper in Iran. Graffiti is costly and demands economic resources. A can of domestic spray paint costs US$5–6. As Goldoust, another graffiti artist, says, "It is expensive—a simple work like a Throw Up may cost up to 5–6 US$." For an active artist, this totals US$60–100 per month (half a worker's salary). Graffiti artists usually possess expensive digital devices, cameras, smart phones, and laptops. Uploading their images on Facebook requires high-speed Internet connections, costly in Iran.

The expansion of graffiti among Iranian youth would not have been possible without the Internet. Almost all graffiti artists have personal blogs, Facebook pages, or websites. The Internet offers a space for graffiti artists to show their works across time and place. Streets walls are linked to Facebook walls. Pictures of new graffiti are uploaded on Facebook walls soon after they show up on city walls. Thus a digital archive of street art is created. Thanks to digital media, graffiti images can be preserved on the Internet, even though they may have been erased from the wall in Tehran.[3] In the summer of 2010, *Stylewars*, the first online magazine dedicated to Iranian graffiti, was started. The name comes from a documentary by Tony Silver and Henry Chalfant on hip hop culture in New York in the early 1980s. Iranian graffiti artists have been growing in number. In early 2014, there were around forty-five identifiable, active graffiti artists throughout the country, of whom twenty-seven were based in Tehran. To name just the best known of these, A1one, Nafir, Black Hand, STONE, Khamosh, Hodak, BigChiz, Tajassom, and Dej Chiz are active in Tehran; STOP in Ahvahz; Goldoust in Ardebil; SG BOX in Shiraz; and NIKO in Mashhad. After the post-election protests in 2009, some graffiti artists, such as A1one, Ck1, and Icy & Sot, left Iran and started working in the diaspora.

A1one

My interest in graffiti started when I was searching for a cover image for *Young and Defiant in Tehran*. It was 2007, and Iranian graffiti had just started flourishing. What became the cover image of the book was a work by A1one, a young man in his mid-twenties whom I later found was recognized as one of the pioneers of graffiti in Iran. The tag "A1one" can be read "alone" (*tanha* in Persian) or "first one." The story of A1one is the story of the 60-generation. He grew up in the unsettled 1980s, during the war, and came of age in the reform era of Khatami (1997–2005). After several years studying art at a university, he was expelled after a dispute over artistic restrictions. Interestingly, the main figures of the counterculture, such as Mohsen Namjoo and Shahin Najafi, both musicians, or Omid Mehregan, journalist and author, have all been expelled from universities. These young artists and intellectuals take pride in having been expelled from universities that represent the oppressive system.

In the eyes of these young intellectuals and artists, academia reproduces official culture and the parental generation's values. A1one's first email responding to my request for an interview was short: "I hate academics." Despite his dislike, I could interview him. A1one preferred to be faceless and gives interviews only by email or telephone. He, like other graffiti artists I have contacted, prefers not to be seen: this is a way to protect himself from getting caught. While still a student, Alone started doing graffiti around his university. In 2003, he made a stencil of Munch's *The Scream* and sprayed it on the walls to protest oppression of the students. His expulsion from the university resulted in the expansion of his work on Tehran's walls. Like many intellectuals and artists of his generation, A1one found inspiration outside what he prefers to call "Univerzoo." As his main sources of inspiration, he mentions David Alfaro Siqueiros and Diego Rivera, two Mexican muralists, as well as Nietzsche, probably the most popular philosopher among young Iranians. He also established Kolah studio, a studio for the documentation of Tehran's graffiti and so-called underground art.

Digital media facilitate the graffiti artists' access to the global youth culture, which is expressed in some of the themes in the works, such as cult icons Kurt Cobain used by BigChiz or Bob Marley by A1one. Although using the Latin alphabet and nonlocal codes is prevalent in graffiti, several artists, particularly A1one, have been working on creating an Iranian style of calligraffiti, a fusion of hip hop graffiti and Persian typography. As in New York, Iranian graffiti is intertwined with hip hop culture A1one was influenced by his friend Hichkas (literally, nobody), Tehran's most famous underground hip hop artist. In March 2011, I interviewed Hichkas, whose tag has been the theme of many graffiti. He has never been allowed to perform or release his music inside Iran. As a friend of A1one, he said that they aim to give hip hop and graffiti in Iran a unique sound and style; "otherwise, it will be only a copy of the Western version." Hichkas and A1one were both born in the mid-1980s and grew up, as Hichkas puts it, in a "closed society, in which we had no choice than to create our own style." An Iranian hip hop genre is emerging as graffiti is also taking on a more Iranian character. For example, A1one has made a series of graffiti using Persian calligraphy. Calling it "Persian graffiti" (*gerafiti-ye farsi*) A1one creates a colorful composition of a word written repeatedly upon each other. A1one's Persian graffiti is influenced by *Siyahmashgh* (literally, black writing), a recent style in modern Persian calligraphy. Calligraffiti turn letters, which otherwise convey audible meaning, into visual art. A1one's political engagement is explicit in his choice of words in his calligraffiti: *edaalat,* (justice) and *solh* (peace), to name two. His stencils are also highly politicized. One is Lady Justice with scales in one hand and a grenade launcher in the other. Another, found on the walls around Tehran University, is an image of a sheep with a dotted line (a scissor-cutting symbol) around its head. Sheep (*gosfand*) are traditionally sacrificed in rituals. *Gosfand* is also used as slang for docile and submissive persons. The graffiti can also be read as a critique of universities, as a space of subjugation, where students are turned into obedient bodies. A1one is also famous for his "eye-tags." Tags of a single eye symbolize, in his own words, the presence, attentiveness, and power of a gaze. In contrast to the panoptic gaze of the leaders portrayed in the murals, the small, single eye-tags posted on traffic signs, in telephone booths, on billboards, and on official posters, symbolize the presence of the observant people.

Nafir

Nafir (literally, scream), also from the 60-generation, is another active graffiti artist in Tehran. His works started showing up on walls in 2008. Referring to his nickname, he states that he is "just a scream on a wall." Paraphrasing Sohrab Sepehri (a celebrated contemporary poet, who wrote "Wherever I am, the sky is mine") Nafir's slogan is "Wherever I am, the wall is mine." He reclaims the right to city walls in order to have a direct channel to communicate his art with the people. On his Facebook wall, he states:

> My gallery is the street. On the walls there is no need for sponsors, of being chic, or for the presence of the artist. . . . No need of invitations or heavy expenses. The people and the walls face each other without any intermediator. . . . [Graffiti is] an art born in the street for the people.[4]

Alienation, loneliness, and social marginalization are recurrent themes in Nafir's works. He has several main figures who appear in different sizes on many places, such as walls, traffic signs, and telephone booths. One is a young man standing with his hands in his jacket pocket and with a sign of a cross on his head. Does the cross indicate rejection and denial of his existence? On his Facebook page, Nafir presents this work with the title "I stand alone." Another of his recurrent figures is a male body, where the head is replaced with a megaphone, shouting "man bough nistam," which literally means "I am not a horn." *Bough* is also a slang word for fool. So the man/megaphone shouts, "I am not a fool." A third figure is also of a male body with a computer monitor instead of a head. The man holds a placard in his hands, saying, "I am under control." The graffiti express feelings of constantly being the object of mass surveillance. His figures, like A1one's single eye, are a declaration of witnessing.

Like A1one, albeit in a different style, Nafir's graffiti targets mainly social injustice. A common theme in his works, like in Icy & Sot's work, is children and their imagination and desires. A laughing boy, representing the tens of thousands of homeless children in Tehran, appears from time to time in various sizes and different places. Nafir is aware of the significance of the location of his graffiti. A large-size laughing boy appeared on the Faculty of Economy at Tehran University on Amirabad Street in December 2013. A few months later in April 2014, the boy appeared on a huge billboard along Chamran Freeway, northbound. Visualizing the neglected and the "invisiblized" poor children in locations that represent the power of capital brings on stage those who should not be visible or audible. Graffiti interacts with its physical location. It calls attention to the link between the neoliberal economic regime (symbolized by the Faculty of Economy and billboards) and urban poverty, embodied by the homeless boy. When one is erased, another shows up on a different place. The image of the homeless boy moves from one wall to another wall throughout the city. Rather than being fixed and rooted, it is nomadic and follows a rhizomatic mode of presence (Deleuze and Guattari 1987). Like a rhizome, the power of graffiti is in its repetitive production. The repetition and replication of messages on walls are the "method of hope" (Miyazaki 2004) practiced by street artists.

Another example: In January 2014, a twenty-five-year-old subway vendor committed suicide in Tehran Underground (see Chapter 7). He was a poor immigrant from the Kurdish province who had been exposed to systematic bullying and harassment by agents of the Tehran Underground. A few days after his death, stencil graffiti by Nafir showed up on the walls close to several underground stations depicting a man hanging from the logo of Tehran Underground, attesting to the hopelessness marginalized groups face in their daily lives in the metropolis. One more example: In a similar way, A1one brings Haj Ghorban Soleimani (a marginalized musician from the northeastern fringes of Iran) to the capital's walls. Originally from a Turkish-speaking minority, Soleimani was not recognized as part of mainstream culture. Wheat pastes of the musician, depicting him sitting on the ground and playing his *dotar* (an "ethnic" instrument), brings Soleimani from the margin into the center of urban space.

Graffiti visualizes not only marginalized bodies but also censored memo-ries. Nafir's portrait of Golshifteh Farahani is one example. Farahani is a cele-brated young actress who became a controversial figure after she posed nude in the French magazine *Madame Figaro* in January 2012. As expected, she was classified as *mamnoo ul-tasvir* (literally, forbidden to be pictured), that is, she would not be shown in media such as cinema, television, or the press. Nafir's wheat paste of her image in several places in Tehran was an attempt to resist the imposed forbidden-ness of her image. Another recurrent stencil by Nafir in 2014 is also of a woman with long, black hair hanging over her shoulders. An image of a woman and her long hair in the city, where female hair is sup-posed to be veiled, brings censored parts of female body into the public scene: it shows the "unshowable." Together with some of the images of the woman with long hair, there are words from poems by Forough Faroukhzad (1935–1967), a celebrated poet and feminist iconoclast. Her poems were censored after the Revolution due to themes of erotic love. Also classified as *mamnoo ul-tasvir*, Faroukhzad's name and poems have been classified as unmention-able in the official media and school curricula. Nafir's graffiti inscribes "should-be-forgotten" memories of Forough on the walls of Tehran. This makes graffiti preeminently political since it redistributes the sensible and thereby offers an alternative narrative. Broadcasting images of unveiled women on walls is an explicit protest against gender segregation in public places.

Moreover, graffiti not only inscribe memories but also envision a different future scenario. In contrast to the official nature murals, depicting idyllic green landscapes, dystopic graffiti illustrate an apocalyptic future of a poison-ously polluted Tehran. The spray paint graffiti pieces depict people in gro-tesque figures wearing gas masks and a smog-darkened sky. For instance, Black Hand has sprayed a stencil that is supposed to give a sense of nature under a bridge on a highway. It reads: "This is not a part of nature. This is a lie." Black Hand reveals the ideology behind concealing the environmental disasters in Tehran with adding "nature" to the urban landscape.

Emotions on Walls

Since authorized public culture tolerates no signs of mundane love and pas-sion, it is not surprising that a large mural illustrating *Khosro o Shirin*, the epic Persian love story, has been whitewashed from walls along Valiasr Avenue.

Not even murals related to the national epic *Shahnameh* are tolerated. In early June 2011 a huge mural in Mashhad in northeast Iran, depicting a dramatic story from *Shahnameh*, was erased by conservative forces. Nevertheless, walls increasingly display love and passion. A stenciled graffiti by Nafir depicts a young man who opens his body to show his red heart. The name of this work is "Love is our resistance." Another work is *Bi tou mahtab shabi*, a piece written on a water tower, referring to Fereydoon Moshiri's poem *Koocheh* (The Alley), a celebrated love poem. Walls are also used by ordinary young people to express their love and passion. A regular type of wall writing that has appeared in recent years consists of the name, or sometimes only the initials, of someone, and then "... doset daram" (... I like you) or "eshqeh-e man ..." (My love is ...). These are often written by young men and can be found near the neighborhood in which the desired young woman lives. One writing, close to a high school for girls in Karaj (a town near Tehran) reads:

> I am the one who drove a Peugeot and gave you my telephone number on Saturday. I will be waiting for you on Monday ... at 6 p.m. in the same place.

Another one reads:

> I wouldn't trade you for the world! You are my love.

Homosexuality is a taboo subject in graffiti globally. However, Black Hand, a young man in his early twenties, challenges this taboo in his works, as seen in a series called *Homofobia* that appeared in April 2013 on walls in Tehran. One example in the series is a wheat paste depicting a young man wearing a black T-shirt, red lipstick, and blue eye shadow, smiling at the viewer. The caption above him says, "Tarsnak nistam" (I am not scary). Another is a spray-painted stencil that shows a young man painting a rainbow (symbol of gay pride) on a wall. However, Black Hand's most subversive work is a series of tags showing same-sex acts in public spaces. Posted on parking signs, between the big "P" and an image of a car, the tags depict two men having sex in different positions. These words bear testimony to love and passion in a city where all public expressions of passion, affection, and heterosexuality, not to mention homosexual sex, are illegal. Using the walls to express passion and affects challenges the imposed imaginaries of the public places. Affects change the "solid things," the walls, from being parts of a "striated space," which is measured and regulated, into a "smooth space," which is the space of affects (Deleuze and Guattari 1987).

Apolitical Politics on Walls

To avoid problems with the authorities, graffiti artists try to present their works as apolitical. Graffiti is still new and, as A1one puts it, "is not taken seriously." According to A1one, making graffiti is not defined as a crime in Iranian law. "They [the authorities] may not care about your art or even the issue of vandalism on public property before thinking about it in terms of being political."[5] To protect themselves, graffiti artists emphasize, either on the social media, their blogs or in interviews, that their works are "non-political" and are only about art and "social issues" (*masael-e ejtemie*). For example, Hodak writes on the first page of his blog, "I shit on politics." Goldoust answers my question about his themes by saying they concern "many issues but [not] political ones." In their view, while "political" issues deal with anti-regime activities, "social" ones highlight the everyday anxieties, poverty, and problems of young people. Despite their tactic of denying that they do not touch on political topics, their urban practices of using walls to redistribute the sensible is indeed political. Rather than representing a post-political generation, graffiti artists are post-ideologically political. This strategy of being "nonpolitical" enables these artists to navigate through the complexities of Iranian society. Imprinting words on the walls is more risky than drawing on the walls. Writing slogans on walls was a form of "minor media" (Fischer and Abedi 1990: 337) or "small media" (Sreberny-Mohammadi and Mohammadi 1994: 143) that was a powerful political tool during the 1979 Revolution. During the post-election uprising in 2009, walls were a central scene for the protest. The Green Movement used wall writing, spray-painted graffiti, and even writing on banknotes as modes of communication.

Like political murals in Northern Ireland (see Sluka 1992), walls have become battlefields where authorities and protestors have been "fighting" since June 2009. The Green Movement protestors vandalized official murals, advertising billboards, and traffic signs by throwing green paint bombs at them. New slogans and graffiti appeared on walls in support of the Green Movement. The proregime forces whitewashed the protesters' wall writings or simply wrote their own slogans over them. There are layers upon layers of graffiti and countergraffiti (cf. Chelkowski and Dabashi 1999: 108) on Tehran's walls.

This makes walls a medium not only for expression of one's opinion but also for communication between the opposite groups—just like my own experience that I narrated at the beginning of this chapter. For instance, one of the slogans of the post-electoral protestors was "Ma hastim" (here we are), written in green all over the walls. By adding a few letters, in black, the slogans were altered into a proregime ones: "Ma ba emmam hastim" (we stand beside the imam), referring to the supreme leader. Another example was written in black, in Ekbatan: "We are not criminals." A few months later, in October 2013, it was changed into "We are criminals" by the addition of a few letters in red to the last word. The play with words in graffiti brings attention to the criminalization of the youth culture. That graffiti is continuously altered, removed, remade, and layered over turns the walls into a site of ongoing debate (Schielke and Winegar 2012). Ideas, images, and contestations flow over the surface of the solid walls. Written words, spray-painted figures, tags, and wheat paste materialize the unfinished contentions. Graffiti is expressive and immediate, and it is an unauthorized communication (Peteet 1996). It does not ask for permission and denies the state's authority over public places. Middle-class youths' as well as poor people's use of walls is informal interventions upon urban spaces and, thus, subversive.

Scribbling on Walls

While graffiti are linked to the art world and slogans on walls are regarded as part of political movements, there are other forms of writing on walls that are not easily classified and are even more transgressive. One form is *yadegari neveshtan*, "leaving a trace." Among young Iranians, this is a form of putting one's mark on city walls, from school walls to walls in the ancient places. They put their names and the date, sometimes followed by a short notice, a message confirming their presence. It is a way to inscribe the self onto, often, protected and inaccessible sites of "cultural heritage" (*miras-e farhangi*). What young people write on the walls is sometimes unreadable, merely illegible scrawls. Words and lines are there but do not transmit a message. It is nothing more than *khat-khati kardan* (scrawling). *Khat-khati kardan* just occupies a space on the wall, and, like pixação in São Paulo (see Caldeira 2012), it is an anarchic intervention in public places. While graffiti (materialization of street art) and political wall writings are signs that relate to other signs in a system as a whole, scrawling is "empty of meaning" and "isolated." Opposite to the "meaningfulness" of graffiti and to political wall writings, *khat-khati kardan* is condemned by the authorities as well as the general public, who see it as vandalism, damaging historical sites (heritages), defacing public places, and making the city ugly. It disturbs and disrupts a certain moral and aesthetical orders of things. Nevertheless, the power of scrawling, or the "value" of scrawling as a signifier, stems from its emptiness.

Scrawling and *yedegari nevisi*, leaving a trace on walls, are considered to be the handiwork of "uncultured" lower-income groups, particularly those who are on the move: soldiers, seasonal workers, or immigrants from rural areas. People on the move, in Deleuze's and Guattari's (1987) terminology, nomads, are inhabitants of the "smooth spaces." With a declaration of their presence on the solid and rooted "cultural heritage," these uprooted, migrating, and deprived groups, who apparently are not part of the "cultural heritage" (palaces, museums, history) and have not been given any share of it (resources, oil, land, water), reclaim recognition and their share of history. To leave a trace is to lack a place. While the "heritages" look back in time, lines and words scrawled on them by marginalized youth record their presence and leave a message to be read in time to come. Similar to what Caldiera observed among marginalized youth in São Paulo, the Tehrani subalterns not only affirm their existence in the city but also start to master the production of signs (2012: 400). Leaving a trace, as well as scribbling on walls, challenges the system of signs and produces new ones. Through imprinting their traces on walls (interventions in public spaces), the subalterns earn visibility and expose the spatial inequalities that they daily face. Scribbling on walls, even though they are empty and meaningless signs, is related to young people's *belataklifi*, protracted unemployment, and marginalization. Stuck in *belataklifi* means to be confronted with the "thickness of time, with impossibility as materialized in emptiness, boredom, and desperation" (Menoret 2014: 58). Interestingly, a sentence scrawled on walls I saw many times was the Persian saying "In niz bogzarad" (This too shall pass). It signifies a hope for a future beyond the untoward presence.

"The Wall Is Mine!"

This is how Nafir expresses his claim to the city. As has been discussed, graffiti in Iran, as elsewhere, are a struggle over urban space, a struggle between, on the one side, political authorities (official murals) and consumerism (billboards) and, on the other, youth counterculture (graffiti) and the urban poor (informal labor announcements). Graffiti is one example of how the young generation is finding its place in the city and reclaiming urban space. A graffiti artist in Ahvaz, a city in southwestern Iran, sees his work as reclaiming urban spaces from the proliferating "advertising toxin that rapes citizens' sight." For him, graffiti is a way to take back city walls from those who have monopolized them for their own political and economic purposes. Graffiti, like political demonstrations, is a way to express one's presence, one's being there. In Baudrillard's (2005) understanding, graffiti is a way of saying "I live here" and "We exist, too." Graffiti signifies the existence of a young generation that challenges the political authorities by making their presence vociferous and flagrant. Through graffiti, the young generation expresses anxiety and visualizes positions. STONE sees no other way to express his "loneliness, anger, or protest" than writing "them on the wall," while, for A1one, creating graffiti articulates a "passion to talk loud." Graffiti becomes a "democratic venue for enacting a personalized urban citizenship" (Lee 2013: 307). Walls become sites where the people are representing themselves and talking back as one to the state. Slogans like "Here we are" come from a citizenry discourse representing a "weness" (ma) and people's strength and endurance (hastim). Another piece of graffiti, "We are not criminals," reclaims the people's agency as citizens and "answers back" to the state's criminalization of youth. Peteet shows that graffiti in the West Bank is a "dramatically graphic and visible way of simultaneously responding to and resisting an assignment of public space that attempted to exclude them" (1996: 148). Similarly, graffiti for young Iranians is a subversive means of protesting the political (murals) and financial (billboards) powers that aim to control the urban space by means of violence and capital. The contrast cannot be more obvious. As a counterpoint to state-sponsored beautification, in form of well-painted figures and ethical codes written in classic calligraphy, graffiti artists and also deprived "nomadic" groups (soldiers, migrant workers who scribble their presence) create unreadable words and meaningless figures that say nothing at first sight. Many graffiti are simply tags. They do nothing but occupy space, declaring their makers' existence, claiming, "This is my city."

Graffiti expresses the reclaiming of what Bayat calls "youthfulness," embodying a desire for autonomy, individuality, joy, and spontaneity (2010: 138). Graffiti as a form of visual communication produces meanings and circulates them instantly. It is visual so does not require literacy. Words and images on walls circumvent barriers and the strict censorship other media face.

Facebook and some other social media are filtered in Iran. Moreover, Internet speed is kept very slow to limit Iranians' access to it. Strict state control over social media makes walls more accessible means of communication, encouraging people to take part and take a stand. The ability to illustrate objects and subjects neglected by other media makes wall writings and wall paintings subversive, challenging the state's monopolization of visibility. Graffiti is part of a counterculture offering a different narrative from that of the official murals. While the latter praises war and martyrdom, the former conveys an antiwar message, for example, by broadcasting the word *soleh*, "peace." While the latter uses conventional motifs and icons, the former disseminates youth culture on Tehran's walls. While the latter supports violence, using images of blood, skulls, and death, the former decorates urban spaces with symbols of nonviolence and social justice, protesting poverty and child labor. While the latter conceals the environmental disaster in Tehran, the former makes it public. While the latter discriminates and excludes undesirable marginalized groups, the former brings them onto the stage. While the latter looks back (night dreams), the former is future oriented (daydreams), pointing toward possibility that has "not-yet" become (Bloch 1996 [1959]).

The battle between state-sponsored political murals and the young generation's graffiti is not only a contest over place but also over its definition (cf. Peteet 1996), a battle over who defines "Iranian-ness." While official murals depict Iranians as "the martyr-making nation," representing a properly veiled, desexualized femininity and sacrificial masculinity, graffiti depicts images of a generation claiming the right to its youthfulness. Walls offer an alternative visual representation of the Iranian people. The battle between images in urban Iran is a battle between generations, classes, worldviews, and ideologies. The struggle over these urban spaces is indeed a struggle over the definition of identities, social relations, resources, and aesthetic values. Like other urban practices discussed in the previous chapter, writing and drawing on walls are attempts to reshape and re-create the spaces of the city. Words and drawings on walls ask questions: "What kind of city is this? Whose city is it?" (Lee 2013: 324).

One neglected and "invisiblized" subject in the official distribution of the sensible is the urban poor, "unshowable" victims of aggressive neoliberalism in Iran. Yet the urban poor dominate these walls, either as actors in using this space to make a living in the informal sector, recording their names on them, or as main characters in the works of graffiti artists. In either way, the urban poor's presence on the walls articulates their claim to the "right (to survive) in the city" (Kusno 2010: 4, quoted in Lee 2013). As I showed in the previous chapter, among the middle-class Iranians, *khiyaban* (street) evokes an "uncultured" space for the poor. Thus, not surprisingly, street art (*honar-e khiyabani*) deals mostly with people of the street and their claim to the right to survive. It should be mentioned here that the socioeconomic conditions of urban youth are characterized by informality as well. The presence of young Iranians in the streets and their mobility, as elaborated in the previous chapter, is related to their social (and temporal) immobility. Protracted unemployment and a general social precarity push middle-class urban youth increasingly into the informal labor market, housing, and banking systems (loan from moneylenders).

Conclusion

This chapter has aimed to show how wall writing and graffiti, as examples of new forms of urban practices by young people and the urban poor, render visible signs, voices, ideas, and imaginations that are supposed to be invisible and unheard, by bringing on the stage new objects and subjects (Rancière 2004). Walls offer an alternative partition of the sensible and thereby create a space for alternative political subjectivities. They reflect a large part of the social life of Iranians. To paraphrase Lefebvre (2003: 19), the wall is alive. It informs. It surprises. Walls tell us the story of everyday life in Iran, the unfinished and ongoing political struggles, love stories, the local debates on modernity, alternative narratives of the past and the future, environment issues, and low-income groups' struggle to make a living. Walls also reflect the high mobility of the young, who suffer from social immobility. The circulation and flow of signs and words on walls show the mobile presence and visibility of both middle-class and working-class youth throughout the city.

The tension between the urban practices employed by the state and by the youth can be explored with help of Gilles Deleuze and Felix Guattari's analysis of differences between *striated space* and *smooth space*. The former is fixed, arranged, and disciplined according to a *sedentary* order. It is the space of "solid things," of the state, regulated, monitored, and controlled. The latter, in contrast, is *nomadic*, slippery, heterogeneous, and defiant. Unlike striated space, which is space of "being," smooth space is space of "becoming." Striated space is hierarchically structured and culturally rooted in opposition to smooth space, the space of movement and a rhizomatic mode of being. The modern state has sought to "draw tight" and "striate" space (Deleuze and Guattari 1987: 385) and transform smooth space into places where everything is ordered, numbered, monitored, and controlled (Halsey and Young 2006: 295).

The officials' city is built on "linear" and "solid things," highways, towers, billboards, and railings that separate the sidewalks from the streets (see Chapter 4). Likewise, official murals represent "solid things" such as cultural heritage, religion, family, and nature. In contrast, graffiti and wall scrawling are parts of the carnivalesque, not of the transcendence but of the transience. They appear on "solid things" (walls) but are removed quickly. Traveling and nomadic images and words, jumping from one wall to next throughout the city, turn the "striated" urban space into a "smooth" space. By expressing emotions (love, grief, and rage) and needs on walls, urban youth and the poor transform the space of "metric," of "properties," into "a space of affects" (Deleuze and Guattari 1987: 479), of movement and of communication (smooth space). "Solid things" express the aesthetics of authority. The official murals, whether extolling politics or nature ones, are "beautifully" constructed. Graffiti or scribbling scrawls (*khat-khati kardan*) are made fast and often are unclear, unreadable, and tumultuous. Adding signs of emotions, words, color (e.g., green or pink), and images to the "solid things" makes graffiti and wall writing subversive. The power of signs on walls resides in their repetition and replication and indicates hope. Walls in Tehran and other large cities in Iran host layers upon layers of slogans, graffiti, love messages, job notices, traces, and scrawls. They are constantly removed and constantly remade. A single sign or inscription does not last long on a wall. However, it shows up on other walls very quickly. As Caldeira (2012: 412) puts it, rather than being a struggle over space, imprinting their traces on walls by young Iranians is an attempt to conquer time, through collective presence and repetitive production. Scribbling "In niz bogzarad"—This too shall pass—indicates hope. Repetition and replication beget hope based on anticipation of something still to become, to happen.

▲ Figure 1. Graffiti by Nafir, 2013.
Tehran.

Courtesy of Rozbeh Shahrestani.

▼ Figure 2. *Homophobia*. Graffiti by
Black Hand, 2015, Tehran.

Courtesy of Black Hand.

▲ Figure 3. Stencil graffiti by Nafir, Tehran.

Courtesy of Nafir.

▼ Figure 4. Graffiti in Ekbatan, Tehran 2013.

Photograph by Shahram Khosravi.

▲ Figure 5. An example of using walls for announcement of services in the informal economy, 2016.
Photograph by Shahram Khosravi.

▼ Figure 6. *Instant Loan*. An example of using walls for announcement of services in the informal economy, 2016. Tehran.
Photograph by Shahram Khosravi.

CHAPTER 6

LEARNING TO ENDURE

In the summer of 2009, when streets were shaking under the feet of young protestors and police boots and disputes about election fraud could be heard and seen on every corner of Iran's large cities, another topic discussed among families, sometimes with even more intensity than the notorious election, was *Jumong*, a South Korean historical television series broadcast by the state-run television (IRIB). *Jumong* aired three nights a week and had a loyal audience ranging from early school age children to elderly grandparents who watched not only the first airing but also its replay the day after. Usually the whole family would sit together to watch, women and men, old and young. Each episode would be followed by a heated discussion. Those who did not follow the series, not many, though, would feel upset by being totally excluded from the conversation.

Jumong is a historical drama broadcast first by Munhwa Broadcasting Corporation in South Korea in 2006 and 2007. In eighty-one, hour-long episodes, the series depicts the legend of Jumong Taewang, a young warrior who started a liberation revolt against the Han Empire of China and founded the Korean kingdom of Goguryeo in 37 B.C. It was first broadcast in Iran in December 2008, dubbed into Persian, as have been all foreign films since the mid-1940s. A huge, well-established dubbing industry, with high-quality translation and voice actors, has made foreign films more attractive for the Iranian audience. As I later found out, the fever of *Jumong* was nationwide. Urban Iranians, like people in the rural areas, followed it passionately. Even in the days of the uprising, *Jumong* did not lose its popularity. Not merely as a mediated product but also through "thingification" (Lash and Lury 2007), *Jumong* was materialized in the form of various objects: DVD collections, posters, stickers, toys, school bags, and T-shirts, among others. Fans started blogs about the series, and a man in Isfahan even applied to change his name to Jumong in the summer of 2009. I heard that sometimes *Jumong* was used by the IRIB to pull people back from the streets into their homes.[1] No matter the intention, *Jumong* indeed had a noticeable impact on people's scheduling of their daily lives, their time and mobility. The obsession with the series even caused several human tragedies. Early in May 2009 in Yasuj, a small city and the capital of the province of Kohgiloye va Boyrahmad, a young man from a poor family, had fallen in love with So Seo-No, the heroine of the series, and committed suicide in pure desperation. When he realized that all his family possessed, a handful of goats, would hardly get him to Tehran, let alone Seoul, he decided to end his life.[2]

The popularity of *Jumong* among Iranians can perhaps be explained by the central aspects of the drama, endorsing spirituality and "traditional values" such as family, filial piety, arranged marriages, obedience to parents, and loyalty. Another aspect people reacted to was the natural landscape. *Jumong* was filmed in the stunning landscape of Hwangmaesan Mountain in southeastern South Korea. While watching, people used to comment with envy on the green hills and valleys, forests, and regular rainfall. Several consecutive years of extreme drought had had a strong impact on water resources in Iran. The lush scenery on the television screen nostalgically recalled a time when Iran enjoyed a leafy landscape and rivers flowing with water. The green landscapes in *Jumong* offered visual pleasure for people who live along dying lakes, such as Lake Urmia in north, or drying rivers, such as Zayandeh Roud in Isfahan or Karoun in Ahvaz. For those who look up at the sky waiting for rain, watching these scenes also made them think about their own precarity due to the drought.

Jumong was popular among Iranians because, unlike the series broadcast by Iranian diaspora satellite channels, such as Farsi1, it fit what they enjoyed watching on television. As I frequently heard, *Jumong* was considered "appropriate for families." When watching Latin American television series on Farsi1, parents were concerned about "unethical relationships," nudity, and vulgar dialogue. In the case of *Jumong*, there was no need for censorship. I also heard from people involved in the film industry in Tehran that foreign television series generally are dubbed into more "proper" language.

Jumong is a melodrama with beautiful actors and a compelling love story. The protagonist is as an archetype, recalling images of a collective memory of a good warrior, a brave and generous leader. He embodies an ideal of manliness not only as a heroic warrior but also as a respectable (*bawaqar*) and modest (*najib*) man. Jumong is the opposite of the metrosexual men depicted in, for instance, Latin American television series. People loved *Jumong* for its depiction of "pure love," faithfulness, and devotedness, that is, timeless values lost in modern society. Undoubtedly, *Jumong* was a triumph for IRIB, which otherwise has difficulty capturing Iranian viewers. The head of IRIB at the time, Ezzatollah Zarghami, announced proudly that *Jumong* was watched by over 70 percent of all Iranians. It was a great achievement for the state-operated network, which had consecutively been losing viewers to satellite television channels broadcasting from the diaspora. The popularity of *Jumong* among Iranians was undoubtedly also linked to the popularity of South Korean products among Iranian consumers. South Korea is regarded as a modern nation with high standards and advanced technology. Its electronics companies, such as Samsung and LG, as well as motor companies such as Kia and Hyundai, are dominant brands in the Iranian market. Unlike Chinese products, South Korean brands are presented regularly on television as being of good quality, fashionable, and chic. During the 2000s, until the international embargo put an end to it, South Korea was the main supplier of high technology to Iran.

Satellite Waves and Purity

Satellite television channels have been a headache for Iranian authorities since the mid-1990s. They regard them as the main weapon in the cultural invasion, the "soft war" against Iran. In 1992, only a small number of households in wealthy neighborhoods in northern Tehran had receiver dishes on their rooftops to watch the few available channels, none yet in Persian. Since the late 1990s, however, the number of receiver dishes has mushroomed not only in large cities but also in rural areas. In December 2013, culture minister Ali Jannati admitted that 71 percent of Tehran residents watched satellite television. The rate for the whole of Iran is 64 percent.[3]

Meanwhile, the number of channels also increased. In 2011 more than four thousand satellite television channels could be received in Iran.[4] In November 2011, around 150 satellite channels broadcast programs in Persian. The popularity of satellite television among Iranians, together with a decreasing audience watching IRIB programs, has made the Iranian state sensitive about this issue. Watching illicit television programs has become the most controversial cultural issue since the late 1990s. The Majlis (parliament) passed bill after bill banning and criminalizing satellite dishes. Over the past two decades, a battle against illicit satellite television channels has been going on both in the political arena and on the rooftops of Iranians' homes. The police have sporadically conducted hunts for receiver dishes on roofs or in courtyards. In October 2011 a new wave of raids on satellite dishes was launched. The police impounded tens of thousands of satellite dishes in a period of less than a month. The state has also used powerful measures to jam satellite signals. These measures were intensified after the 2009 election. The police chief, Brigadier General Esmail Ahmadi Moghaddam, legitimated the operation as a "protection of the virtue" of the nation:

> Satellite networks are a base for operations against our country. Their goal is to spread lies, defame, accuse, and create disturbances and so-cial unrest. Our country is not too vulnerable to the political activities of the satellite programs. It is the moral aspect of their programs that is more destructive.[5]

Apart from news channels such as BBC Persian and Voice of America, two main sources for news, the most popular channels among Iranians are music, fashion, and film, such as the Persian Music Channel (PMC), Manoto, Farsi1, or GEM TV, just to name a few. PMC, launched in 2003, is headquartered in Dubai. It broadcasts Persian and foreign music videos. According to the PMC's official site, the channel is available via eleven million receivers in Iran. Manoto, based in London, was launched in 2010 and is popular for its novel (for Iranian audience) entertainment programs such as *Befarmaeed Shaam* (an Iranian version of *Come Dine with Me*) and *Stage* (a version of the talent contest *Idol*) and political satire shows. The most popular television channel since 2012 has been GEM TV, which broadcasts Turkish series. Farsi1, co-owned by media mogul Rupert Murdoch, was launched in August 2009 and operates from Dubai. It is an entertainment channel broadcasting American and Latin American soap operas dubbed into Persian. The managers claimed in 2011 that the channel had thirty-five million viewers in Iran. Although this figure is probably exaggerated, Farsi1 is widely popular in Iran.

The more popular satellite television channels became, the more state campaigns against them intensified. The authorities' main concern has been the "detrimental effect" of these programs on families. According to the offi-cial discourse, satellite television is a threat to the equilibrium of the Iranian Muslim family, which would be damaged by the visual waves produced merely with the intention to "corrupt the foundation of the family and defuse the effects of morality and religion by introducing new role models."[6] The fundamental social harm caused by the satellite television is believed to be the vanishing of "shame and decency" and "breaking the shamefulness of bad behavior" (*qebh shekani*). The "hidden purpose" of these channels, according to the authorities, is to promote, normalize, and routinize female *bihayai* (women's lack of shame and decency) and male *bigheyrati* (men's lack of zeal to control women's sexuality). The eradication of women's "shame and decency" and men's "honor" will result in the collapse of family and uncontrollable sexuality.[7]

Experts, such as media scholars, sociologists, social workers, psychologists, family therapists, and clerics in abundant conferences, workshops, reports, and talk shows discuss the pathology (*asibshenasi*) of satellite television. The official experts' list of social harms caused by these programs is long: licentiousness; lifestyles that run counter to the traditional society; sexual relationships between young boys and girls; infidelity in marriage; disrespect of parents; extramarital pregnancy and illicit abortions; psychological and mental crises; feminism and the demotion of the role of men in the society; and finally Satanism.[8] One of the most frequently interviewed and quoted experts is Dr. Hossien Baher, a behavioral scientists In an interview with Javan, a news agency, he analyzed *Victoria*, a popular soap opera broadcast on Farsi1. *Victoria*, a Spanish-language soap opera made in Colombia, broadcast for the first time in September 2009 in Iran and soon became the most popular soap opera among Iranians. Dr. Baher's theory went farther than those of other experts: he believed that the soap opera was a project to damage Iranian families. He stated that the scriptwriter of the soap opera had written the story with the intention of disturbing family relations in Iran by encouraging divorce and showing that post-divorce life is sweet. In his view, by having an Iranian audience in mind, the producer and director used every detail, from interior decoration to the soundtrack, to manipulate Iranian viewers. He even states that the actress who plays Victoria was chosen because she looked like an Iranian woman. Thus, Iranian women might easily identify themselves with the protagonist and view her as a role model.[9]

Interestingly, the authorities are almost entirely concerned about women, or rather housewives. In debates, reports, and workshops on the damaging consequences of satellite programs, men are almost never mentioned. Iranian authorities are particularly concerned about the damage of satellite television on "housewives."[10] Media experts explain that these programs are made with "features that attract women" and with "feminine themes" only to target housewives. The programs are believed to incite women to "rebel against their husbands." Farsi1 was even blamed for causing 15 percent of all divorces in the country.[11] Another "damaging" consequence of Farsi1 television series was to persuade the young to instigate generational conflict through stimulating and encouraging *bache salari* (the rule of children) and "insolence" toward parents.[12] The popularity of satellite channels in Iranian society is mirrored in the official reactions against it. Frequent raids to confiscate satellite dishes have been unsuccessful. After the extended wave of raids on satellite dishes in October 2011, the police admitted that only 16 percent of those whose dishes had been confiscated ceased watching satellite television programs, meaning that 84 percent have installed new dishes.[13] Unable to stop a steadily increasing stream of visual waves entering the private sphere, the IRIB decided to produce and broadcast attractive programs and television series to win back the Iranian audience.

Voice and Visage of the State

Television in Iran started in the late 1950s. As a symbol of progress, it was part of the shah's plans to take Iran to the "gates of civilization." Rather than a means of communication, National Iranian Radio and Television (NIRT) became a symbol to show other states Iran's greatness (Khiabany 2008). With up to 80 percent of all broadcast programs coming from the West, mainly from the United States, NIRT promoted the "alluring manifestations of western culture, with little consideration of the urgent needs and demands of Iranian society" (Mohammadi 1995: 373). After the Revolution, NIRT was renamed Seda va Simaye Jomhoriye Eslami, literally, the Voice and Visage of the Islamic Republic. Internationally it is called IRIB (Islamic Republic of Iran Broadcasting). Based on a nativist ideology (a yearning for a cultural purity that had been demolished by Westernization), the Islamic Republic aimed to create its own "people" who would differ from the prerevolutionary "Western-oriented people." Television became a significant part of the project of constructing a new nation. IRIB expanded drastically in the late 1980s and throughout the 1990s. Personnel increased from eight thousand to fourteen thousand. It currently broadcasts fifteen national television channels, ten international news channels, six satellite channels for international viewers, and thirty-four provincial television channels all over Iran. Unlike the shah, the revolutionary state provided television access to rural areas as a means of educating the people. The IRIB reaches almost all corners of Iran and has played a signifi- cant role in integrating the country's minorities. As in the case of television in Egypt, Iranian television has aimed to integrate the audience into the national consciousness as well as to mobilize and "modernize" them (Abu-Lughod 2005: 11). The network invested heavily in "developmental" programs, such as science, health, family relations, literacy, and religion.

Prosocial TV

IRIB has invested heavily in producing domestic TV programs to attract view- ers. Since the Revolution, up to seven hundred television series have been produced and broadcast by the state network (see Table 4). Domestically pro- duced shows are divided into three main groups: historical and religious per- sonalities; comedies; and shows that focus on social issues. Watching television series has become a significant part of Iranians' leisure time. Educational and developmental projects have been the main features of the IRIB. The state television network has produced and broadcast prosocial programs to pro- mote "desirable" cognitive and behavioral activities and to construct a na- tional habitus (Abu-Lughod 2005:26). As Antonio Gramsci argues, "every relationship of 'hegemony' is necessarily an educational relationship" (1971: 350, quoted in Crehan 2002: 157). Televisions shows are not only entertaining but preeminently didactic, a means to foster a good nation.

Through television, the IRIB has attempted to (re)produce images of the ideal Iranian Muslim revolutionary man and woman. Prosocial television se- ries promote "proper models" for building a family life. A vital and common

Table. 4. Broadcast Iranian Television Serials, 1961–2013

Year	Number
1340-1349 (1961-1970)	6
1350-1359 (1971-1980)	64
1360-1369 (1981-1990)	76
1370-1379 (1991-2000)	342
1380-1389 (2001-2010)	225
1390-1392 (2011-2013)	50

Source: IRIB.

feature of these series is the reproduction of a national habitus and aesthetics of modesty, through praising attributes of endeavor, hard work, "contentment" (*qenaʿat*), "endurance" (*sabr*), and "shame and decency." Interestingly, the IRIB representation of the family stands in total contrast to how the family is shown by the independent cinema. The former aims to endorse family values through reproducing the image of the traditional, virtuous, and well-functioning Muslim family in talk shows, educational programs, and television series. The cinema casts light on family crises. To state that family crises have been the main themes of the Iranian cinema since the early 2000s is not an exaggeration. The independent cinema has illustrated the transience, ruptures, contradictions, and conflicts of the precarious situation of families. Unlike the romanticized ideal family model broadcast by IRIB, the family depicted in the cinema has collapsed and is scattered, dysfunctional, and full of lies and deceptions. The prosocial television depiction is based on a dichotomization of the purity of "home" and the peril of "street," the virtue of "family" and transgression of the single lifestyle. Bullying single youth and so-called *arazel owbash* is very common on television shows. The stereotyped image of single youth is usually unmarried men or women, struggling with identity crises, having no families. They are homeless and constantly and aimlessly on the move, as, for instance, in *Kalantar*.

Kalantar, a television series first broadcast in the autumn of 2006, was the first show that focused mainly on youth delinquency. It depicted the friendship between two girls, Neda and Shima, and how they ended up in trouble in a criminal gang. Neda is from a "traditional and religious" lower-class family. Shima is from an affluent, Westernized but torn family. Post-revolutionary Iranian television series have primarily been based on a simple dichotomy between two sorts of families: a Westernized, sometimes corrupt (financially and sexually) wealthy family with low morals versus a poor family with high morals and devoted to tradition and religion (Azadarmaki and Mohamadi 1385/2006). *Kalantar* has this very structure. Shima's parents are divorced. Her father is careless and greedy. Neda's parents, in contrast, are "good" people who got into trouble because of Neda's friendship with Shima. The problems become more complex when Shima befriends a young man in a park and runs away from home. The man is an *arazel owbash* who deceives young women. Shima is kidnapped, and the rest of the story is about the search for her by Neda's family and the police. The series ends with the arrest of the *arazel owbash* and Shima's death. She has been "polluted" by the street and street people, bodily and morally. Because she has lost her purity and chastity, she could not be returned home. The family is sacred and an assurance for social well-being. Since Shima has "no family" (divorced parents), she has not learned how to follow the rules and respect the norms of families, thereby an easy prey for criminal gangs. The main theme of *Kalantar* is respect for authority: the family and the state. There is nothing in between. Young people's problems can be solved only by one of these sources. Outside the realms of the family and the state, only peril, disorder, and darkness persist, waiting for young people. Public spaces, streets, squares, and parks are depicted as spaces of wilderness, outside the control of the family, spaces of "wolves" and *arazel owbash.*

Hegemonic morals are naturalized in the television series, and crises/crimes/sins are caused when individuals disobey the family, religion, or the state. The television series is explicitly educational in terms of promoting spirituality, religious values, and moralities. The central themes in many of the spiritual television series are sin (*gonah*), repentance (*tobeh*), divine punishment (*mokafat*), and redemption (*rastegari*). Spiritual series are more frequently broadcast during Ramadan. These are based on the Manichean dichotomy *kheyr/shar*, good/evil. In several series, Satan is embodied as a human character, as in *Ou yek fereshte bod* (She Was an Angel), broadcast during Ramadan 2005, or *Soghote yek fereshte* (The Fall of an Angel), broadcast during Ramadan 2011. In these shows, evil is the main cause of society's social problems. There is certainly a link between the ubiquitous reference to evil in the series and generally in the official political discourse and the proliferation of the occult imagination in society (see in Chapter 7). Needless to say, the stories always end when evil is defeated by the forces of goodness (usually represented by the police). When sin and crime become indistinguishable, determining and performing divine punishment are jobs delegated to the state. The series depict the police (representing the state) as the only actor capable of destroying evil. While evil is ubiquitous, as Azadarmaki and Mohamadi put it, "the solution is in the hands of the state, which as a caring father, protects his immature children" (1385/2006: 82). It is not surprising that the police and intelligence services support and have been involved in the production of more than twenty television series between 2004 and 2013. They show "the authority of the state" and the power of the police and thereby that the authorities ensure social justice and the safety of the nation.[14] As Abu-Lughod shows in her study of Egyptian television, a function of television series is to persuade the people that "Those in authority . . . are there to ensure social justice, to help those in need, and generally to improve society" (2005:

91). As in Egypt, Iranian pedagogical series aim to contribute to the hegemony of the state. By focusing merely on evil as the source of social problems, the real problems such as unemployment, gender discrimination, marginalization of youth, or domestic violence are concealed. The good/evil dichotomy in Iranian television is of course gendered. While "improperly veiled" women represent evil and alienation, women veiled in a full-body black cloak represent goodness and authenticity. In their study of *Marg tadriji yek roya* (The Gradual Demise of a Dream, broadcast in 28 episodes in 2010) Chanzanagh and Haghpors (2011: 1920) show that the television series was

> based on a serial of binary opposition including goodness /evil . . . modern/ traditional woman, religious/nonreligious woman. . . . The features of women with positive roles are: covered, academically educated and satisfied with the role of being a mother and housewife. They are women with religious and traditional inclination, and have a great respect for their husbands and are dependent on them. On the contrary, women with negative roles have the following features: first, they are self-alienated . . .; second, they are against the traditional roles of women in Iranian society: They are against patriarchy and consequently they are rejected by society and family.

To preserve traditional values is the central motif in all television series. Women are seen as the "carriers" of the collectivity, transmitting traditions, values, and culture to the future generation (Yuval-Davis 1992). Anxiety about the loss of traditions is preeminently a concern about losing control over Iranian women as well as the next generation. One function of the series is, thus, to keep women in their place in the gender hierarchy. In their study of gender stereotypes in Iranian television series, Fasai and Karimi (1384/2005) show that women are presented as passive and inferior, while men are portrayed as wise, active, and superior. Even in the series in which women are presented as "active" outside their homes (they are educated and have a job, drive cars, and so forth), the gender stereotypes of Iranian women as weak and dependent is reproduced. While the female characters are teachers, managers, or doctors, they are not shown working but are shown as "active" only in the private sphere. Therefore, the image of the Iranian man as the real trustworthy axis of the family is reproduced (cf. Abu-Lughod 2005: 92). For instance, in *Ham-ye farzandan man* (All My Children), broadcast in the spring of 2009, the mother is a university teacher, but we never see her at her workplace. She is shown busy managing the household and family life. Similarly, Raana in *Chahr Khone* (Four Houses), a comedy-drama aired in 2007 and 2008 in 107 episodes, is a flight attendant, but she is never shown at work. She is depicted as passive, irrational, and dependent, as is her sister Parastoo, a psychologist who only talks about her profession to create ridiculous, funny scenes. Like women, "villagers" (*dehatis*) and migrants (domestics and Afghans) are also depicted in television series as irrational and ridiculous. These three categories are the very antithesis of what is constructed as mainstream Iranian-ness. The "rational" and "responsible" urban middle class is constructed in opposition not only to women but also to non-urban masculinity (see Khosravi 2014).

Television Series and Consumption

Television has played a significant role in the ideological shift from early revolutionary ideals to neoliberalism. The aggressive marketization of the society, particularly in the 2000s, can also be seen in the new television series produced and broadcast by IRIB. IRIB is a mixture of public and commercial television, with a US$ several hundred million annual budget. The worlds and lifestyles that television brings to Iranians homes are infused with the ethos of consumption (cf. Abu-Lughod 2005: 199). The glitter of urban, modern middle-class life is shown directly in commercial advertisements and also indirectly in television series, written and produced by educated people living in Tehran. The majority of Iranian television series are apartment series (*seriyalha-ye apartemani*) based on the consumption of the urban middle class. The setting is usually a small, well-organized, calm, and cozy apartment in Tehran.

In these apartments, life is sweet and free from the insecurities the majority of Iranian people face in their daily lives. The nuclear families in the series have no major financial difficulties, the aged parents come only on sporadic visits from their retirement home, and the children are hardworking university students. Unlike in real life, water runs constantly through the pipes, and electricity never goes off. The television series are full of the signs and means of modern life: Internet, cars, mobile phones, modern interior design, jargon, and transnational connections (for example, personal links to the Iranian diaspora). The television series are based on the urban pattern of consumption. As Abu-Lughod states, "Television may be both an index and an instrument of participation in the larger world of mass consumption, disseminating images that people, as audience, consume" (2005: 223). A popular series back in 2009 was *Shamsulemareh*, which depicted the story of a wealthy young woman living in a luxurious, large house with several domestic servants, waiting for an appropriate suitor. The main protagonist was played by Haniyeh Tavassoli, an attractive young woman and an Iranian superstar in recent years. Her look, clothes, house, lifestyle, and personal connections to abroad all promoted a culture of consumption. In the summer of 2014, the series *Setayesh* was the most popular show on television. It depicted the life of a wealthy patriarch in a huge house in northern Tehran. His wealth, house, cars, properties, and comfortable life were a recurrent theme in discussions around the television set. Furthermore, a huge "celebrity" industry, mainly in the press but also in social media, amplifies the appeal for a celebrity lifestyle. In addition, commercials, advertising commodities, comfort, and pleasure, aim to turn Iranians into consumer citizens. Every month between five hundred and seven hundred ads (depending on the season) are broadcast on Iranian television channels. Slightly above 40 percent of them are ads for food and household consumption, such as furniture, refrigerators, microwaves, ready-made vegetables, cheese puff snacks, bottled water, soft drinks, and washing detergent.[15]

Both the television series and the commercials promote nutritious and hygienic manufactured food products. Beside several food shows, there are numerous ads involving middle-class families sitting around tables eating "tasty," "healthy," and "nutritious" food. Food consumption has drastically changed in Iran. For instance, until two decades ago, almost all dairy products were locally produced. Today, dairy products found in stores in cities and rural areas are manufactured. People hear and see on television that "good" food is made of Basmati rice from India, frozen meat and chicken from Brazil, or Italian pasta. For people who cannot afford meat more than once or twice a month, all the ads on the screens for rich foodstuffs are only a reminder of their marginality and precarious situation. Here is a typical example, an advertisement for Pemina food products broadcast by IRIB in June 2014. Thirty-six seconds long, it shows a young, middle-class couple with two children in a cozy living room with modern furniture and, next to the living room, an open kitchen. The young woman in the kitchen asks what the children want for dinner. They want cheesy croquettes and chicken fillets. In a short time and in a supermodern kitchen, the mother has prepared a dinner full of salads and colorful food dishes. The ad ends showing the nuclear family of four, sitting together around the dinner table.

Series and commercials promote the pleasure of consumption. Television promotes an urban middle-class lifestyle that promises health, security, and comfort, a life unreachable for the majority of the Iranian people. Advertisements aired on satellite television channels are even further beyond the reach of many Iranians: migration to Dubai through investment (at least several hundred thousand dollars); citizenship in a Caribbean country (which sells citizenship permits); expensive colleges in Europe; five-star hotels along the southern beaches of Turkey; or real estate in Toronto.

Precarious Lives: A Biographical Vignette

During one of my regular visits to my village in the Bakhtiari region, a few hundred kilometers west of Isfahan, I visited Rostam, a man around thirty years old. His older brother was a good friend of mine, and, as a boy, I spent a lot of time in their house. Rostam has been unemployed since he lost his last job in a restaurant in Isfahan three years ago in 2012. For the past three years, he has been living on bank loans. Rostam, his wife, and two school-aged children still live in his parental house, where a younger brother (also unemployed) and his family also live. His father passed away a long time ago, and his old mother had a stroke two years earlier and has been in need of constant nursing. She can neither move nor communicate.

On the evening I went to visit Rostam, he took me to the small room in the corner of the yard where his mother was lying on a bed. He said in a loud voice that Shahram had come to visit her. His mother, unable to talk or move, looked at me for a long time before Rostam took my arm and asked me to sit down. Close to the door, opposite her bed, was a small, cheap television set on a wooden box. An Iranian television series was on. I asked Rostam about a job he had been promised in a city along the Persian Gulf. He shook his head and answered in a complaining tone.

Rostam: There is no job.
I said: *Inshallah* something shows up soon for you.

He just smiled. The series was one of the many about a nuclear family living in a convenient apartment somewhere in modern-day northern Tehran. The mother was preparing dinner in an open kitchen, talking to the young daughter, who had just arrived from the university, tired and hungry. She started setting plates on the dinner table and called her father to ask where he was.

He was still at work. Rostam handed me a cup of tea and said, "There will be no jobs unless foreign companies come back."

A couple of times the series stopped for advertisements. The commercial I found most bizarre was an ad for the bottled water *Damavand*. Showing the snow-covered top and green slopes of the Damavand Mountains in northern Tehran, the commercial proclaimed the high quality of the water and recommended that people drink it daily for a healthy body: "Revitalize your body with Damavand." Rostam's village and the whole valley it is located in suffer from a several-year drought. People and the land in their valley are thirsty. For them, who in the middle of summer have only a few hours per day of flowing water in the pipes, and for the farmers, who have been severely hit by the drought, ads for mineral richness of the fresh bottled water are only a reminder of their precarious situation. When I tried to communicate with Rostam's mother, he pointed out that she was unable to talk or move. He said, "The television is on all the time, so she watches TV but I am not sure if she understands anything. She just stares on the screen."

The series was showing the mother talking with her daughter about a male distant relative who was studying at a university abroad. She looked at her daughter and said his parents had called and asked if they could come for a marriage proposal ceremony (*khastegari*). The daughter said that she did not want to emigrate. She wanted to stay in Iran and take care of her parents. They hugged. The mother stretched her hands upward and thanked God for "having such a good daughter." The husband arrived, and all sat around a table full of colorful food dishes. The contrast between what the episode showed and the life-world of Rostam and his mother was huge. I asked Rostam what he thought about the television series. First, he shrugged and then only said "*Chonom?*" (What do I know?) Then, after a short silence, he looked up, as addressing God, and satirically said, "*Ino bandehasen, moam bandesom!*" (These people are his creatures. I'm also his creature).

We both laughed. The frustration in his ironic complaint, as in many other comments I heard in my village, came from the discrepancy between the expectations of modernization and goals in life (created partly by television series) and the real means to reach these goals. I left Rostam and his mother with a pain in my heart. She passed away a few months later. The image of her I recall from my childhood was when she walked back from her farm in evenings with a shovel or sack on her shoulder. For sixty or seventy years, she worked both on the farm and in her house every day, but had nothing left when she died. A long life working hard on a farm in a remote valley ended with watching day and night the middle-class Tehranis' pattern of consumption, transnational connections, and pleasure of life. In her last months she watched the promises of hard work, the fruits of endurance, the significance of being responsible and a good mother disseminated through television. Her life on the farm and sad death in front of a television set testified very well to the falsehoods of neoliberal promises and assurances.

The Noble Endurance

As I discussed in a previous book, pain (*dard*), suffering (*ranj*), and endurance (*sabori*) have been used as the hallmarks of "high human values" in official discourse (Khosravi 2008). The IRIB has played a crucial role in building up a romanticized image of noble, enduring poor people. In the first decade after the Revolution, the "dispossessed" (*mostaz´afin*) were praised, and deprivation was glorified. While the "oppressors" were depicted as greedy, decadent, and corrupt, the "dispossessed" were portrayed as the repository of innocence, possessing genuine human values. If unbridled pursuit of material wealth had rendered the elite heartless lackeys of capitalism, the suffering of the dispossessed had humanized them (Dorraj 1992: 221). The first director of IRIB after the Revolution, Sadegh Gotbzadeh, declared that IRIB would be for "barefoot people." He even invited the barefooted to participate in media production (Sreberny-Mohammadi and Mohammadi 1994: 169–70). In many television series, poor people are represented as noble, modest, and honest, people who resist the temptation of bribes even while they are mired in financial problems. The modest and noble dispossessed appear on television screens at the same time as financial corruption soars among high-ranking officials. In recent years, several cases of embezzlement, each worth several US$ billion, have been revealed. While television series pedagogically attempt to persuade people that greed leads to immorality and illegality, financial corruption has infiltrated almost all segments of the bureaucracy. Rather than being contradictory, institutionalized corruption, occult imaginaries, a gamble-like economy, consumerism, and teaching the poor to endure are all features of post-revolutionary neoliberalism in Iran. After the war, endurance was conflated with the idealization of consumerism. The neoliberal-oriented television programs are Janus-faced, promoting consumerism and an urban middle-class lifestyle, while at the same time aiming to persuade poor people to endure hardship, be content, and not seek to change their situation.

To foster and educate the nation to persist and endure and endeavor harder, the IRIB found East Asian television series useful. The aforementioned *Jumong* was one of many East Asian series broadcast by IRIB. Japanese and several Chinese series broadcast in the 1980s and the 1990s were followed by the "Korean wave" in the early 2000s. East Asian series suit "Iranian ethics and values." However, the most popular and controversial television series in post-revolutionary Iran has undoubtedly been *Oshin*, a Japanese serialized morning television drama produced in 1983. *Oshin*—or, as renamed by IRIB, *Salhaye dor az khane* (The Years Away from Home)—depicted the life of the fictive woman Shin Tanokura (or Oshin) from the late nineteenth century to the early 1980s. Born in a poor rural family, through hard struggles, she triumphed over difficulties and became a rich and successful entrepreneur. IRIB started broadcasting *Oshin* in 1986, during uncertain times. The Iranian nation was still shaken by political turbulences, financial insecurities, and an ongoing war. The series instantly won Iranians' hearts and became a phenomenon. The audience rating in Iran rose to almost 90 percent (Singhal and Udornpim 1997: 171). Perhaps the absence at that time of alternative television channels (through satellite) and the Internet played a role in its popularity. Like the name Jumong for boys in 2009, Oshin became a nickname for girls in the late 1980s. I was told half-jokingly that not even Iraqi missiles could move Iranians from watching *Oshin*. The Japanese television series penetrated the houses of even high-ranking religious leaders. Ayatollah Khomeini watched the series himself, and his successor Ayatollah Khamenei praised it for "showing the reality" of poor people's suffering and endurance.[16] The current head of the national security forces, Esmail Ahmadi-Moghaddam, admitted he was also a fan of *Oshin*.[17] *Oshin* entered Iranians' lives at the same time a neoliberal state capitalism did, led by Hashemi Rafsanjani, known as "the commander of constructiveness." A symbol of the persistence and success of Japan after the Second World War, the protagonist Oshin was supposed to become a role model, as a risk-taker and entrepreneur. The educational aspect of the series was that, through endurance, hard work, and determination, even a "poor woman" can reach success and fame.

Precarious Lives: Another Biographical Vignette

Mahzadeh is a woman in her late fifties from my village. I always saw her with a generous smile, which made her irresistibly charming. But, behind her calm and charming face there is a history of a rough life. Not even twenty-five, she became a widow with two children. Poor and alone, she moved to Isfahan and started working as a domestic servant. She could not say how many years she worked as a maid, but after some calculations we came to thirty years, approximately. She stayed with many different families, cooking, cleaning, and washing, and brought up her two children by herself. She worked seven days a week. Her son started working at twelve, and her daughter married at fourteen or fifteen (she did not remember exactly). Mahzadeh's work was informal, which means thirty years of unregistered and undocumented work. Her work was invisiblized. After thirty years without insurance and pension, she returned to her village in 2005 when the pain in her legs, probably the result of a harsh and long working life, became unbearable. Her son is now a worker in Tehran, and her daughter, with three children of her own, live with her in the village. Her son-in-law is a worker in Bandar Boushehr along the Persian Gulf and, from time to time, sends a little money to his wife. Like many other poor people in rural areas, Mahzadeh voted for Ahmadinejad in 2009. In Tehran I regularly heard the arrogant comment that only village people (dehatiha) voted for Ahmadinejad. Mahzadeh had put up a picture of him in her room. To my question why she liked him, Mahzadeh said he was the only one ever who cared about them. I challenged her and asked if he really did. Her answer was sharp and compelling: "Even if he did not, he was the only one pretending." No one else even cared to pretend, she said. Next to the picture of Ahmadinejad on the wall was a picture of Oshin. When I asked her why she liked Oshin, Mahzadeh said, "Her life is like mine. When I worked in Isfahan, I was a stranger like her. I was alone and poor."

When I told her that what she had done was not less than that of Oshin, Mahzadeh cast her eyes down as if she was ashamed. She stretched her hands forward, showing the palm of her hands, and said sadly, "Pa che mene dastome? Hoof!" (But what is there in my hands? Puff, nothing!)

Mahzadeh is disappointed and frustrated about being poor despite thirty years of hard work. Contrary to facing a promising future (as a result of that work) as put forward by neoliberal rhetoric and television series—such as Oshin—she is still poor. The success and comfort Oshin enjoyed in the latter part of her life never arrived for Mahzadeh and many like her. Another popular South Korean television series, Jewel in the Palace (broadcast in 2003), depicted the life of Jang-Geum, an orphaned kitchen cook, who, again through hard work, reached her aims and desires and became a physician in the royal court. Mahzadeh talked admirably about Jang-Geum: "She was wonderful.

She was a simple worker but studied hard and worked hard to achieve her aims. I have heard that it was after this series that Korean women started to work outside the home."

Mahzadeh admired this character even for her modesty and her restraint in her love for an officer. Mahzadeh saw these as signs of Jang-Geum's shame and decency. We never talked about it, but perhaps being single almost the whole of her adult life (apart from seven or eight years), Mahzadeh could recognize herself in or even identify with how Jang-Geum suppressed her passions and sexual desires. *Oshin, Jewel in the Palace,* and even *Jumong,* romantic dramas, in which love is platonic, foster and endorse emotional endurance. As elaborated in other chapters, enduring pain, poverty, and suffering is seen as a virtue. In line with Iranian neoliberalism, East Asian television series depoliticize poverty. Through the romantization of poverty and the idea that it can be defeated through individual efforts, the neoliberal state attempts to individualize and personalize poverty and aims to foster responsible, prudent, entrepreneurial citizens. East Asian series are used by IRIB to make Iranians believe that even unprivileged and poor individuals can succeed and reach their dreams through endurance and hard work.

Broadcasting East Asian television series alongside Iranian ones has become part of the technologies of citizenship, constituting a moralizing and "responsibilizing" project that aims to turn citizens into responsible, risk-taking, entrepreneurial, and ethical subjects. While the Iranian poor recognize their own suffering and endurance in the East Asian television series, the Tehran-produced counterparts, paradoxically, seem unfamiliar and foreign. While Mahzadeh talked passionately about Oshin and Jang-Geum, she was silent most of the time when I brought up Iranian TV series. The distance she felt toward these programs was obvious in her comment when I talked about *Shamsulemareh* and its rich and attractive superstar Haniyeh Tavassoli:

God makes rich people pretty. If you are poor, you are ugly too.

The contempt for the poor and marginalized people embedded in post-revolutionary neoliberalism is explicit in some of the Iranian television series depicting rural people as "ridiculous" and "ignorant." Like mobbing of the urban poor (*arazel owbash,* vendors, and homeless people), systematic bullying of rural people has been done by the state-run television that marks a person from the rural areas as *dehati. Dehati,* which literally means "a villager," generally signifies deprived and "uncultured" persons. Moreover, *dehati* (portrayed in the television series as a labor migrant in cities) has become synonymous with an unskilled worker. This is part of the alienation Rostam and Mahzadeh felt toward Tehran-centric television series.

Sabori, endurance, is about emotions. Television, particularly melodramatic series, trains and directs emotions. Indeed, the manipulation of emotions is pivotal in the television series. As Abu-Lughod states, series are not only about moral order, but they also provide an education in sentiments. Suffering and pain in everyday life are interpreted in relation to the dramas aired on television, and this may lead to the "melodramatization of consciousness." It may explain the "pull" (*keshesh*) of the series. They not only pull in viewers but also play on people's feelings (Abu-Lughod 2005: 117–18). The series *Jumong*, depicting the Korean people's collective pain, helplessness, and resentment under the siege of a brutal oppressor (Mickler 2009), plays on the feelings of Iranians who find themselves in a similar situation. It plays on the same feeling an interlocutor expressed in analogizing life in Iran to life in France under Nazi German occupation. Identifying with the oppressed (*mazlom*) and the creation of a discourse on emotions (sadness, suffering, a sense of guilt) deeply rooted in the Karbala paradigm, have been crucial in constructing a post-revolutionary subjectivity. The "emotionalization" of politics in order to generate a sense of guilt has been instrumental in establishing the authority of the post-revolutionary state (see Khosravi 2008). Enduring pain and suffering became hallmarks of dignity and inner purity (*safa-ye baten*). Emotional pain is associated with inner purity, conscience, and responsibility. The "cultural shareablity" of *Oshin*, *Jewel in the Palace*, and *Jumong* can be explained by three archetypes: 1) their ability to reshape their own world through endurance and heroic struggles; 2) their self-sacrificing; 3) their desexualized "pure" love, respect for old people, and family-centric values.

What made *Oshin* and *Jumong* popular among Iranians was the "culturally shareable" values of enduring pain and suffering. Many marginalized people incorporated the meanings of the television series into their daily lives to unfold and demystify their own precarity. Iranians used to compare the series with their own real-life experiences and thereby created meanings through engagement with the audience and conversation during and after the series were shown (cf. Fiske 1986). Perception of the East Asian series has not always been what the authorities had wished. A side effect of *Oshin* and *Jewel in the Palace* has been an increasing interest in women's rights. Oshin's popularity also comes from her successful combination of traditional values and modern life. The character "showed" that women in traditional societies can live a modern life, be independent, work outside the home, and achieve big goals. Oshin embodied the archetype of "self-seeking individuation, the disobedient female, and the heroic struggle" (Singhal and Udornpim 1997: 175). Oshin turned into a political issue when she was once mentioned instead of Fatemeh, the daughter of the Prophet Muhammad. On Women's Day in Iran (the birth of Fatemeh) in February 1989, a radio reporter asked women on the streets on a live program who their role model was. The answer, given by many women, was of course Fatemeh. One young woman's answer enraged the clergy: she said Oshin was a better role model for Iranian women than Fatemeh. The answer shocked the authorities, and four people involved in the broadcast were arrested. Similarly, *Oshin* is believed to have had a "positive influence in the process of female emancipation" in Bangladesh (see Singhal and Udornpim 1997: 171). Even if it didn't directly influence the women's rights movement in Iran, *Oshin* has had an impact on how women's position and role in society are discussed in Iran.

Another unintended perception of the television series *Jumong* was how Iranians incorporated the legend of Koreans' freedom struggles against the oppressor, the Chinese emperor, into their own contemporary political contestations. The feeling of "living under occupation," expressed by a young interlocutor, induced Iranians to identify with the drama even more. The bad guys in *Jumong* were the Chinese, portrayed as brutal oppressors. When *Jumong* was broadcast, young Iranians were involved in protests against the election result. China was the first state to congratulate Ahmadinejad on his reelection in 2009—making China unpopular among youth. Moreover, the "bottomless import of cheap Chinese products," as Iranians put it, has undermined domestic industries. I frequently heard that Ahmadinejad opened the door for Chinese "low-quality" products in exchange for their political support in the international arena. Revenues from the Iran-China trade increased drastically from US$3.5 billion in 2000 to US$30 billion in 2010 and were expected to reach US$50 billion by 2015.[18] Many believe that importing Chinese products resulted in bankrupting domestic entrepreneurs. When people watched the series, their cheers at Chinese defeats on the battlefield were juxtaposed to comments that they deserved it since they betrayed the Iranian people. Anti-Chinese sentiments expressed in front of television were soon turned into anti-Chinese slogans in the post-election protests on the streets during the summer of 2009.

Conclusion

Television in general, both satellite and regular broadcasting, has permeated the daily life of the Iranian nation and has become a fundamental element of public culture in which social identities and social relations are constructed. Television series are used as means to educate and foster the nation. They are didactic as well as entertaining. They construct not only a "national imagination" (Anderson 1983), but also a national habitus (Abu-Lughod 2005: 26). Although they endorse "traditional" values such as supporting the nuclear family, honoring the older generation, and upholding patriarchy, the series promote assimilation of the nation into a modern, urban middle-class lifestyle. Similar to Indonesian proletarian theater in the late 1960s (Peacock 1968), the themes and structure of Iranian television series encourage the audience to be modern. The logic of drama in these shows is structured linearly with a climax and finally a goal in form of an individual achievement (see also Abu-Lughod 2005: 131). Television series function as "rite of neoliberalization." Neoliberal messages implicit in East Asian series such as *Oshin* and *Jewel of the Palace* are strikingly obvious: individualizing and personalizing poverty. The neoliberal messages in the series promote the entrepreneurial self, risk-taking, individual responsibility and a belief in individual volunteerism.

An uncanny combination of commercials and "revolutionary anti-capitalism" features of IRIB productions has resulted in an ambiguous policy. On the one hand, the state-run network has reproduced the romanticized image of the noble dispossessed, while, on the other, it has, since the mid-1990s, promoted consumerism and an urban middle-class lifestyle. The change of IRIB from public-service television to a commercial medium reflects the general ideological shift in Iran since the late 1990s. Grounded on a progressive narrative of development, the "development realism" in domestic and East Asian television series aims to persuade the audience that education and hard work lead to success. It fosters a faith in education as a key to progress and social mobility. Consequently, young people in both urban and rural areas have been enticed by the education industry, in which private companies promise "guaranteed achievement" through Konkur (the university entrance exam) in exchange for a high fee. Both IRIB and satellite television channels broadcast abundant advertisements for education companies, private schools, and universities abroad.

The reality of life for many people in Iran petrifies them in "a situation in which improving one's standard of living through linear progress is no longer possible (Mains 2007: 666; see also Ferguson 2006). The young Boyrahmadi shepherd committed suicide when he realized he could not reach the beautiful So Seo-No in *Jumong*. Unlike what the television series *Jumong* presented, strong will and diligence were not enough. Mahzadeh sees Oshin's life as similar to hers, but after thirty years of hard work, Mahzadeh is still poor, unlike what the series had promised. Rostam, unemployed and heavily in debt to banks and moneylenders, watches "the good life" available on the television screen but unreachable for him. Television changes something in people's subjectivity. Television, and particularly the television series, creates a shared language and emotion. Television includes them and at the same time excludes them. Through an "exclusionary inclusion" television, integrates people as consumers but excludes them as equal citizens. Television series have been part of a nation-building project after the Revolution. The series, however, do not give answers to how the nation-state can be transformed into "a more equitable and just place" (Abu-Lughod 2005: 245). Abu-Lughod in her brilliant and rich ethnography of Egyptian television shows how "Television offers goods and evokes dream worlds that, even if they have become part of a familiar cognitive or imaginative landscape, are unevenly realizable" (223). The uneven distribution of hope and precarity is the main focus of the next chapter.

CHAPTER 7

PRECARIOUS IRAN

In April 2013, a short video clip was uploaded on YouTube by Ali Molavi, a twenty-six-year-old Tehran-based artist. The short clip is about a wish (*arezoo*). Molavi asked fifty randomly selected people in central Tehran what their wishes were. Young and old, men and women looked into the camera and talked about their wishes.[1] The answers varied. Some wished for money, others for peace in the world. A recurrent wish was to be somewhere else, or rather, not to be in Iran. One wished to die. Another wished to "be sent to another world." A couple said it was too late for them to wish for anything. The hesitation, silences, and perplexity in their faces when hearing the question and not knowing how to express their wishes—if they had any at all—demonstrated the sense of precarity, insecurity, and vulnerability sensed and lived by many Iranians today. A precarious and insecure life eradicates hope. Precarity prevents hope from being generated and wishes from being imagined. Perhaps the most striking answer was given by a young woman who disclosed the political dimension of "lacking" wishes. She said, "They [the authorities] have not left any space for us to wish anymore."

The Pressures of Life

The "pressures of life" (*feshar-e zendegi*) is a common term used by Iranians to express the precariousness they sense and live. The pressure has been increasing in recent years. According to official sources, between 31 and 40 percent of Iranians live below the poverty line, and 10 percent live below the extreme poverty line, a condition characterized by severe deprivation of basic human needs.[2] In January 2016, the minimum cost of living for a family of four in Tehran was 3,200,000 toman (US$850) per month, while the average monthly income for a worker in Tehran was a quarter of that, 800,000 toman (US$220).[3] According to this calculation, "up to 90 percent of all workers live below the poverty line."[4] The working poor, whose wages are not enough to provide basic needs, chase after extra incomes. In 2014, seven million, or up to 30 percent of the people in the labor force, had at least two jobs.[5] To give a picture of the situation, here are a few examples from July 2014. A clerk works as a taxi driver after he finishes his day job in an office in Tehran. When he finishes his second job and comes home, his children are asleep. He meets his children only on Fridays, the weekend in Iran. A middle-aged caretaker in a hospital in Isfahan works as a personal assistant to elderly people in their homes. He often sleeps in his employers' homes. His wife and two children often go back to his wife's parents in a small town in northern Iran so he can work more. A woman in her mid-forties works as a call-in maid for 3,000 toman (slightly under $US1) per hour. She usually works ten to twelve hours a day, six days a week. The list can go on. Precarious labor means less time for family relations. When more and more people have to spend twelve to sixteen hours working, it means a family life without interpersonal relations and, as expressed in a report, "home is reduced to a place only for sleep."[6]

Another form of precarity is the irregularity of employment. Iran's Ministry of Labor and Social Affairs stated in mid-June 2014 that eleven million employees, almost 50 percent of everyone employed in the country, had irregular employment: half the whole labor force falls into the irregular workforce category. The situation was even worse for the working class, among whom short-term and irregular employment is above 90 percent.[7] In the private sector, the rate was 100 percent.[8] Irregular employment means that workers have temporary, short-term, or often informal jobs and are usually not covered by health or unemployment insurance. Between ten and thirteen million Iranians are entirely excluded from the insurance system.[9] Of the workers who lost their lives working on construction sites in 2013, only 10 percent were insured.[10] Informal and irregular employment also means absence of protection against employers' exploitation. Delayed salary payments, sometimes up to six months, are not unusual for those who are irregularly employed. Every week there is a news report about workers somewhere in Iran going on strike and protesting against not having been paid for months. Almost all young workers I met during my extended fieldwork since 1999 have been in irregular employment and testified that they have rarely been paid on time. The situation is even harsher for workers in rural areas. Several months-delayed payments mean that employees have to take loans from banks. The less fortunate ones who are not eligible for bank loans turn to moneylenders who demand high interest rates. In January 2016, new hand-written announcements on walls in the central and southern parts of Tehran caught my eye: "*vam-e fori*" (instant loans), followed by a cell phone number. Informal moneylenders demand an incredible annual interest rate, between 70 and 100 percent. Irregular employment with irregular salary payment means that workers lose part or all of their wages on the interest they have to pay to the banks or moneylenders. Sometimes these workers are trapped in a hostage-like situation. The employer agrees to pay part of the delayed payment if the worker agrees to work for a few more months. This kind of extortion can continue for years. Another common feature of short-term employment is that employers do not always pay social security contribution for the whole period of employment. Short-term workers, usually migrant workers from rural areas, discover later that their employers paid their social security contribution only for the first weeks or months. Getting regular employment today, for those who have no "inside connection" (*parti bazi*), is almost impossible. The rate of unemployment among youth is twice the rate for the whole population, and it is even higher among young people with higher education (40 percent). The prognoses indicate that the number of educated but unemployed young people will increase from 5.7 million in 2015 to 10 million in the coming years.[11]

As shown in Chapter 2, unemployed and underemployed youth belong to an increasing generation kept in waiting, in suspension, *belataklifi*, a precarious condition characterized by invisibility, immobility, uncertainty, and arbitrariness. This generation feels that they are not fully in command of their lives. Their precarity is best shown in how they are viewed by others. Similar to Allison's study, which shows that Japanese youth are blamed for the precarity of the recent economic (dis)order and "unproductivity" of Japan (2013: 30), the young generation in Iran is blamed for being a "burden" (*sarbar*) on the family and society. The stigma, *sarbar*, is used to describe youth living off their parents, which resembles how young Japanese are called "parasite singles" (30). Regarded as a "burden" on the family and society, the youth are reduced to a *thing*: a form, a load, a mass. Unable to build their own families, they are also regarded as "impotent" to reproduce the life they are supposed to reproduce. As I explored in Chapter 3, single youth are blamed for not participating in reproduction, whether economic or demographic. The declining marriage rate, increasing divorce, financial difficulties, and transformation of the ideal lifestyle among youth have caused a demographic precariousness in the country. The authorities declare that a low birth rate is a serious concern for the well-being of the society in the coming twenty years.[12]

As shown in Chapter 3, the "unproductivity" of young people makes them the target of criminalization and, subsequently, of systematic bullying and mobbing. Unemployed, irregularly employed, or underemployed, young Iranians are stuck in various forms of immobility. First, temporal immobility: waithood and the condition of *belataklifi*. Second, spatial immobility: inability to move out of the parental home. Their mobility in the streets, automobility, and strolling are criminalized. Third, social immobility: un(der)employment and loss of ability to improve their socioeconomic status.

This young, immobilized generation constitutes a class in the making: young, single, un(der)employed, immobile, with no hopeful prospects for a better future stuck in the multiple precarity. Echeverri Zuluaga finds his interlocutors in in Dakar in similar situation, suffering from suspension, that prevent them from crossing social and geographical borders:

> Suspension . . . refers to the interruption of social ties . . . as well as to a temporal slowing manifest in the absence of plans in the present, plans deferred to the future, prolonged waiting, and the inability to improve one's life condition. (2015: 593)

The prevalent sense of an insecure life, a precarious life, among Iranians, particularly among the youth, is the focus of this chapter, which also aims to encapsulate the main themes of the book. Here I use "precarity" not as existential precariousness, the general shared vulnerability of life, but as political and legal regulations, manifested in a differential distribution of insecurity, danger, and hope. I do not focus on the precariousness of life, shared by everyone, but use precarity as an analytical tool to explore the politically induced condition in which certain categories of people are discriminated against, marginalized, excluded, and exposed to danger. Precarity as a symptom of neoliberalism, a socioeconomic condition (Standing 2011), is characterized primarily by job insecurity. However, when financial insecurity slips into other dimensions of life, precarity expands, and one's whole human condition becomes precarious (Lazzarato 2004, in Allison 2013: 9). The term *precarity* is useful to conceptualize the relationship between precarity as a socioeconomic condition and as an ontological experience (Millar 2014; Molé 2012; Neilson and Rossiter 2005). Nevertheless, following other anthropologists, I use the term "to conceptualize the labor condition as inseparable from issues of subjectivity, affect, sociality, and desire" (Millar 2014: 35; see also Molé 2012 and Allison 2013).

Disconnectedness

Boridim dige. This is what I have frequently heard young Iranians saying. *Boridan* literally means "cut off," but is used here to express extreme fatigue and exhaustion, a lack of motivation and will to do something. *Boridim dige*, "We have become exhausted." Being cut off metaphorically also conveys a sense of disconnectedness and detachment from both home and homeland, a common feeling among young Iranians. The widespread precarity sensed and lived by Iranians not only shows financial insecurity and social instability, but also indicates a deterioration of family-oriented identity, a disruption in the linear life cycle from adolescence to adulthood, and a weakening sense of belonging to the nation and to the state. Sensing precarity is linked to a prevalent moral panic regarding a series of "collapses": collapse of the family, of ethics, and of society. As discussed in Chapter 1, the panic about these collapses is based on anxieties about weakening family ties, vanishing filial piety, increasing divorce rates, growth of domestic violence, and intensified generational conflicts.

The pain of being cut off among Iranians can be compared to the similar experience among the Japanese. Anne Allison's ethnography of precariousness in Japan is gripping:

> When family as a source of life and a life resource dissolves, it is not only the country's low birthrate but its slow death of humanism—of people dying from abandonment, lack of care, simple "disinterest"— that feeds a collective sense of a dwindling soul. (2013: 40)

I heard many time that, under the pressures of life, morality and family values are vanishing in Iran. Murdering family members, splitting up, abandoning parents, and inheritance conflicts among siblings have become common. As a young man put it, "Here it is not the human being who is killed but humanity." Among the older generation, there is a longing for the past that "was more human." I often heard people nostalgically say that in the past people showed more respect to each other and took much more care of each other. For both older and younger generations who express a feeling of disconnectedness and abandonment, the present time is characterized as

a state of not-ness: not feeling quite right, not sufficiently secure, no-
ticeably not human. A slippage from a time when things were (remembered or fantasized to be) better. When home meant social
security—the stable job, a steady income, middle-class lifestyle, a place
in society, and a future. (Allison 2013: 175)

Losing *family* is followed by a sense of losing *home*. The feeling of being cut
off is a sense of disbelonging, being removed from context, being out of place.
As Bachelard (1964) shows, home is a space for safety and imagination, a
space for sheltering soul. When the parental home is turned into a space for
oppression, fails to protect and support the children, and becomes a space
where youth become a "burden," young people take refuge in the streets, in
coffee shops, in automobility (see Chapter 4), where they can create alternative forms of sociality and find greater autonomy. Similar to the garbage dump
for *catadores* (garbage pickers) in Rio de Janeiro (Millar 2014) and cafés for
the young poor in Japan (Allison 2013), streets have become a "refuge" for
young Iranians.

Hope is materialized in home(land) (Bloch 1996 [1959]). The "liquidiza-
tion" of home(land), that is, that home(land) is no longer experienced to be
safe, protective, or hospitable, generates a sense of homelessness and, subsequently, of hopelessness. When hope(lessness) is differentially distributed
among citizens, belonging to the state becomes uncertain and the homeland
is experienced as "a land under foreign occupation." The proliferation of this
sense of home(land)lessness and the elusiveness of life have permeated young
Iranians' literature, music, and cinema. For instance, the movie *Asabani nistam* (I Am Not Angry, by Reza Dormishian, 2014) illustrates how home(land)
lessness is sensed and lived by Iranian youth. The main protagonist is Navid,
a young migrant from the Kurdistan province living in Tehran. For being a
political activist during the protests after the 2009 election, he is expelled from
the university. He is stuck in *belataklifi*, oscillating between diverse irregular
employments and unpaid salaries, waiting to marry the woman he loves. His
landlord orders him to evacuate because he plans to build a *borj*, a tower
building. When Navid refuses to collaborate in corrupt businesses, he loses
his jobs. He is an outcast in all its meaning. Throughout the film, we see him
being exposed to systematic bullying conducted by the police, employers, his
landlord, wealthy people, his girlfriend Setareh's father. The film shows the
excluded and marginalized young men and women who are immobilized in
time (waithood) and space. They are turned into quasi-citizens who have lost

the right to have rights. An interesting scene in the film is when we see Navid and Setareh sitting between parked cars on a heavily trafficked street to commemorate their friend who was killed there during the protests of 2009. As I discussed in Chapter 4, that they leave the sidewalk to occupy a place in the street, where they are not supposed to be, is a replication of political behavior. Navid's rage and disappointment are diagnosed as major depression and are medicated. His mental condition is characteristic of his generation, a Prozac generation, as Orkideh Behrouzan writes about (2016). Reducing his economic and political problems, the results of systematic oppression, to a mental disorder is how Iranians' precariousness is depoliticized. The poverty, discrimination, and exclusion the protagonist is experiencing are personalized and individualized. Navid's frustration gradually turns into aggression, and, when he feels he is losing his last hope and love in the world, Setareh, in a moment of rage and deeply drugged by heavy medications, he kills her father. The film ends with his execution by public hanging, just like an *arazel owbash*, surrounded by a mob.

Seen as a "burden" or parasites who are living off their parents, the young are kept biologically alive, sent back and forth between the state and the family. The feeling of disconnectedness and disbelonging was expressed explicitly by one interlocutor this way: "I try to spend as little time as possible at home. For me it is like living at a hotel. I go there only for sleep." A sense of *boridegi*, detachment, that is, not being recognized or accepted by others, is the main challenge for the young precariat (cf. Allison 2013: 65). *Boridegi*, detachment from home, can lead to *biganegi*, alienation from homeland. Alienation, a feeling of being a foreigner, or rather finding Iran a foreign land, is not uncommon among middle-class urban young Iranians, as if one lives "in a country occupied by foreign forces, like when France was occupied by Nazi Germany." This partly explains growing desire to be somewhere else, expressed by several people in the video clip with which I opened this chapter. This desire for elsewhere recalls young Togolese longing for displacement, a longing for a future that replaces untoward pasts, both political and cultural. They are ready to "jettison their past and commit themselves to a future without a telos and be willing to evacuate a space they call home" (Piot 2010: 20). The desire for elsewhere among young Iranians is associated with the feeling of being rejected in their own home and by the homeland. It originates in boredom and a condition of suspension (Echeverri Zuluaga 2015). While not seeing any "future" here, where the prospect of a better life will not be actualized, they seek it elsewhere. Iranians' longing for elsewhere has somehow led to tragic destinies: migrant illegality, hazardous journeys, long-term confinement in camps and detention centers, deportation, and sometimes death (see Khosravi 2010). Many interlocutors gave voice to their sense of disconnectedness, like this one:

> I just want to be away from these people. . . . I want to flee from everyone, even from myself. . . . People's culture has changed. They are not Iranians anymore, but Arabs and Afghans.

When the state fails to foster hope in the nation, a "paranoid nationalism" (Hage 2003) emerges that blames social exclusion on other marginalized groups. This explains the progress of nationalism, expressed in forms of anti-Arab sentiments (blaming all current problems on the invasion of Arabs around fourteen hundred years ago that brought Islam to Iran) or blaming Afghan migrants for "stealing jobs" from Iranians. The paranoid nationalism of Iranians was demonstrated on International Workers' Day 2015. When, after many years, Iranian workers got permission to celebrate their day, the main target of their manifestation was "foreign workers." Tens of thousands of workers gathered in front of the Labor House in Tehran with banners and slogans against foreign workers, particularly Afghan migrant workers. Instead of directing their anger and protest against the structures that reinforce their marginalization, the working poor blame migrants who are in a similar situation to theirs. What paranoid nationalism conceals is indeed this very similarity of precarity that citizens and noncitizens share. A differential distribution of precarity has turned a large number of young Iranians into quasi-citizens, whose rights can be deferred, suspended, and denied. Precarity can make citizenship rights inaccessible for citizens, as in the case of Abbas.

Precarious Lives: A Biographical Vignette

Abbas was born in 1965 in a small village in the Bakhtiari region. He is the second of seven children and has two brothers and four sisters. Abbas started helping his father on the small land they owned when he had not even reached school age. He was only ten when his father died of a stroke at fifty-five. And then drought came, and with it their revenue vanished. Drilling a deep well required a lot of money they did not have. So he and his brothers started a circular migration lifestyle. They went to near and far places in search of jobs, always short-term, low-paying ones: day labor on construction sites in nearby cities during the winter, cleaning potatoes for plantations in late spring, working on irrigation projects in summer, or harvesting on farms in early autumn. One late fall day in 1984, he was going to Borojen, a small town about one hundred kilometers north of his village, where his brother, who was working in Borojen, had found a job for him on a construction site. The job was to last several months, his longest so far. Early in the morning that day, he paid his fare to a driver and found a place next to other men and women in the back of a pick-up truck. Some were going to work, some to visit a doctor, others to obtain a dowry for their daughter. Approaching Borojen, the vehicle was stopped by the police. It was *sarbaz giri* (literally, soldier catching, arresting runaway soldiers and those who have not done their military service). Abbas was nineteen years old and had, like many other young men in the region, ignored call-ups from the military. The war with Iraq, now in its fourth year, was harvesting lives. The police asked for his papers. Abbas had none. Consequently, he was detained and soon sent to a military base in Isfahan to start his compulsory military service. After only ten days' training, he was sent to the war front. He got some instructions and became a deminer at the front, where he served for twenty-eight months. People were dying incessantly in the war. In the winter of 1986, the Iraqi army, facing heavy losses, used chemical weapons in large quantities. Abbas remembered details, confirmed by the documents in his medical dossier. It was a Monday, 17 February 1986, around noon, when the gates of hell opened. The mustard gas paralyzed the unequipped Iranian soldiers. The chemical weapons used by the Iraqi army killed around 20,000 and damaged 120,000 others. Survivors developed severe chronic complications. Many faced a slow and painful death. Others are still suffering. Abbas is one of them. He, like other soldiers, got primary treatment first after one day. Abbas says he still smells the gas, "like rotten eggs." According to official sources, there are 550 000 *janbaz* (disabled veterans), of whom 120,000 are registered as chemically injured veterans.[13]

The medical files he showed me said that his lungs are seriously damaged, his skin is burnt, and he suffers from depression. The Foundation for War Veterans classified him as the lowest rate of war-disabled veteran (*janbaz*), that is, at the 10 percent level. For 10 percent, he received an insignificant compensation. To feed his four children, Abbas became once again a circular laborer, moving from one informal job to another. His damaged lungs force him to sit down to take a breath after a short walk; his eyes get more irritated when working in dust; and his burnt skin makes working in the sun unbearable. Working long days on farms under the sun and in dust means incessant, insufferable pain. For more than two decades he has been engaged in negotiation with various military organizations and medical institutions to raise his percentage of disablement and suffering compensation to 25 percent. He said,

> If I had an inside connection in the system, I could get it. I was told there are people in Tehran who fix it for 10 million toman [about US$6,000 in 2011]. If I reach 25 percent, I get 600,000 toman [US$375 in 2011] per month for the rest of my life. I could get a bank loan without interest, and my family would be insured.

Abbas said that he knew many who had been injured just like him, on the same day, at the same place, from the same bomb, but received 25 percent disability. They were, however, Persian-speaking, literate residents in large cities with access to information. Abbas's class and minority status denied and delayed his access to the citizen rights enjoyed by his peers. I witnessed this once when I accompanied him to a medical institution in Isfahan. He was sent back and forth between different floors and offices. When he opened his mouth, unveiling his status as a "villager" with Bakhtiari accent, he was ignored and treated badly. When I involved myself and talked on his behalf, in Tehrani-accented Persian, the situation suddenly changed for the better. His struggle is for rights to benefits in the form of social welfare. Abbas indeed is struggling for his citizenship rights, for the right to have rights. He is in Adriana Petryna's term (2002) a "biological citizen." Petryna coined the term to show how the Chernobyl victims used their biological injury to be included in the state's welfare system: "The damaged biology of a population has become the grounds for social membership and the basis for staking citizenship claims" (2002: 5).

The first time I met Abbas was in the summer of 2002, and for thirteen years I have witnessed his struggle with the intricate and corrupt bureaucracy. Doctors, officers, bureaucrats, and individuals took his money to give him a signature, a letter, a name, an address, advice. All to no use. Every year I met him his dossier (parvandeh) was thicker than the previous year's. He collected documents over documents; that made him even more dependent on brokers. In the governance of papers he is lost, abandoned, and extorted. As an illiterate poor man from an ethnic minority, living at the fringes of a remote province, Abbas has no chance against the state apparatus. His physical and psychological suffering is not observed, registered, or recognized. Nevertheless, like "biological citizens" in Petryna's study, Abbas's suffering and pain are the sole way for him to be included in the realm of the state. The last time I met him, in June 2016, he was still "10 percent," 10 percent included, 10 percent citizen.

While Hamed, the undocumented Afghan-Iranian young man with whom I started this book, has no citizenship rights at all in the country he was born and grew up in, Abbas has access to only 10 percent of his citizenship rights. The case of Abbas is an example of how citizens are turned into quasi-citizens or "denizens" (Hammar 1990). Somehow similar to illegalized non-citizens, young Iranian citizens are stigmatized and criminalized not for what they do but for who they are: single, poor *arazel owbash*, "unproductive," or a "burden." Categorized as such, youth are treated as illegalized persons, exposed to arbitrary extrajudicial punishment. As in the case of undocumented noncitizens, young Iranians experience institutionalized bullying and mobbing in daily life. They are daily stopped, interrogated, controlled, and detained. Being treated like noncitizens in their homeland, they not surprisingly feel like they are living under "foreign occupation." This is a graphic example of how precarity can be sensed and lived. The "governmental precarization" not only destabilizes life through insecuritization of wage labor but also through destabilization of ways of living and, hence, of bodies (Lorey 2011).

Ungrievable Lives

Once a young woman said to me, "We don't live. We are the walking dead." Death, the image of death, or the risk of death is palpable in in Iranians' daily lives. With more than twenty-three thousand car crash fatalities every year, Iran tops has the highest number of traffic deaths in the world. Moreover, Iran has the highest number of executions in the world after China. Many of them take place publicly. For those who are exposed to extreme precarity, death by disease or lethal incidents is more commonplace. The fragility of life and the risk of death are more tangible for marginalized people:

> This sense of an insecure life and the sense that it could, and some-
> times does, turn quickly to death. . . . Precarity that registers deeply in
> the social sense: of an affective turn to desociality that, for many, feels
> painfully bad. . . . And this is part of the pain of being precarious and

part of the precariat: having a life that no one grieves upon death and living a precariousness that no one cares to share with you in the here and now. (Allison 2013: 15)

For instance, in my village in the Bakhtiari region (see Chapter 6), lives can turn quickly to death. These deaths are caused directly or indirectly by the state. Sepeher, a young teacher in my village whom I wrote about in *Young and Defiant in Tehran* (2008: 172), was killed in a car crash in the autumn of 2013. A talented and engaged teacher in the village, he was respected and liked by all. According to the police report, the crash was caused by nonstandard roads—constructed by the state. In the same year, a teenage boy from the same village who was sent by the school on a Rahian Nour trip (visiting battlefields of the Iran-Iraq war) lost his life when he walked on a mine. These trips are arranged by the state propaganda apparatus. In August 2014, a twenty-four-year-old man shot dead another man, both from my village, in a fight over water. The state's promises from a decade ago to solve the water problem for the village have never been fulfilled. Death is also a daily issue in big cities. A young Tehrani man put it this way:

People's lives are worthless. . . . Death is everywhere around us in this city. If you drive a car, I guarantee you will see corpses every single day in Tehran. If not dead in a car accident, you can see public hangings or death because of public fighting. You see more death than life in this city.

If life has no "worth," it can quickly turn to death. That life is "worthless" makes it, in Judith Butler's words, "ungrievable," since it is not regarded as a life. In her analysis of how, in modern wars, certain lives are represented as more or less worthy of grief, she writes:

This differential distribution of precarity is at once a material and a perceptual issue, since those whose lives are not "regarded" as potentially grievable, and hence valuable, are made to bear the burden of starvation, underemployment, legal disenfranchisement, and differential exposure to violence and death. (2009: 25)

In her view, the worth of life is differentiated through war, racism, discrimination, and social inequalities. Following Butler, I will show below how the lives of the urban working poor are not seen as being in danger, injured, or lost, simply because they are not recognized as lives at all.

Precarious Lives: Biographical Vignettes

Unknown, Twenty-Six Years Old

On 21 January 2014, a young street vendor who had migrated from Kurdistan province to Tehran committed suicide by throwing himself under a train in Tehran's subway. That day at the Golbarg Station in East Tehran he had been exposed to harsh humiliation and hassling by municipal agents before all the passengers. His merchandise, which was supposed to support his family back in his village in Kurdistan, was confiscated. His scanty wares were not worth more than a handful of dollars. It was not first time he had been bullied. His multiple marginalities—being poor, belonging to an ethnic minority, and being a migrant from a rural area—made him easy prey for the municipal agents. Harassment continued on the platform. He pleaded with the agents to give back his merchandise but was ignored. He threatened to kill himself and was ignored again. He jumped, and his young body was smashed under the train arriving the station.

Ali Cheraghi, Forty-One Years Old

In recent years, the municipality of Tehran has launched a mission of "removal of barriers of crossings" in order to "alleviate traffic congestion" and enhance the mobility of cars. In collaboration with the police and private companies, a new semi-official body has been formed whose main task is bullying the urban working poor, particularly vendors. Bullying vendors on the streets and in the metro is part of the structural bullying of urban poor, for example, so-called *arazel owbash* and single youth (Chapter 3), as well as of homeless people and residents of informal settlements (Chapter 4).

Protected by their relative anonymity and lack of accountability, these private agents have been extremely violent toward street vendors. They are often equipped with batons, tear gas, and brass knuckles. For Abolfazl, a fourteen-year-old, mid-August was still halfway through the summer vacation—if we can call it a "vacation" after all. Like many other children of poor families, Abolfazl used to work with his father during the summer. The father, Ali Cheraghi, was a forty-one-year-old street vendor. On that day in mid-August, Abolfazl and his father loaded their truck with stuff gathered from dumpsters and drove to Tehran's Pars neighborhood in the northeastern section of the city. Around 10 a.m., Ali had just parked his truck near the Bagheri Highway when it happened. Abolfazl witnessed the whole incident from inside the truck:

> A car from the "street congestion" committee turned in front of us and blocked our way. Then four guys got out and told my dad to step out. He told me to stay seated, and then he got out. One of them told my father that the truck would be confiscated, and my father said he would call the police. But when he began dialing, the man pounced on him. One of them grabbed my father's hands and held them behind him and others beat him. When I got down from the truck, I saw one of the men hit my father on the side of the head with a set of brass knuckles. That was when he fell to the ground.[14]

Ali was taken to a hospital but died a few days later from injuries to his head. No one has been charged for his death. Eight months later, Abolfazl, who witnessed the brutal murder of his father, experienced structural discrimination against the vendors again. After the death of his father, he started to sell fruit on the streets of Nemaat Abad, a poor neighborhood in south Tehran. On 7 April 2015 the municipal "street congestion" agents attacked fifteen-year-old Abolfazl, destroyed his cart, and threw the fruit on the ground to "alleviate traffic of the citizens."[15]

Younes Asakereh, Thirty-Four Years Old

On 15 March 2015, Younes Asakereh, a thirty-four-year-old street vendor in Khoramshahr, a city in southwestern Iran, set himself on fire in front of the municipal building. Younes, who belonged to the harshly discriminated Arab minority, had sold fruit in the street for fifteen years. When municipal agents in a program to "clear" the city from street vendors confiscated his cart and wares, all he possessed in the world, and prevented him from doing business, he poured gasoline on himself and struck a match. He suffered from burns over 70 percent of his body, and, after a few days, died.[16]

Three vendors' lives were precarious and their deaths were ungrievable. Such lives cannot be apprehended as injured or lost if they are not first apprehended as living (Butler 2009: 1). Precarious-ization of lives and making deaths ungrievable means human beings are seen as nonhuman. As shown in the case of *arazel owbash*, dehumanization of young working-class people, which aims to turn them into *human animality*, represents their lives as "not-human" lives and therefore ungrievable. Dehumanization means fading humanity, and with it solidarity and compassion. On 20 March 2010, an old man, apparently poor, jumped off a bridge on Jomhori Street to end his life. Before the jump, still hesitating and scared, he looked down at the crowd who had gathered to watch his death. They were filming him with their mobiles and screaming, "Jump! Jump!"[17] Somayeh Tohidloo, a sociology Ph.D. student at Tehran University and an activist who witnessed the tragedy, wrote later that day on her blog:

> I do not know these people. A people for whom another's death is entertainment, something to be recorded by their mobiles and cameras. The old man's pain and grief had no effect on the crowd. Instead I saw joy. . . . I do not know what has happened with this society. Social capital has vanished and humanity and ethics are gone. . . . We live in a society in which the death of a poor old man has become an issue for amusement. . . . This society is in danger.[18]

Social capital in this context refers to collective resources based on mutual trust, reciprocity, cooperation, and participation. Social capital is thus fundamental for political participation, transparency, and democracy. A survey of social capital in Iran shows that the situation has been worsening, from position 82 in 2009 to 120 in 2013. Social capital is measured by a series of philanthropic behaviors: trust in other people, helping unknown persons, volunteering, giving money to people in need, to name but a few. In the survey, conducted in 140 countries, Iran was ranked 120.[19] Many commentators interpret this lack of trust and compassion, decreasing social capital, as an indicator of social collapse. Said Moidfar, a sociologist at Tehran University, believes Iranian society has already "collapsed" when it comes to social relations in the public arenas:

> When you go to the public places, you see that there is no rule. It is chaotic. Anyone can do anything he or she wants to do. There is no civility, no ethics, no respect. . . . An aggressive competition is among the people. . . . [Iranian society] is an abandoned society, in which everyone is looking out only for his or her own interests. . . . Public space in Iran is a space of alienation and extreme individualism.[20]

His dystopian scenario depicts a society in which public spaces have collapsed and soon private spaces will also. In his view, Iran will, in the near future, be a divided society, characterized by riots, lawlessness, and people's isolation.

The collective sense of insecurity is conspicuously expressed in the ways urban people try to protect themselves from real or imagined threats. The fear of burglary and violence cannot be expressed better than in how houses are enclosed behind high walls, often with spiked fences on the top and security frames on windows. In middle-class neighborhoods, more and more closed-circuit television systems have been installed. Vigilant methods to ward off burglars are sometimes violent. It is not unusual to see walls with razor wire or broken glass cemented on top surrounding houses. Many city dwellers also use brake and steering wheel locks in their cars. Needless to say, this collective sense of insecurity has created a lucrative market for security businesses. In more affluent neighborhoods, private guards are hired, and gates are installed to create a sort of gated community, which protects the residents not only from burglars but also from the state. Gated neighborhoods are less monitored and controlled by the police and therefore offer relatively more free space for youth. Houses that look like bastions and cars that are literally chained materialize the fear and insecurity sensed by Iranians. There is a general anxiety about the decollectivitization and growth of *fardgarai* (individualism). A young female interlocutor expressed her anxiety this way:

> In Iran, everyone cares only about herself or himself. . . . When we should be collective, we are individuals, and when we should be individuals, we are collective. Look at our traffic. Everyone just thinks about herself or himself, just to go a few centimeters forward, just to win a few seconds. Mercy, compassion, and kindness belong to history.

Her anxiety about the growing incivility and indifference to the pain of others stems from an idea about an "epistemic shift" (Allison 2013: 128) in Iranian society, a shift away from collectivity, solidarity, togetherness, and prioritizing a collective social whole toward individual interest. "People have changed. Time has changed." By saying this, people refer to a basic shift in society. This "epistemic shift" in Iran, Japan, or other societies, is a consequence of the biopolitical dimension of global neoliberalism. In the absence of the state as protective and assuring and when the future becomes uncontrollable and unpredictable, fear replaces hope. This fear engenders a shift from "convivance," a way of "harmoniously living together" beyond individual interests (Abélès 2010:10) to individualism. Abélès calls it the "politics of survival" in the global neoliberal era, which is characterized by insecurity, uncertainty, and vulnerability. For precarious groups, the politics of survival is a response to the "persistent anguish concerning the durability of our world and our possible future" (102). In the shadow of the epistemic shift, desires are replaced with anxieties and hope is replaced with fear. The fear and the uncertainty of a possibly futureless tomorrow intensify indifference, decollectivity, and individualism. Facing an insecure future and living in the unstable present, survival has come to mean caring about one's own interest.

Individualism has turned life into an arena of competition. *Moafaqiyat* (achievement), that is, a better education, more wealth, a successful marriage, social status, is the goal of the competition. It provides one with a feeling of being special, chosen, and elected. Competition, the belief that life is itself a race, has become deeply rooted in young Iranians' habitus. A principal notion in Iran is *cheshm ham cheshmi*, competition between families, neighbors, people who know each other, over being more successful than others. Another notion frequently heard is *doshman shad shodan* (one's foe becomes pleased). The failure to achieve means for many that one's foe, one's rival, becomes glad. Not making real or imagined foes glad is a main motive for achievement. Higher education has become a competition. *Konkur* (the entrance exam to universities), with its ranking system, publishing the names and pictures of the best students, is today more about competition than education. For some, academic credentials are a matter of life and death. Headlines about young people's suicides after failing to enter a university appear more and more often. Furthermore, after road accidents, suicide is the second most common reason for death among students. Schools, universities, and life itself are turned into battlefields, where young Iranians struggle for *jolozadan*, to outpace their rivals. *Jolozadan* is also commonly used for passing another car when driving. The will to surpass others, to be first, has generated what Iranian sociologist Abbas Kazemi calls *farhang-e ajaleh*, a culture of haste. Focusing on the factors behind such an intense haste in daily life, Kazemi argues that the "culture of haste" arises from a series of lacks: lack of confidence, lack of certainty, and lack of security. Kazemi is right when arguing that *ajaleh* is seizing others' time for one's benefit: "In a society with no collective solutions for problems, haste is the easiest individualistic way to solve the problem."[21]

Ajaleh is a way to create or secure individual advantages, a tactic to win over time, to capture opportunities (before they disappear or others grasp them), to find goods (before they are gone), or to purchase (before prices go up again). Thus, daily life is turned into a race and urban spaces into competition fields in schoolyards, the moments before a traffic light changes, on queues inside and outside stores or banks. The conjunction of insecurity, hurry, and competitiveness is best manifested when driving. One young woman behind the wheel, while trying to change lanes in Tehran, told me:

> Look, people are willing to expose you to danger only to gain one meter from you. . . . People here attempt to take other people's rights, because they cannot take them from the state.

The state's failure in providing access to citizenship rights leads to the collapse of sociality, pushing society toward decollectivization. In such a society, other citizens are turned into rivals. Characteristic of this shift of life into a competition are the promotion of self-interest and indifference (bi-tafavoti) to others' pain and suffering. There is a general belief that incivilities in everyday life have increased. People recurrently mention "lack of compassion and sympathy" among Iranians toward other Iranians. Is the interest among people to participate in the mobbing of arazel owbash and watching their public executions or in turning a suicide attempt into entertainment an indicator of such a lack? Whose life is counted as valued, and whose death is regarded ungrievable? State violence normalizes and stimulates aggression and antagonism among people. The violence practiced by the people is logically an extension of the state violence they have been exposed to. Their aggression is just a replication of the state violence (cf. Fanon 1963; Taussig 1986).

Everyday Emergencies

Life for many Iranians is felt as if it is continuously interrupted. I draw on Penglase's (2009) and Millar's (2014) concept of "everyday emergencies" to show how insecurities and systematic disruptions of life have become normalized and routinized. Pervasive irregularity destabilizes life for many Iranians. Irregular jobs, irregular incomes, temporary housing, and waithood, all encapsulated in the notion of belataklifi, make life precarious. Furthermore, the police are the main actors in creating this state of insecurity. Young women are detained for "improper veiling." Young men are arrested on suspicion of being arazel owbash. Concerts, exhibitions, and other events are canceled just minutes before they were to start. The police invade parties of middle-class youths, as well as those of the poor, in search of "cultural crimes." Because it is unprotected by the law, a young life can be destabilized by everyone. Single tenants can be forced by their landlords to leave at any time. For the irregularly employed, that is, the majority of young people, dismissal from a job without notice is a constant danger. Moreover, the prices of basic needs change daily. Unstable and unfixed prices mean that financial planning is almost impossible. And there are more insecurities. Shrinking water reserves cause regular water shortages and even power outages. Every day Iranians are reminded that their country is heading toward collapse. Dystopian headlines and reports in the main newspapers are not rare. The most popular term is *tsunami*, used as a warning of the anticipated catastrophes. Opening any newspaper, one can read "alarming" statistics: on public violence; on "escalating spouse killing"; on a "red alert signal of divorce: 18 divorces per hour"; on "Iran tops the list of brain drain"; on a "catastrophe of water scarcity."[22] The society is felt to be shrinking more and more. In an interview with *Shargh* newspaper, Hossein Raqfar, a well-known economist, said Ahmadinejad's core tactic was to create constant feeling of unsteadiness in order to push through his controversial and unpopular policies.[23]

Uncertainties in Iran's international relations are another factor that contributes to how radical insecurity is sensed and lived by Iranians. In the late spring and summer of 2015, the whole nation followed the nuclear negotiations between Iran and the permanent members of the UN Security Council, minute to minute, with hope, fear, and anxiety. They knew well that each word coming out of the negotiations could change their lives drastically for worse or better. The international embargos and sanctions affect prices of basic needs, employment, and travel and transaction restrictions. They, above all, generate a sense of powerlessness and marginalization. When I write these words, in early June 2016, sanctions are lifted, but the Iranian nation is still stuck in *belataklifi*. Being sanctioned begets a sense of humiliation and a sense that one's life, destiny, and future are in the hands of other states. Hearing American and other Western states repetitively declaring that "the military option certainly will remain on the table" is a main source of everyday emergencies; under these circumstances, the scope of life can quickly turn into the scope of death. It intensifies the sense of precarity, that Iranian lives are not valued and their deaths ungrievable. All these big and small "everyday emergencies" disrupt and unsettle life for a majority of Iranians. Everyday emergencies undermine primarily the life of youth and deprived groups. However, it is the young people who are blamed by the parental generation and in the official discourse for their situation. The fear of an uncertain, unstable, insecure future makes Iranians feel that being in a constant "state of exception" has become the norm. The precarity sensed and lived by Iranians was expressed vividly by a middle-aged man in Tehran who depicted the life of Iranians as floating pieces of a boat on the sea:

> Our situation here is like being in a broken boat on the sea. We hold ourselves onto floating pieces so as not to sink and wait for a boat coming to rescue us from this hazard.

Constant disruptions, daily emergencies, and ephemeral life projects have become a political scheme. As Penglase (2009) showed, everyday emergencies caused by either the police or drug traffickers in favelas in Rio de Janeiro, Brazil, suspend normality but can also constitute it. Precarity, existential insecurity, has become normalized, and the everyday emergencies, in Walter Benjamin's words, are no longer exceptions but the rule (Benjamin 1999 [1940]: 248). Michael Taussig correctly states that some states naturalize their power and reproduce their stability by generating instabilities and uncertainties and exposing society to constant disruption. The states foster an "illusion of order congealed by fear" (Taussig 1992: 22). By fostering forms of fear and everyday emergencies, the state strengthens its sovereignty. In the shadow of fear of working-class masculinity (*arazel owbash*), of middle-class single men and women, of the street and street people, the authorities represent their brutality in terms of "caring and saving."

Everyday emergencies, uncertainties, and a possible futureless tomorrow (Abélès 2010) forces people to take refuge *from* the oppressor *in* the oppressor, in the same way one takes refuge in God from the fear of him. We should understand the Iranian state in terms of political theology, not because it is an Islamic Republic but, as Carl Schmitt states, because "all significant concepts of the modern theory of the state are secularized theological concepts" (1985 [1934]: 36). Political theology, the divine sovereignty of the state, with the power to distinguish which life is grievable and which is not, was captured in an image taken at the public hanging of two young men (labeled *arazel owbash*) in Tehran in January 2013 (see Chapter 3). Two young men, twenty-one and twenty-three years old, were hanged for stealing around US$25. The image captured by photojournalist Amir Pourmand moments before the noose was put around the twenty-one-year-old's neck shows the devastated young man crying and laying his head on the shoulder of his executioner. The executioner in a black mask put his arm around the young man's shoulder to console him. The image clearly shows what Taussig calls the "illusion of order congealed by fear" (1992: 22). It shows how the oppressed have no option other than taking refuge from the state's aggression in the state, since the power of the state is so petrifying and omnipresent. It is an image of a state fostering insecurity and uncertainty to reproduce its own authority. The state demonstrates its divine sovereignty by showing its ability to decide which life is livable and which is not, which death is grievable (for example, martyrs) and which is not (by transforming death into a public event, a spectacle, a show). Precarious life, in a society in which the scope of life can quickly turn into the scope of death, becomes open to mystification and occult imaginaries.

Occult Economies

Fear and insecurity, collapse of trust in the economic and political system, growth of corruption, and fading prospects for the realization of hope have resulted in a proliferation of interest in occult imaginaries (see Doostdar 2013). Uncertainties in life and feelings of hopelessness have begotten new forms of "spiritual" practices. Underground churches, popularity of New Age cults, and (re)invention of religious rituals have grown tremendously in the past two decades. It is said that almost 10 percent of Iranians regularly seek assistance from a "prayer writer" (do'anevis), a fortune-teller, or a "geomancer" (rammal), trying to increase their chances for success, in education, in business, or in marriage. A survey among students in Tehran shows that 68 percent of young women between eighteen and twenty-six have sought magical help at least once. Although the survey is gender biased and associates superstition primarily with women, it shows, interestingly, that those who seek help from occult specialists are mostly educated middle-class Tehranis.[24]

Furthermore, a large part of the new forms of occult activities take place online. The clients of occult brokers are from the urban middle class, people who have access to computers and the Internet, and who can afford the fees between $US10 and $US100. According to the Tehran police department, the occult is a hundred million dollar business.[25] Although occult imaginaries and practices are not new and have a long history in Iranian society (see Rahnema 2011), the proliferation and penetration of occult into different segments of the society are new. Both classic and contemporary anthropologists believe occult and magic activities are social technologies that seek to impose a measure of control when the world appears most chaotic. Bronisław Malinowski in his classic study of magic in the Trobriand Islands in the early twentieth century stated:

> All this shows the wide diffusion of magic, its extreme importance and also the fact that it is always strongest there, where vital interests are concerned; where violent passions or emotions are awakened; when mysterious forces are opposed to man's endeavours; and where he has to recognize that there is something which eludes his most careful calculations, his most conscientious preparations and efforts. (1922: 395–96)

While Malinowski studied non-Western, small-scale societies at the beginning of the twentieth century, in their study of the global capitalism at the millennium, Jean and John Comaroff (1999, 2001) come to similar conclusions. They argue that the proliferation of occult economies, for instance, in South Africa, is rooted in the uncertainties of contemporary capitalism:

> This, after all, is an age in which the extravagant promises of millennial capitalism run up against an increasingly nihilistic, thoroughly post-modern pessimism; in which the will to consume outstrips the opportunity to earn; in which, relatively speaking, there is a much higher velocity of exchange than there is of production. As the connections between means and ends become more opaque, more distended, more mysterious, the occult becomes an ever more appropriate, semantically saturated metaphor for our times. (Comaroff and Comaroff 2001: 27)

Witnessing the flow of the vast wealth passing through society into the hands of a few people generates the belief that the promises of the neoliberal capitalism are attainable through "magical technologies and mysterious modes of accumulation" (Comaroff and Comaroff 1999: 284). Current occult imaginaries in Iran come not from traditions or superstitious beliefs but from witnessing the mysterious mechanisms of the market through which some reach unimaginable wealth. Getting rich quick and effortlessly, in the eyes of Iranians, seems more magical than anything else. The occult imaginaries proliferate at the same time that "unimaginable riches" become more visible.

Since the early 2010s, Iranians started to see an increasing number of cars worth fifty times the average car price. Buildings whose price per square meter is equivalent to three years of a worker's wage have mushroomed. Ice cream covered in edible gold, which costs almost a worker's monthly salary, has entered the menus in luxury restaurants. Fast wealth creates suspicion of corruption but also of mystery. Rumors swirl around persons who have gotten rich fast. To make sense of how they could make it, many talk about treasure hunting, usury, corruption, speculation, and chance. The hunger for fast wealth has involved Iranians in various forms of mysterious ways of getting rich, such as pyramid schemes, antique treasure hunting, or occult activities. Occult economies have penetrated the whole society. Occult economies not only are the product of traditional beliefs and practices but are also generated by secrecy and the opacity of modern bureaucratic technologies and practices (James 2012: 57). Occult economies operate through illicit and unregulated traffic in commodities and capital between mysterious and hidden hands:

> Occult economy may be taken, at its most general, to connote the deployment of magical means for material ends or, more expansively, the conjuring of wealth by resort to inherently mysterious techniques, whose principles of operation are neither transparent nor explicable in conventional terms. (Comaroff and Comaroff 1999: 297)

People talk about treasures as a quick way to get rich. A market of treasure hunting has emerged, including guides, "maps of treasures" and metal detectors. Young men, usually poor and unemployed ones in rural areas, dig deep in the earth, searching for a fortune they cannot find on the surface. Another form of underground economy is informal loans. In rural areas and among the working poor in urban areas, loans from private moneylenders have become regular. For the working poor, the local informal credit system is an agreement between individuals, thus, easier, more accessible, and faster than bank loans. It requires no paper work and no collateral. Since usury is regarded as immoral and sinful, the whole process is wrapped in secrecy. The identity of the moneylender is kept secret, and the total amount paid back by the client is also concealed. Loans from moneylenders mean high interest rates, as they can demand an incredible interest rate, as mentioned above.

Stories of "unimaginable riches" are also wrapped in secrecy. Shahram Jazayeri and Babak Zanjani, two notorious entrepreneurs who accrued unimaginable riches during a short time in the 2000s through corruption and connections with influential officials, are full of secrecy and mystery. After several years of investigations and trials, the volume and origin of their wealth are still unknown. How the rich get rich is always wrapped in secrecy and mystery in Iran. A prevalent form of occult economies is the pyramid scheme. The first pyramid scheme appeared in Iran at the turn of the millennium. GoldQuest, a Hong Kong-based multilevel marketing company, promised Iranians wealth for enrolling other people in the scheme. GoldQuest has been followed by many other pyramid schemes. The function of the schemes is based on mystery and secrecy. The agents use fanciful PowerPoint presentations of get-rich-quick narratives full of foreign words, signs, and symbols. In the video clips uploaded on the Internet, some agents' presentations are more like sermons, a mishmash of religious arguments that Islam praises wealth and wealthy people and reasons condemning wage work. They promise wealth unreachable by wage labor. GoldQuest and many other pyramid schemes, due to a widespread preference for getting rich quickly, have enrolled many people, from the lower-middle and working classes and from urban and rural areas.

Another prevalent form of occult economies is speculation—buying properties, gold, cars, or foreign currencies and hoping to sell soon at a profit. High inflation, market bubbles, and unstable markets often mean that such risky investments are also lucrative. In post-revolutionary Iran, gambling and betting have been classified as sins and therefore illegal. Nevertheless, it seems that economic behavior in Iran is based more on betting, speculation, and risky investments than on productive labor. Moreover, banks offer prize-linked savings accounts and run lotteries. While more and more people believe that wealth is the outcome of chance, just like gambling, and as more and more speculation, betting, and gambling have become mainstreamed into everyday economic and social behavior (cf. Krige 2010), Iranian economic practices become more and more casino-like. Although pyramid schemes are banned and have gone underground, their multilevel marketing strategies have penetrated other segments of society by turning citizens into speculators and gamblers. Iranians' participation in high-risk gambling-like speculations has turned everyday life, not only economic behavior but also driving, education, and migration, into something governed largely by chance. Drawing on the Comaroffs, I believe Iranians' engagement in occult economies is

a response to a world gone awry, yet again: a world in which the only way to create real wealth seems to lie in forms of power/knowledge

that transgress the conventional, the rational, the moral—thus to mul-
tiply available techniques of producing value, fair or foul. (2000: 316)

Turning citizens into speculators, involved in various mysterious, get-rich
schemes, adopting a "casino relationship to the world," changes the moral
valence and undermines social capital and trust, and thereby shrinks the political sphere (Hilgers 2011). The political sphere started shrinking as magical
practices were expanding. During the presidency of Ahmadinejad (2005–
2013) occult imaginaries, economies, and activities penetrated deeper into
politics. In September 2005 he claimed that, during his speech at the UN
General Assembly, he was enshrouded in a "halo of light" and his audience
was hypnotized. This was the beginning of a wave of "supernatural" phenom-
ena during his time as president (see Rahnema 2011). Ahmadinejad's apocalyptic politics, based on a messianic faith i the return of the Twelfth or Hidden
Imam, made him different from former presidents. Twelve Imam Shiite Muslims believe that the final imam, the ultimate savior of humankind, has been
in occultation since the ninth century. Ahmadinejad's government invested
more than any other Iranian government on propaganda of the "Return" and
stated that the main task of his government was to facilitate the imam's return.
Tens of millions of American dollars have been earmarked for building roads
and the huge complex of the Jamkaran Mosque, where it is believed the Hidden Imam lives. On the outskirts of Qom, the small unknown village of Jamkaran has been turned into a popular attraction for pilgrimages. Thousands
of Iranians visit the mosque each year to write their wishes and requests on a
piece of paper and throw it into the well. Moreover, Ahmadinejad put sorcery
and witchcraft in the context of political conflicts in the global arena. In September 2011, Ahmadinejad said that "all Satans in the world are mobilized
against Iran."[26] One of his speeches in 2009 announced that he had evidence
that showed the main reason for the American invasion of Iraq was to prevent
the imam's return. However, in May 2011, charges of using sorcery and witchcraft to manipulate people and events for particular political ends were raised
against Ahmadinejad and his government. Several of his collaborators were
arrested for being involved in magical activities and "involving jinns" in domestic and international politics. Furthermore, according to an arrested "sorcerer," several high-ranking government officials had visited him for advice
and for a look "into the future." The "sorcerer" stated that he had been con-
sulted for international relations, such as information about Israel's plans to
attack Iran or neighboring countries' politics. He also claimed that he had

given Ahmadinejad a ring to protect him from the spirits his political adversaries used against him.

Anthropologists have shown that witchcraft and sorcery do not belong to "rural," "traditional" societies but have been used by "modern" political elites in different countries. Magic in itself is always intensely political (Bubandt 2006: 421). In several modern African and Asian states, witchcraft and sorcery have been intertwined with political and economic changes (Geschiere 1997; Bubandt 2006). For instance, Ahmadinejad's government exercised sorcery and magic at the same time as the nuclear power program and other advanced military technologies were expanding in Iran. Witchcraft is a discourse that focuses on evil. A look at the political discourse in Iran shows that it is full of metaphors and vocabularies about Satan and *shar*, evil, which may explain the proliferation of political witchcraft in the country. The perception of a rise in evil's strength makes the need for magic and witchcraft more intense. Not surprisingly, sorcery and witchcraft became an issue for the government when political isolation and economic sanctions against Iran increased drastically. The rise in sorcery expresses widespread precarity sensed both by the nation and by the state.

Another aspect of political sorcery is corruption. As Bubandt shows, sorcery and corruption are part of the same political imagination: "Significantly . . . the sense that sorcery is on the increase is often accompanied by a perception that corruption is also on the rise" (2006: 414). In recent years, international watchdog groups have ranked Iran as a highly corrupt state. Transparency International, the global civil organization leading the fight against corruption, ranked Iran 144th in corruption out of 177 countries in its Corruption Perceptions Index in December 2013.[27] During the same period as the arrests of Ahmadinejad's inner circle for sorcery, a series of corruption scandals among high-ranking officials became a huge national issue. The largest embezzlements, each several billion U.S. dollars, happened under Ahmadinejad's presidency. There has been an extended liaison between criminal businessmen and agents of the state. Unlike the common view of sorcery as incompatible with the modern world, there are symbioses between modern forms of financial corruption and sorcery. In Iran, like many other countries in Asia and Africa, magic and sorcery have been "used" as means for accumulating more economic and political power (cf. Geschiere 1997; Bubandt 2006). Media reports on corruption among high-ranking officials have been increasing. In early 2015 an official source declared that the amount of contraband over the past year was over $20 billion, that is, double the country's development budget. For many commentators, the huge amount of contraband indicates state complicity in smuggling. Very similar to what Daniel Smith (2007) observed in his study of corruption in Nigeria, Iranians commonly not only mistrust the state's intention and capability to combat corruption and crime, but they also believe the state is one of the main actors in smuggling and corruption. Corruption has reached academia as well. Like occult economies, there is a huge multimillion-dollar market for writing theses, ranging from undergraduate to doctoral levels.[28] So-called "academic corruption" is displayed best on the streets around Tehran University, which are full of firms and individuals who "write theses" on all academic levels. Moreover, every now and then, there is also news about scandals of academic plagiarism among high-ranking scholars or politicians. So-called "academic corruption" is a consequence of the privatization of education, as well as the marketization of a society that turns anything into commodity.

Corruption infuses everyday experience. Many Iranians believe that "no one does anything for you until you pay." In a wide range of daily activities, Iranians start with seeking an "insider connection"—from visiting a doctor in a clinic or going to a court to enrolling in a school. For many Iranians, meeting with the bureaucracy starts with several calls to friends and relatives to see if they know someone "inside." Connections and bribes can move a file languishing in "negligence or intentionally withheld from circulation file" (cf. Hull 2012: 156). Expectations of and participation in corruption are symptoms of dysfunctional citizenship, experiencing the absence of the right to have rights, the absence of access to citizenship rights. The combination of academic, financial, and political corruption has intensified occult imaginaries and practices. During these times of multifaceted state corruption, political witchcraft, and individual and national precarity, both the nation and the state seek their prosperity and security from the occult. This is evident in the mushrooming of New Age groups, of various kinds of East Asian spirituality, of fortune-telling businesses, of training centers for "inner energies," of "doctors" who heal serious illnesses with their "inner power," of the attraction of the Jamkaran Mosque, of treasure hunting, and of the popularity of pyramid schemes. As a result of the privatization of health care, making medical services inaccessible for underprivileged groups in the society, alternative occult healing practices have blossomed. The interest in occult forms of social imagination conveys Iranians' precariousness in the world, shadowed by insecurity, corruption, "political pessimism" (Bubandt 2006), lack of transparency, and increasing inequalities (cf. Piot 2010).

Dreams

Ahmadinejad's apocalyptic politics, based on a messianic faith that engendered political pessimism, made his successor Hassan Rohani appear as a hero and rescuer when he presented his plan for a government of "prudence and hope" (*tadbir va omid*). *Omid* (hope) was what persuaded Iranians to vote. The youth's vast engagement in the election in June 2013, despite anticipated defeats and despite recurrent political disappointments over the past decades, staged the "return of hope."

The older generation, referring to the 2009 election fraud, believed that the youth's hope was a naïve and false one. Many middle-aged men and women said that the young lived in "dreams and imagination" (*khabo khiyal*). Regarding young people's political hope, false hope or just "dream and imagination" is in line with how youth are generally represented as a spoiled generation stuck in passivity, *belataklifi*, and daydreaming. What the parental generation neglects is the vibrancy and potentiality of youthful daydreams. Daydreaming for German Marxist philosopher Ernst Bloch is an expression of hope. As Bloch showed in contrast to night dreams, which look back, daydreams are oriented toward future and possibilities that have "not-yet" become:

> The daydream projects its images into the future, by no means indiscriminately, but controllable even given the most impetuous imagination and mediatable with the objectively possible. *The content of the night-dream is concealed and disguised, the content of the day-fantasy is open, fabulously inventive, anticipating, and its latency lies ahead.* It comes itself out of self-and world-extension forwards, it is wanting to have better, often simply wanting to know better. (1996[1959]: 99, emphasis in original)

Bloch's magnificent work on daydreaming and hope is of relevance here. Not surprisingly, interest in his ideas on hope and daydreaming first appeared among young Iranian intellectuals after the crackdown on the 2009 election protests, at a time when there was no hope left. In similar way, Bloch's major work *The Principle of Hope* was written between 1938 and 1947, a time when all hope was gone from Europe. For Bloch, daydreaming is not passive wishful imagining but rather an actively constructed "anticipatory consciousness" that includes engagement and transformation. The consciousness that operates in the field of hope for Bloch is anticipatory and not messianic. It is mobilizing rather than therapeutic (Giroux 2002). Anticipatory consciousness provides potentialities for individuals to go beyond the here and now. A daydream is "a space of concrete anticipation, only here is the volcano of productivity to be found pouring out its fire" (Bloch 1996 [1959]: 127). Daydreaming youth construct future-oriented social imaginaries and a subjectivity living in the future, containing both fear and hope. A key concept in Bloch's theory is the "not-yet-conscious," disposed and directed forward to the future, rather than backward to the past. Driven by hope, the "not-yet conscious" scratches at the inadequacies, frustrations, and hardships of present life (Allison 2013: 80). For Bloch, the "not-yet-conscious" is a characteristic above all of youth. It is related to youthful aspirations, desires, and excitement for change. This is a "conscious in its act." Longing for this "not-yet" experience is an expectation of possibilities for a different and better future (144). As Allison argues, hopeful imaginaries of the future are shaped into images of a proper home(land) with a future of collectivity, an

> image of a home that, nesting the imagination of a world and time
> beyond, prods the daydreamer to remake the here and now, to remake
> a hopeful home, a home that (day)dreams of the future. (2013: 81)

The collective daydreaming of young Iranians performed in their urban practices, like strolling around a street, hanging around squares, sitting in coffee shops, driving back and forth, leaving traces on walls, combined with the urban poor's "quiet encroachment," is an attempt to go beyond the here and now. Unlike those who criticize the young for "unproductivity" and passivity by associating them with dreams and the imagination, I argue that daydreaming and the imagination are social practices that are constitutive features of modern subjectivity. Collective daydreaming and imagination are the prelude to expression and can fuel social actions (Appadurai 1996: 7).

In this book, I have attempted to explore the paradoxes in Iranians' everyday life. On the one hand, there are the multiple precarities: a sense of disconnectedness, imaging a futureless tomorrow, home(land)lessness, intense individualism, and growth of incivilities. On the other hand, there is hope, performed in the repetition and replication of political engagement. There is also the proliferation of civility and solidarity manifested during political protests and street carnivals and within social movements. While young Iranians describe themselves as being stuck in *belataklifi*, purposelessness and endless waithood, forced to endure; and while they are regarded as "unproductive" and a "burden"; and while they find themselves forced into a petrifying immobility (both social and spatial), they are full of aspirations and inspiration. If there is indifference to the suffering of others, manifested in watching the public shaming of *arazel owbash* and public executions, and if there is a sense of political detachment and lack of engagement, there are, at the same time, signs of the opposite. If many young Iranians express hopelessness, they still perform hope at the same time. For instance, there is a recent but forceful engagement with environmental movements and protests against public punishment. If a forced "immobility" is imposed on youth and their mobility on streets and public places is criminalized, they show, as I have shown in Chapter 3, that they are a generation of mobility (strolling, automobility, migration). If they are supposed to be invisibilized by legal and political processes, they are more visible than any generation before. This book has been an attempt to juxtapose these paradoxes in Iran in the first decade of the twenty-first century. Hirokazu Miyazaki (2004) believes that, to understand hope, one should enact hope. Following him, I have attempted in this book to employ hope as a method of analysis. Through ethnography and storytelling, one of my aims has been to replicate and transform hope. Echoing my Iranian interlocutors' words, the words ending this book, thus, should be from Bloch, a German Jew who lived in a dark time in the last century and who certainly experienced his homeland "under foreign occupation." *The Principle of Hope* was originally written in the late 1930s, a time when Kafka, another European Jew, said there was hope but not for everyone: "So let a further signal be set for forward dreaming. This book deals with nothing other than hoping beyond the day which has become" (Bloch 1996 [1959]: 10).

NOTES

Introduction

1. www.radiozamaneh.com/196626, accessed 19/3/2015.

2. http://www.mehrnews.com/news/2581988, accessed 18/5/2015.

3. www.radiozamaneh.com/196151, accessed 7/1/2015.

4. http://www.ilna.ir/223862, accessed 19/3/2015.

5. http://www.ilna.ir/38/199694, accessed 19/3/2015.

6. aftabnews.ir/fa/news/255252/, accessed 19/3/2015; see also http://www.salamat news.com/news/149743 accessed 14/5/ 2016.

7. *Tehran Times*, 26 April 2015, http://www.tehrantimes.com/news/246326/Insurance -to-reach-to-10-million-slum-residents, accessed 12/5/2016.

8. http://www.tabnak.ir/fa/news/473318, accessed 6/4/2015.

9. http://science.time.com/2013/10/18/the-10-most-polluted-cities-in-the-world, accessed 5/8/2014.

10. http://jdtums.ac.ir/news/display/353, accessed 23/3/2015.

11. http://www.bbc.co.uk/persian/iran/2015/03/150306_u14_iran_slum_mahjoub, accessed 2/4/2015.

12. http://www.irna.ir/fa/News/81351492/ accessed 19/3/2015.

13. See special issue of *Tejarat Farda* magazine on informal settlement, Mordad 1392 (July 2013), 50. http://tejarat.donya-e-eqtesad.com/fa/packagestories/all?package=w50, accessed 2/4/2015.

14. http://www.radiofarda.com/content/f16-iran-ahmad-janati-friday-prayers/2682 1953.html, accessed 13/3/2015.

15. http://fararu.com/fa/news/187567, accessed 28/3/2015.

16. http://www.ilna.ir/3/286071, accessed 7/6/2016.

17. http://www.khabaronline.ir/detail/301824/Politics/government, accessed 16/3/2015.

18. http://news.gooya.com/politics/archives/2012/08/144858.php, accessed 17/3/2015.

19. http://www.bbc.co.uk/persian/iran/2011/03/110308_l39_iranian_students_outside _theses.shtml, accessed 16/3/2015.

20. http://weekly.ahram.org.eg/2006/797/special.htm, accessed 17/5/2015.

21. http://www.bbc.com/news/world-middle-east-24435408, accessible 23/2/2015.

22. http://www.ohchr.org/EN/NewsEvents/Pages/DisplayNews.aspx?NewsID=1570
4&LangI=E, accessed 28/3/2015.

23. http://aftabnews.ir/fa/print/251802, accessed 27/3/2015.

24. http://alef.ir/vdcdxs0xfyt0oo6.2a2y.html?24txt, accessed 27/3/2015.

25. For the semiotics of politics and funerals, see http://www.bbc.co.uk/persian/
iran/2015/03/150325_l39_analysis_political_funerals, accessed 31/3/2015.

Chapter 1. The Precarious Family

1. http://womenrc.ir/News/66693.htm, accessed 7/4/2012.

2. http://www.servat.unibe.ch/icl/ir00000_.html, accessed 6/6/2012; see also Ramezani (1980).

3. http://paaknahad.ir/ accessed 30/5/2012.

4. Some believe that the official version of the account is partly fictional and was part
of the state propaganda; see Kelly (2005).

5. http://www.mercatornet.com/demography/view/5365, accessed 15/2/2013.

6. http://www.guardian.co.uk/world/2006/oct/23/iran.roberttait, accessed 5/6/2012.

7. http://www.usatoday.com/news/world/story/2012-07-29/iran-baby-boom/56576
830/1, accessed 6/9/2012.

8. http://www.khabaronline.ir/detail/245290/, accessed 3/10/2012.

9. http://www.qudsonline.ir/NSite/FullStory/News/?Id=72933, accessed 2/11/2012.

10. http://www.tabnak.ir/fa/news/367550/, accessed 6/1/2014.

11. *Jam-e Jam*, 21 Aban 1391 (11 November 2012), 17.

12. http://www.mardomsalari.com/Template1/News.aspx?NID=175404, accessed
12/11/2013. http://www.asriran.com/fa/news/308235, accessed 4/1/2013.

13. http://www.bbc.co.uk/persian/business/2015/04/150411_l57_iran_women_unem
ployment, accessed 16/4/2015.

14. http//www.digarban.com/print/14522, accessed 21/9/2013.

15. http://khabaronline.ir/detail/159347, accessed 11/8/2013.

16. www.eghtesadonline.com/fa/content/8451, accessed 8/1/2013.

17. javan.hmg.ir/index.php/segment/SN/item/208, accessed 2/2/2013; see also Shahrokni and Dokouhaki 2012.

18. http://www.isa.org.ir/session-report/4526, accessed 21/11/2013.

19. http://www.roozonline.com/english/news3/newsitem/archive/2012/august/06/
article/77.html, accessed 7/10/2012.

20. http://farsnews.com/newstext.php?nn=13921007000193, accessed 5/1/2014.

21. http://www.aftabnews.ir/prtg739q7ak9nq4.rpra.html, accessed 5/11/2012.

22. http://www.tabnak.ir/fa/print/261977, accessed 5/9/2012.

23. http://www.magiran.com/npview.asp?ID=1717515, accessed 21/1/2013.

24. http://www.ebtekarnews.com/Ebtekar/News.aspx?NID=74463, accessed 7/6/2012.

25. http://www.jamejamonline.ir/paperctgs.aspx?SID=254, accessed 10/6/2012.

26. http://womenrc.ir/?lang=fa&&action=news&type=2&keyword=&key=41052, accessed 7/6/2012.

27. http://fararu.com/fa/print/112946, accessed 6/6/2012.

28. http://www.sabteahval.ir/Default.aspx?tabid=4773, accessed 8/4/2012.

29. http://www.tabnak.ir/fa/print/279662, accessed 23/2/2013.

30. http://khabarfarsi.com/ext/640120, accessed 8/10/2012.

31. http://www.zanestan.es/issue2/06,03,22,05,56,43, accessed 13/10/2012.

32. http://ilna.ir/news/news.cfm?id=7096, accessed 13/10/2012.

33. http://www.aftabnews.ir/vdch6knw.23nqvdftt2.html, accessed 8/4/2012.

34. http://www.afkarnews.ir/vdcgzt97.ak9wx4prra.html, accessed 8/4/2012.

35. http://www.etemaad.ir/Released/91-05-04/93.htm, accessed 25/7/2012.

36. http://www.aftabnews.ir/vdciqpaz3t1aqq2.cbct.html, accessed 20/7/2012.

37. http://www.aftabnews.ir/vdcb80b8arhbg5p.uiur.html, accessed 12/6/2012.

38. http://www.khabaronline.ir/detail/127882/weblog/ferdousi, accessed 12/6/2012.

39. *Shahrgh* (newspaper), 12 Ordibehesht 1391 (1/5/2012), 11.

40. http://www.asriran.com/fa/print/230904, accessed 9/9/2012.

41. http://yalasarat.com/vdce.w8xbjh8wp9bij.html, 24/2/2013.

42. http://www.mashreghnews.ir/fa/38481, accessed 26/2/2013.

43. Hossein Bahonar in *Etemad* (newspaper), 12 Ordibehesht 1391/ 1/5/2012, 13.

44. http://www.jahannews.com/prthvvnzi23nkxd.tft2html, accessed 27/1/2012.

45. http://www.jamejamonline.ir/newstext.aspx?newsnum=100888879247, accessed 27/1/2011.

46. http://www.fararu.com/prtcpxqe.2bqix8laa2.html, accessed 27/1/2011.

47. isna.ir/fa/news/91080200996, accessed 23/10/2012.

48. http://www.css.ir/?p=418, accessed 14/6/2012.

49. http://www.nytimes.com/2008/05/28/business/worldbusiness/28iht-ihousing.4.1 3287657.html, accessed 14/6/2012

50. http://www.radiofarda.com/content/f10-iran-house-rent-price-60-percent-increase /24707004.html, accessed 1/10/2012.

51. http://www.shasa.ir/newsdetail-85091-fa.html, accessed 14/6/2012.

52. http://www.womenrc.ir/News/57752.htm, accessed 15/6/2012

53. http://www.asriran.com/fa/print/168953, accessed 27/3/2012.

54. http://www.khabaronline.ir/detail/202120, accessed 16/6/2012.

55. http://www.inn.ir/newsdetail.aspx?id=108021, accessed 14/6/2012.

56. http://www.fardanews.com/fa/print/116144, accessed 22/5/2012.

57. http://www.tabnak.ir/fa/print/184510, accessed 15/6/2012.

58. http://www.digarban.com/node/1815, accessed 15/6/2012.

59. http://www.tebyan.net/newindex.aspx?pid=299611, accessed 1/11/2015.

60. http://www.digarban.com/node/658, accessed 9/4/2012; http://www.atynews .com/fa/print/50252, accessed 27/3/2012.

61. See, for instance, http://www.iranian.com/main/2012/jul-34, accessed 20/7/2012.

62. http://www.ashenaye-mahboub.com/main.php, accessed 9/4/2012.

63. http://www.pbs.org/wgbh/pages/frontline/tehranbureau/2011/09/video-sex-educa tion-in-the-islamic-republic.html#ixzz1q2OfyBBG, accessed 9/4/2012.

64. http://www.1oo1nights.org/index.php?page=1&newsitemId=5815&contentFilter
Time= 2011, accessed 12/6/2012.

Chapter 2. The 1360 Generation

1. http://sheikheshahr.blogspot.se/2012/09/blog-post.html, accessed 21/3/2013.
2. http://derazleng2.wordpress.com/2011/02/, accessed 7/12/2013.
3. http://offscreen.com/view/shahram-mokri, accessed 24/12/2015.
4. http://www.mehrnews.com/fa/NewsDetail.aspx?NewsID=1718068, accessed 1/1/2013.
5. http://www.rahesabz.net/story/64674, accessed 10/17/2013.
6. www.eghtesadonline.com/fa/content/8451, accessed 8/1/2013.
7. www.eghtesadonline.com/fa/content/8451, accessed 8/1/2013.
8. http://khabarfarsi.com/ext/7470972, accessed 10/12/2013.
9. http://www.mardoman.net/success/patlife, accessed 20/7/2012.
10. http://www.khabaronline.ir/detail/227864/politics/military, accessed 20/7/2012.
11. http://www.iqna.ir/khouzestan/news_detail.php?ProdID=456095, accessed 20/7/
2012.
12. www.radiozamaneh.com/196626, accessed 19/3/2015.
13. http://www.ilna.ir/news/news.cfm?id=91376, accessed 27/7/2013.
14. www.isna.ir/fa/news/92053017589, accessed 6/1/2014.
15. http://www.khabaronline.ir/news-71133.aspx, accessed 9/6/2012.
16. http://www.khabaronline.ir/detail/244460, accessed 8/1/2013.
17. http://www.sahamnews.info/1391/06/241963, accessed 24/9/2012.
18. http://www.farsnews.com/newstext.php?nn=13911227000890, accessed 10/4/
2013.
19. http://www.jamejamonline.ir/newstext.aspx?newsnum=100831547858, accessed
8/1/2013.
20. http://sharghnewspaper.ir/Page/Paper/91/03/21/19, accessed 15/7/2012.
21. http://fararu.com/prtf11dj.w6dvcagiiw.html, accessed 5/5/2010.
22. http://khabaronline.ir/detail/227883, accessed 27/7/2013.
23. www.dw.de/dw/article/0,,16045824,00.html, accessed 6/1/2013.
24. http://www.khabaronline.ir/detail/6586/ accessed 6/1/2013.
25. See http://www.behzisti.ir/services, accessed 20/12/2015.
26. http://www.salamatnews.com/printNews.aspx?id=48517, accessed 9/8/2012;
http://khabaronline.ir/detail/268630/society/health, accessed 6/1/2013.
27. http://www.hrw.org/reports/2012/12/13/why-they-left, accessed 20/7/2013.

Chapter 3. Ephebiphobia, the Fear of Youth

1. www.aftabnews.ir/prteno8zpjh8wei.b9bj.html, accessed 20/6/2011.
2. http://aftabnews.ir/vdci5uaz3t1aqz2.cbct.html, accessed 11/1/2013.
3. http://www.farsnews.com/newstext.php?nn=13920406000711, accessed 24/7/2013.
4. http://kerman.isna.ir/Default.aspx?NSID=5&SSLID=46&NID=22336, accessed
24/7/2013.

5. http://www.aftabnews.ir/vdchqwnzw23nmwd.tft2.html, accessed 16/6/2012; http://www.iribnews.ir/NewsText.aspx?ID=133517, accessed 28/3/2015.

6. I wrote about technologies of citizenship and "anti-citizens" in a different context, undocumented immigrants in Sweden, but there are striking similarities in the processes of excluding and criminalizing young people in Iran and illegalized immigrants in Sweden (Khosravi 2010).

7. http://www.tebyan.net/index.aspx?pid=193635, accessed 17/6/2012.

8. Interview with Dr. Mohammad Said Zukai, *Shargh* (newspaper), 5 Aban 1390, 4, http://sharghnewspaper.ir/Page/Vijeh/90/08/05/7, accessed 18/6/2012; see also Statistical Center of Iran 1391/2012.

9. http://www.womenrc.ir/News/48458.htm, accessed 17/6/2012.

10. *Shargh* (newspaper), http://sharghnewspaper.ir/Page/Vijeh/90/08/05/7, accessed 18/6/2012.

11. http://www.fararu.com/prtjyiei.uqemxzsffu.html, accessed 27/17/2011.

12. http://www.khabaronline.ir/news-109418.aspx, accessed 27/1/2011.

13. *Rah-e Nou* 3, 19 (Azar 1381/December 2002).

14. See Fatemeh Aliasghar in *Shargh*: http://sharghnewspaper.ir/Page/Vijeh/90/08/05/7, accessed 18/6/2012.

15. http://www.farsnews.com/newstext.php?nn=13910727000037, accessed 18/10/2012.

16. http://www.mehrnews.com/mobile/detail/2112861, accessed 14/8/2013; see *Shahrgh* (newspaper), 16/8/1394, 17.

17. http://fair-family-law.eu/spip.php?page=print&id_article=10242, accessed 27/8/2013.

18. isna.ir/fa/news/92042313760, accessed 6/11/2013.

19. See Fatemeh Aliasghar, in *Shargh*, http://sharghnewspaper.ir/Page/Vijeh/90/08/05/7, 12, accessed 18/6/2012.

20. http://www.roozonline.com/persian/news/newsitem/archive/2012/december/30/article/-b61c83d9bb.html, accessed 10/8/2013.

21. http://www.mehrnews.com/FA/NewsDetail.aspx?NewsID=1761501, accessed 7/3/2013.

22. http://fararu.com/vdcee78w.jh8eni9bbj.html, accessed 17/6/2012.

23. http://radiozamaneh.com/society/khiyaban/2012/08/23/18620, accessed 24/8/2012.

24. http://sharghnewspaper.ir/Page/Vijeh/90/08/05/7, accessed 18/6/2012.

25. In June 2016 the monthly *Zanan-e Emrooz* (Today's Women) published a special issue on single women. *Zanan-e Emrooz*, Khordad 1385/2016, No. 18.

26. Kosha Vatankhah, *Shahrgh* (newspaper), http://sharghnewspaper.ir/Page/Vijeh/90/08/05/7, 9, accessed 18/6/2012.

27. *Andishe Pouya*, 4 (Aban/Azar 1391/2012): 36–41.

28. See also *Zanan Emrooz* (magazine), special issue on "white marriage," No. 5, October 2014. The magazine was banned later that year for "encouraging and justifying white marriage."

29. http://www.baztab.net/fa/news/21274, accessed 19/1/2013.

30. http://www.iranhumanrights.org/2013/01/thugs, accessed 11/1/2013.

31. http://www.aftabnews.ir/prtbz5b8frhbwfp.uiur.html, accessed 7/1/2013.

32. http://www.entekhab.ir/fa/news/87660, accessed 23/12/2012.

33. http://www.asriran.com/fa/print/212924, accessed 17/6/2012.

34. http://www.tebyan.net/newindex.aspx?pid=212416, accessed 27/12/2012.

35. Recently, tattoos became popular among the young middle class. Different from traditional *khalkoobi*, young men and women today have tattoos of nationalist signs or satanic symbols of death or flowers.

36. http://awalnews.ir/vgld.x0o2yt0f9hf62yyal.html, accessed 31/8/2012.

37. https://www.youtube.com/watch?v=wMPVlkqemq8, accessed 10/1/2016.

38. http://www.entekhab.ir/fa/print/38163, accessed 1/8/2012.

39. http://www.ihrv.org/inf/?p=271%22%22, accessed 3/8/2012.

40. http://salamatnews.com/viewNews.aspx?ID=64809&cat=12, accessed 19/1/2013.

41. http://news.gooya.com/politics/archives/2012/07/143706.php, accessed 2/8/2012.

42. http://www.youtube.com/watch?feature=player_embedded&v=YMWuH6LXrnU, accessed 15/4/2013.

43. http://www.ebtekarnews.com/Ebtekar/News.aspx?NID=108559, accessed 15/4/2013.

44. www.tabnak.ir/fa/news/291330/, accessed 22/12/2012.

45. http://fararu.com/fa/print/118686, accessed 6/9/2012.

46. http://www.ihrv.org/inf/?p=271%22%22, accessed 14/4/2013.

47. www.ghanoononline.ir/News/Item/52487/108/, accessed 23/12/2012.

48. http://saeedshabani.blogspot.nl/2012/07/blog-post_16.html, accessed 2/8/2012.

49. http://www.khorasannews.com/News.aspx?type=1&year=1391&month=3&day=22&id=4318649, accessed 17/4/2013.

50. http://www.hamshahrionline.ir/details/183651, accessed 17/4/2013.

51. www.radiofarda.com/articleprintview/27323255.html, accessed 2/11/2015.

52. http://aftabnews.ir/fa/print/331677, accessed 18/11/2015.

53. http://www.hindustantimes.com/world-news/tehran-beggars-make-1-500-a-month-iran-official/article1-539343.aspx#sthash.UZTyeTe5.dpuf, accessed 29/12/2013.

Chapter 4. Streets

1. Krista Mahr, "Neda Agha-Soltan," *Time*, 8 December 2009, see http://content.time.com/time/specials/packages/article/0,28804,1945379_1944701_1944705,00.html, accessed 23/5/2016.

2. http://tehranreview.net/articles/7695, accessed 21/8/2013.

3. These debates were primarily published on a progressive and intellectual site called *Rokhdaad* (Event), which was closed down in 2009 and the primary writer on the site, Omid Mehregan, imprisoned.

4. http://www.entekhab.ir/fa/news/65100, accessed 1/3/2014.

5. www.tabnak.ir/fa/news/292767, accessed 24/8/2013.

6. http://aftabnews.ir/fa/news/129456, accessed 20/6/2011.

7. http://khabaronline.ir/detail/200607/society/judiciary, accessed 22/3/2014.

8. http://www.economist.com/news/americas/21595011-youngsters-gathering-shop
ping-malls-want-attention-not-political-change-kids-are-all, accessed 22/3/2014.

9. http://blog.qeh.ox.ac.uk/?p=536, accessed 22/3/2014.

10. http://www.beitolabbas.com, accessed 6/3/2014.

11. http://www.aftabnews.ir/prtg7q9qtak9nz4.rpra.html, accessed 10/4/2012.

12. http://archive.radiozamaneh.com/society/haftkoocheh/2012/01/06/9758, accessed
23/8/2013.

13. http://www.etemaad.ir/Released/91-02-25/97.html, accessed 15/5/2012.

14. http://www.peykeiran.com/Content.aspx?ID=99842, accessed 16/12/2015.

15. http://archive.radiozamaneh.com/society/haftkoocheh/2012/01/06/9758, accessed
23/8/2013.

16. http://khabaronline.ir/detail/294301, accessed 20/10/2013.

17. http://www.hamshahri.org/print-43936.aspx, accessed 28/1/2011.

18. http://www.isna.ir/ISNA/NewsView.aspx?ID=News-1829567, accessed 19/8/2011.

19. http://anthropology.ir/node/8659, accessed 14/6/2012.

20. http://www.sharaghnewspaper.ir/Print/90/08/03/15086.html, accessed 25/10/2011.

21. isna.ir/fa/news/93091911771, accessed 11/1/2016; see also http://khabaronline
.ir/%28X%281%29S%28xb3prytaezw0xpxpmupoktmkgy%29%29/detail/327835/society
/4015, accessed 10/2/2014.

22. http://www.hamshahrionline.ir/print-125329.aspx, accessed 19/1/2011.

23. www.ilna.ir/ 9/262727, accessed 3/4/2015.

24. Meidaan.com/archive/17116, accessed 7/6/2016.

25. http://www.isna.ir/fa/news/93100602112/40, accessed 2/4/2015.

26. http://khabaronline.ir/detail/476747, accessed 11/1/2016.

27. http://55online.ir/print/37214, accessed 11/3/2015.

28. http://www.shahrwandan.ir/news/28380, accessed 2/4/2015.

Chapter 5. Walls

1. http://www.entekhab.ir/fa/news/158442, accessed 27/4/2014. See also http://www
.newsweek.com/2014/03/28/choking-death-tehran-248027.html, accessed 23/4/2014.

2. See *In Yek Sonyist*, a short documentary by Saman Salur, 2002.

3. See, for example, http://nikoart.blogfa.com; http://ahwazgraffiti.blogfa.com; http://
www.goldoust.com; http://irangraffiti.blogspot.com; http://tehranwalls.blogspot.com; and
http://www.gaff.ir, accessed 10/4/2015.

4. https://www.facebook.com/nafirart, accessed 8/4/2014.

5. http://zine.artcat.com//2008/07/interview.php, accessed 2/2/2011.

Chapter 6. Learning to Endure

1. Similarly, many claimed that American pop star Michael Jackson's sudden death
on 25 July 2009 had been arranged by Iranian authorities to shift the focus of the

international media from the Iranian Green Movement. His death certainly had some impact on what was called Iranians' "Twitter Revolution." When the news broke, "Michael Jackson Tweets" climbed to a hundred thousand per hour and pushed "Green Movement Tweets" out of the top topics.

2. http://jamejamonline.ir/newstext.aspx?newsnum=100906023882, accessed 4/10/2011.

3. http://www.bbc.co.uk/persian/iran/2013/12/131217_l39_satellite_ban_jannati.shtml, accessed 22/5/2014; http://www.khabaronline.ir/detail/178892, accessed 19/10/2011.

4. http://www.entekhab.ir/fa/news/40716, accessed 8/10/2011.

5. http://www.entekhab.ir/fa/news/40604, accessed 2/11/2015.

6. http://www.isna.ir/ISNA/NewsView.aspx?ID=News-1824997, accessed 4/10/2011.

7. http://www.womenrc.com/News/61979.html, accessed 5/12/2011.

8. http://www.tabnak.ir/fa/pages/?cid=82728, accessed 11/10/2011; see also http://www.tebyan.net/Politics_Social/Media/Radio_TV/2010/8/7/132710.html, accessed 11/10/2011.

9. http://www.javanonline.ir/vdchmqnxv23n6qd.tft2.html, accessed 3/12/2011.

10. http://www.mehrnews.com/fa/newsdetail.aspx?NewsID=1417970, accessed 8/10/2011.

11. http://www.fararu.com/prtdjn05.yt0jx6a22y.html, accessed 1/6/2011.

12. http://www.khabaronline.ir/print-84325.aspx, accessed 21/1/2011.

13. http://www.kaleme.com/1390/07/26/klm-77335/?theme=fast, accessed 8/12/2011.

14. http://www.tabnak.ir/fa/news/330619, accessed 5/6/2014.

15. http://mediaarshiv.com/fa/?current=home&Sel=120, accessed 3/5/2015.

16. http://www.mashreghnews.ir/fa/news/214076/, accessed 29/5/2014.

17. http://www.tabnak.ir/fa/news/330619, accessed 30/5/2014.

18. http://old.tehrantimes.com/index_View.asp?code=221174, accessed 17/10/2011.

Chapter 7. Precarious Iran

1. http://www.alimolavi.ir/?p=24; or watch it on You Tube, https://www.youtube.com/watch?v=vzcF_BXVoPA, accessed 29/7/2014.

2. http://www.sharghdaily.ir/Modules/News/PrintVer.aspx?News_Id=40282&V_News_Id=&Src=Main, accessed 3/8/2014; http://www.tabnak.ir/fa/print/413231, accessed 30/7/2014.

3. http://www.isna.ir/fa/news/94101508141, accessed 13/1/2016.

4. http://ilna.ir/news/news.cfm?id=192832, accessed 13/8/2014.

5. http://khabaronline.ir/detail/368253/Economy/market, access 4/8/2014.

6. http://khabaronline.ir/detail/368253/Economy/market, access 4/8/2014.

7. http://www.mehrnews.com/TextVersionDetail/2305685, accessed 6/8/2014.

8. http://aftabnews.ir/fa/print/168133, accessed 5/8/2014; Mehrnews.com/mobile/detail/2305685, accessed 8/4/2014.

9. http://fararu.com/fa/print/170651, accessed 6/8/2014.

10. www.dw.de/a-17846310, accessed 13/8/2014.

11. http://www.nividar.com/news/538568f09c89e9747b91e963, accessed 13/8/2014;

see also http://www.mehrnews.com/news/2581988, accessed 18/5/2015; see also http://www.irna.ir/fa/News/81749005, accessed 13/1/2016.

12. http://www.dw.com/fa-ir/18975946, accessed 14/1/2016.

13. http://www.defapress.ir/Fa/News/4855, accessed 13/1/2016; see also http://www.medanthrotheory.org/read/5774/medicalization-way-of-life, accessed 13/1/2016.

14. http://www.theguardian.com/world/iran-blog/2014/sep/15/iran-tehran-pedlars-survival, accessed 31/3/2015.

15. www.ilna.ir/ 9/263881, accessed 7/4/2015.

16. https://hra-news.org/fa/guilds/a-188, accessed 15/3/2015.

17. http://30mail.net/news/2011/mar/19/sat/8304, accessed 7/8/2014.

18. http://smto.ir/?p=4690, accessed 7/8/2014.

19. *Ayandepazhohi Iran 1393*, Tehran: Ayandeban, 2013. http://www.ayandeban.ir/iran1393, accessed 27/5/2016.

20. *Zamime haftegi Etemad* 40 (14 Bahman 1392/February 2014), 16–18.

21. http://akazemi.ir/fa/?p=467, accessed 8/8/2014.

22. Ayandeban (literally, future observatory) is a recently established semi-official institute for future research. Its annual reports for 2013 and 2014, based on existing statistics, illustrate a dystopian scenario for Iran in the near future. The main challenges Iran struggles with are 1) the conflict with the West over the nuclear program 2); intensified political tensions within the state; 3) financial instability; 4) drought; 5) air pollution; 6) destabilizing family; 7) growth of mental illness; 8) decrease of social capital; 9) drug consumption; 10) armed conflicts in the region; 11) increase of cancer. See http://www.ayandeban.ir.

23. *Shargh* newspaper, 10 Khordad 1395, p. 15.

24. http://www.irna.ir/fa/News/81320108, accessed 4/3/2015.

25. Ibid.

26. www.rahesabz.net/print/42715, accessed 16/9/2011.

27. http://www.transparency.org/country/#IRN, accessed 11/8/2014.

28. http://fararu.com/fa/news/224800, accessed 14/1/2016.

REFERENCES

Abaza, Mona. 2006. *The Changing Consumer Cultures of Modern Egypt: Cairo Urban Reshaping*. Cairo: American University in Cairo Press.

Abazari, Yousuf. 1381/2002. "Fouropashi ejtemai." *Aftab*, Mehr 1381 19: 32–41. http:// yossif-abazari.persianblog.ir/post/47/, accessed May 25, 2012.

Abazari, Yousuf, Fasai, Soheila, and Hamidi, Soheila. 1387/2008. "Ehsas-e na-amni dar tajrobeh zananeh az zendegi rozmarah." *Pazhohesh-e Zanan*, 6, 1: 75–103.

Abbasi-Shavazi, M., P. McDonald, and M. Hosseini-Chavoshi. 2008. "The Family and Social Change in Post-Revolutionary Iran." In K. M. Yount and H. Rashad, eds., *Family in the Middle East: Ideational Change in Egypt, Iran, and Tunisia*. London: Routledge, 2–20.

Abélès, Marc. 2010. *The Politics of Survival*. Durham, N.C.: Duke University Press.

Abdi, Abbas, and Samira Kalhor. 1388/2009. *Jorm, mojrem, va mojazat dar Iran*. Tehran: Nashre Elm.

Abu-Lughod, Lila. 2005. *Dramas of Nationhood: The Politics of Television in Egypt*. Chicago: University of Chicago Press.

Afary, Janet. 1996. *The Iranian Constitutional Revolution, 1906–1911: Grassroots Democracy and the Origins of Feminism*. New York: Columbia University Press.

Agamben, Giorgio. 1998. *Homo Sacer: Sovereign Power and Bare Life*. Trans. Daniel Heller-Roazen. Stanford, Calif.: Stanford University Press.

Aghajanian, Akbar. 1990. "War and Migrant Families in Iran: An Overview of a Social Disaster." *International Journal of Sociology of the Family* 20: 97–107.

Aghajanian, Akbar, and Vaida Thompson. 2013. "Female Headed Households in Iran (1976–2006)." *Marriage & Family Review* 49, 2: 115–34.

Alikhani, Ali. 1382/2003. *Negahi be padideh gosast-e naslha*. Tehran: Pazhoheshkadeh motaleat farhangi va ejtemai vezarat olom.

Aliverdinia, Akbar, and William Pridemore. 2009. "Women's Fatalistic Suicide in Iran: A Partial Test of Durkheim in an Islamic Republic." *Violence Against Women* 15, 3: 307–20

Allison, Anne. 2012. "Ordinary Refugees: Social Precarity and Soul in 21st-Century Japan." *Anthropological Quarterly* 85, 2: 345–70.

———. 2013. *Precarious Japan*. Durham, N.C.: Duke University Press al-Qtaibi, Abullah, and Pascale Ménoret. 2010. "Rebels Without a Cause? A Politics of Deviance in Saudi Arabia." In A. Bayat and L. Herrera, eds., *Being Young and Muslim: New Cultural Politics in the Global South and North*. New York: Oxford University Press, 77–94.

Amani, Mehdi. 1992. *Les effets démographiques de la guerre Iran-Irak sur la population iranienne*. Paris: Institut National d'Études Démographiques.

Amuzegar, Jahangir. 2003. "Iran's Theocracy Under Siege." *Middle East Policy 10, 19: 135–53.*

Anderson, Benedict. 1983. *Imagined Communities: Reflections on the Origin and Spread of Nationalism*. London: Verso.

Appadurai, Arjun. 1996. *Modernity at Large: Cultural Dimensions of Globalization*. Minneapolis: University of Minnesota Press.

Arendt, Hannah.1994 [1951]. *The Origins of Totalitarianism*. New York: Harvest.

Auyero, Javier. 2011. "Patients of the State: An Ethnographic Account of Poor People's Waiting." *Latin American Research Review* 46, 1: 7–29.

———. 2012. *Patients of the State: The Politics of Waiting in Argentina*. Durham, N.C.: Duke University Press.

Azadarmaki, Taghi. 1389/2010. *Jameshenasi Iran: Jameshenasi monasebate beine nasli*, Tehran: Nashre Elm.

Azadarmaki, Taghi, and Jamal Mohamadi. 1385/2006. "Zanan va serialhaye televizioni." *Pazhohesh Zanan* 4, 4: 67–94.

Bachelard, Gaston. 1964. *The Poetics of Space*. Trans. Maria Jolas. Boston: Beacon.

Bahramitash, Roksana. 2003. "Islamic Fundamentalism and Women's Employment in Iran." *International Journal of Politics, Culture, and Society* 16, 4: 551–68.

———. 2013. *Gender and Entrepreneurship in Iran: Microenterprise and the Informal Sector*. Basingstoke: Palgrave Macmillan.

Bahramitash, Roksana, and Hadi Salehi-Esfahani. 2011. *Veiled Employment: Islamism and the Political Economy of Women's Employment in Iran*. Syracuse, N.Y.: Syracuse University Press.

Bakhtin, Mikhail.1984. *Rabelais and His World*. Trans. Hélène Iswolsky. Bloomington: Indiana University Press.

Balibar, Étienne 2002. *Politics and Its Other Scene*. New York: Verso.

Banakar, Reza. 2016. *Driving Culture in Iran: Law and Society on the Roads of the Islamic Republic*. London: Tauris.

Barker, Joshua. 2009. "Introduction: Street Life." *City & Society* 21, 2: 155–62.

Barseghiyan, Araz. 1390/2011. *Yekshanbeh*. Tehran: Cheshmeh.

Baudrillard, Jean. 2005. *The Conspiracy of Art: Manifestos, Interviews, Essays*. Ed. Sylvère Lotringer. Trans. Ames Hodges. New York: Semiotext(e).

Bayat, Asef. 1997. *Street Politics: Poor People's Movements in Iran*. New York: Columbia University Press.

———. 2010. *Life as Politics: How Ordinary People Change the Middle East*. Stanford, Calif.: Stanford University Press.

Behdad, Sohrab, and Farhad Nomani. 2012. "Women's Labour in the Islamic Republic of Iran: Losers and Survivors." *Middle Eastern Studies* 48, 5: 707–33.

Behrouzan, Orkideh. 2010. "Prozàk Diaries: Postrupture Subjectivities and Psychiatric Futures." Ph.D. dissertation, Massachusetts Institute of Technology.

———. 2016. *Prozak Diaries: Psychiatry and Generational Memory in Iran*. Stanford, Calif.: Stanford University Press.

Benjamin, Walter 1983. *Charles Baudelaire: A Lyric Poet in the Era of High Capitalism*. Trans. Harry Zohn. London: Verso.

———. 1999 [1940]. *Illuminations*. Trans. Harry Zohn. London: Random House.

——— 2006 [1936]. "The Storyteller: Observations on the Works of Nikolai Leskov." In *Walter Benjamin: Selected Writings*, vol. 3, *1935–1938*, ed. Howard Eiland and Michael W. Jennings. Cambridge, Mass.: Harvard University Press.

Berman, Marshall. 1982. *All That Is Solid Melts into Air: The Experience of Modernity*. New York: Simon & Schuster.

Bhabha, Homi K. 1994. *The Location of Culture*. London: Routledge.

Billari, Francesco C., Dimeter Philipov, D., and Pau Baizán. 2001. "Leaving Home in Europe: The Experience of Cohorts Born Around 1960." *International Journal of Population Geography* 7: 339–56.

Bloch, Ernst. 1996 [1959]. *The Principle of Hope*. Trans. Neville Plaice, Stephen Plaice, and Paul Knight. Cambridge, Mass.: MIT Press.

Bollas, Christopher. 1993. *Being a Character: Psychoanalysis and Self Experience*. London: Routledge.

Borneman, John. 1992. *Belonging in the Two Berlins: Kin, State, Nation*. Cambridge: Cambridge University Press.

———. 2004. *Death of the Father: An Anthropology of the End of Political Authority*. New York: Berghahn.

Bourdieu, Pierre. 1984. *Distinction: A Social Critique of the Judgement of Taste*. Trans. Richard Nice. London: Routledge.

———. 1992. *The Logic of Practice*. Trans. Richard Nice. Stanford, Calif.: Stanford University Press.

———. 2000. *Pascalian Meditations*. Trans. Richard Nice. Stanford, Calif.: Stanford University Press.

Bourgois, Philippe. 2002. *In Search of Respect: Selling Crack in El Barrio*, Cambridge: Cambridge University Press.

Bozorgian, Amin. 1391/2012. *Ideha-ye khiyabani*. Paris: Parsbook.

Braun, Jerome, and Lauren Langman. 2011. *Alienation and the Carnivalization of Society*. London: Routledge.

Bubandt, Nils. 2006. "Sorcery, Corruption, and the Dangers of Democracy in Indonesia." *Journal of the Royal Anthropological Institute* 12, 2: 413–31.

Butler, Judith. 2009. *Frames of War: When Is Life Grievable?* London: Verso.

Caldeira, Tersa. 2012. "Imprinting and Moving Around: New Visibilities and Configurations of Public Space in São Paulo." *Public Culture* 24, 2: 385–419.

Chamayou, Grégoire. 2012. *Manhunts: A Philosophical History*. Princeton, N.J.: Princeton University Press.

Chanzanagh, Hamid Ebadollahi, and Mahrokh Haghpors. 2010. "Television and Gender Ideology Training in Iran: A Case-Study of a Popular TV Drama in Iran." *Procedia Social and Behavioral Sciences* 9: 1918–1921.

Chelkowski, Peter, and Hamid Dabashi. 1999. *Staging a Revolution: The Art of Persuasion in the Islamic Republic of Iran*. New York: New York University Press.

Chua, Jocelyn Lim. 2014. *In Pursuit of the Good Life: Aspiration and Suicide in Globalizing South India*. Berkeley: University of California Press.

Clinton, Jerome W. 1987. *The Tragedy of Sohrab and Rostam: From the Persian National Epic, the Shahname of Abol-Qasem Ferdowsi*. Seattle: University of Washington Press.

Cohen, Stanley. 1987. *Folk Devils and Moral Panics*. London: Routledge.

Comaroff, John, and Jean Comaroff. 1999. "Occult Economies and the Violence of Abstraction: Notes from the South African Postcolony." *American Ethnologist* 26, 2: 279–303.

———. 2000. "Millennial Capitalism: First Thoughts on a Second Coming." *Public Culture* 12, 2: 291–343.

———. 2001. "Millennial Capitalism and the Culture of Neoliberalism." In J*Millennial Capitalism and the Culture of Neoliberalism*, ed. Jean Comaroff and John Comaroff. Durham, N.C.: Duke University Press, 1–55.

Crapanzano, Vincent. 1985. *Waiting: The Whites of South Africa*. London: Granada.

Crehan, Kate A. F. 2002. *Gramsci, Culture, and Anthropology*. Berkeley: University of California Press.

Dabashi, Hamid. 2007. *Iran: A People Interrupted*. New York: New Press.

Dadvar, Elmira. 2012. "Madar-e mojarad dar sinemaye moaser Iran." *Iran Nameh* 27, 1: 196–203.

de Certeau, Michel. 1984. *The Practice of Everyday Life*. Trans. Steven Rendall. Berkeley: University of California Press.

Deeb, Lara, and Mona Harb. 2013. *Leisurely Islam: Negotiating Geography and Morality in Shi'ite South Beirut*. Princeton, N.J.: Princeton University Press.

De Genova, Nicholas. 2002. "Migrant Illegality and Deportability in Everyday Life." *Annual Review of Anthropology* 31: 419–47.

Deleuze, Gilles, and Félix Guattari. 1987. *A Thousand Plateaus: Capitalism and Schizophrenia*. Trans. Brian Massumi. London: Bloomsbury Academic.

Dhillon, Navtej, and Tarik Yousef. 2009. *Generation in Waiting: The Unfulfilled Promise of Young People in the Middle East*. Washington, D.C.: Brookings Institution Press.

Doostdar, Alireza. 2013. "Fantasies of Reason: Science, Superstition, and the Supernatural in Iran." Ph.D. dissertation, Harvard University.

Dorraj, Manochehr. 1992. "Populism and Corporatism in Post-Revolutionary Iranian Political Culture." In Samih K Farsoun and Mehrdad Mashayekhi, eds., *Iran: Political Culture in the Islamic Republic*. London: Routledge, 214–33.

Douglas, Mary. 1966. *Purity and Danger: An Analysis of Concepts of Pollution and Taboo*. London: Routledge & Kegan Paul.

Dragićević-Šešić, Milena. 2001. "The Street as Political Space: Walking as Protest, Graffiti, and the Student Carnivalization of Belgrade." *New Theatre Quarterly* 17, 1: 74–86.

Durkheim, Émile. 1951. *Suicide: A Study in Sociology.* Ed. George Simpson. Trans. John A. Spaulding and George Simpson. Glencoe, Ill.: Free Press.

———. 1965. *The Elementary Forms of the Religious Life.* Trans. Karen E. Fields. New York: Free Press.

——— 2014 [1933]. *The Division of Labour in Society.* Trans. W. D. Halls. New York: Free Press.

Echeverri Zuluaga, Jonathan. 2015. "Errance and Elsewheres Among Africans Waiting to Restart Their Journeys in Dakar, Senegal." *Cultural Anthropology* 30, 4: 589–610.

Ehsani, Kaveh. 2009. "Survival Through Dispossession: Privatization of Public Goods in the Islamic Republic." *Middle East Report* 39, 250: 26–33.

Fanon, Frantz. 1963. *The Wretched of the Earth.* Trans. Constance Farrington. New York: Grove Press.

Farastkhah, Maghsoud. 1392/2013. "Dindari khakestari." *Mehrnameh* 29: 122–24.

Farji, Mehdi, and Nafiseh Hamidi. 1385/2006. "Baznamai zendegi rozmareh dar khiyaban." *Motaleaat Farhangi va Ertebatat* 2, 5: 159–77.

Fasai, Sadeghi, and Shiva Karimi. 1384/2005. "Gender Stereotypings in Iranian Television Drama." *Woman in Development and Politics (Women's Research)* 3, 13: 59–90.

Ferguson, James. 2006. *Global Shadows: Africa in the Neoliberal World Order.* Durham, N.C.: Duke University Press.

Fischer, Michael M. J., and Mehdi Abedi. 1990. *Debating Muslims: Cultural Dialogues in Postmodernity and Tradition.* Madison: University of Wisconsin Press.

Fiske, John. 1986. "Television: Polysemy and Popularity." *Critical Studies in Mass Communication* 3, 4: 391–408.

Foucault, Michel. 1990. *The History of Sexuality.* Trans. Robert Hurley. New York: Vintage.

Frisby, David. 1994. "The *Flâneur* in Social Theory." In Keith Tester, ed., *The Flâneur.* London: Routledge, 81–110.

Gatejel, Luminita. 2011. "The Common Heritage of the Socialist Car Culture." In *The Socialist Car: Automobility in the Eastern Bloc,* ed. L. Siegelbaum. Ithaca, N.Y.: Cornell University Press.

Geschiere, Peter. 1997. *The Modernity of Witchcraft: Politics and the Occult in Postcolonial Africa.* Charlottesville: University Press of Virginia.

Ghannam, Farha. 2013. *Live and Die like a Man: Gender Dynamics in Urban Egypt.* Stanford, Calif.: Stanford University Press.

Ghazinezhad, Maryam, and Marya Abasian. 1390/2011. "Motale keifi avamel-e ejtemai hamsar koshi." *Zan dar Tose va Siasat* 9, 2: 77–110.

Ghazi Tabatabai, Mahmoud, and Mehdi Rezai. 1388/2009. "Abaad ejtemai va farhangi tasadofat rannandegi dar Iran." *Majaleh Ensanshenasi* 7, 11: 126–55.

Giroux, Henry. 2002. "The War on the Young: Corporate Culture, Schooling, and the Politics of 'Zero Tolerance.'" In *Growing Up Postmodern: Neoliberalism and the War on the Young,* ed. R. Strickland. New York: Rowman and Littlefield, 35–46.

Goldman, Wendy Z. 1993. *Women, the State and Revolution: Soviet Family Policy and Social Life, 1917–1936.* Cambridge: Cambridge University Press.

Golkar, Saeid. 2015. *Captive Society: The Basij Militia and Social Control in Iran.* New York: Columbia University Press.

Goodstein, Elizabeth S. 2005. *Experience Without Qualities: Boredom and Modernity.* Stanford, Calif.: Stanford University Press.

Graham, Mark, and Shahram Khosravi. 2002. "Reordering Public and Private in Iranian Cyberspace: Identity, Politics, and Mobilization." *Identities* 9, 2: 219–46.

Greenhouse, Carol J. 2010. *Ethnographies of Neoliberalism.* Philadelphia: University of Pennsylvania Press.

Gusterson, Hugh. 1997. *Nuclear Rites: A Weapons Laboratory at the End of the Cold War.* Berkeley: University of California Press.

Hage, Ghassan. 2003. *Against Paranoid Nationalism: Searching for Hope in a Shrinking Society.* Annandale, N.S.W.: Pluto.

———, ed. 2009. *Waiting.* Carlton South, Vic.: Melbourne University Press.

Halsey, Mark, and Alison Young. 2006. "'Our desires are ungovernable': Writing Graffiti in Urban Space." *Theoretical Criminology* 10, 3: 275–306.

Hamidi, Farrideh. 1383/2004. "Tasir sakhte khanevadeh bar farar dokhtaran." *Zan dar tose-e va siasat* 2, 3: 85–101.

Hammar, Tomas. 1990. *Democracy and the Nation State: Aliens, Denizens and Citizens in a World of International Migration.* Aldershot: Avebury.

Han, Clara. 2012. *Life in Debt: Times of Care and Violence in Neoliberal Chile.* Berkeley: University of California Press.

Harvey, David. 2008. "The Right to the City." *New Left Review* 53, September–October, 23–40.

Hasso, Frances Susan. 2011. *Consuming Desires: Family Crisis and the State in the Middle East.* Stanford, Calif.: Stanford University Press.

Hilgers, Mathieu. 2011. "The Three Anthropological Approaches to Neoliberalism." *International Social Science Journal* 61, 202: 351–64.

Hollingshead, August B. 1949. *Elmtown's Youth: The Impact of Social Classes on Adolescents.* New York: Wiley.

Hoodfar, Homa. 1999. *The Women's Movement in Iran: Women at the Crossroads of Secularization and Islamization.* Women's Movement Series 1. Paris: Women Living Under Muslim Laws.

Hoshangi, Tahreh. 1391/2012. *Frahang otomobil dar shahre Tehran.* Tehran: Entesharat Nissa.

Hosseini-Chavoshi, Meimanat, and Fatemah Abbasi-Shavazi. 2012. "Demographic Transition in Iran: Changes and Challenges." In Hans Groth and Alfonso Sousa-Poza, eds. *Population Dynamics in Muslim Countries: Assembling the Jigsaw.* Berlin: Springer, 97–116.

Hull, Matthew Stuart. 2012. *Government of Paper: The Materiality of Bureaucracy in Urban Pakistan.* Berkeley: University of California Press.

Inda, Jonathan X. 2006. *Targeting Immigrants: Government, Technology, and Ethics*. Oxford: Blackwell.

Irving, Mark. 2009. "Vatan (homeland): A Rumination on Territoriality." In H. Amirsadeghi, ed. *Different Sames: New Perspectives in Contemporary Iranian Art*. London: Thames and Hudson, 38–47.

Isin, Engin F., and Greg Marc Nielsen. 2008. *Acts of Citizenship*. London: Zed.

Ismail, Salwa. 2006. *Political Life in Cairo's New Quarters: Encountering the Everyday State*. Minneapolis: University of Minnesota Press.

Jackson, Peter. 1988. "Street Life: The Politics of Carnival." *Environment and Planning D: Society and Space* 6, 2: 213–27.

Jacobs, Jane. 1961. *The Death and Life of Great American Cities*. New York: Random House.

James, Erica C. 2012. "Witchcraft, Bureaucraft, and the Social Life of (US)AID in Haiti." *Cultural Anthropology* 27, 1: 50–75.

Jeffrey, Craig. 2010. *Timepass: Youth, Class, and the Politics of Waiting in India*. Stanford, Calif.: Stanford University Press.

Jensen, Steffen. 2014. "Stunted Future: Buryong Among Young Men in Manila." In Anne Line Dalsgård, Martin Demant Frederiksen, Susanne Hojlund, and Lotte Meinert, eds., *Ethnographies of Youth and Temporality: Time Objectified*. Philadelphia: Temple University Press, 41–57.

Kamrani, Behnam. 1389/2010. "Ham-e chiz arome." *Mehrnameh* 7: 178.

Karimi, Neda and Gharaati, Sepideh. 2013. "Why Do Brains Drain? Brain Drain in Iran's Political Discourse." *Critical Approaches to Discourse Analysis Across Disciplines* 6, 2: 154–173.

Katouzian, Homa. 2010. "The Short-Term Society: A Study in the Problems of Long-Term Political and Economic Development in Iran." *Middle Eastern Studies 40, 1: 1–22.*

Kaur, Ravinder. 2008. "The Politics of Humour in Iran." *ISIM Review* 22: 46–47.

Kazemi, Abbas. 1392/2013. *Parsezani va zendegi rozmare irani*. Tehran: Farhange Javid.

Kelly, Catriona. 2005. *Comrade Pavlik: The Rise and Fall of a Soviet Boy Hero*. London: Granta Books.

Kelly, John D., and Martha Kaplan. 1990. "History, Structure, and Ritual." *Annual Review of Anthropology* 19: 119–50.

Khiabany, Gholam. 2008. *Iranian Media: The Paradox of Modernity*. New York: Routledge.

Khosravi, Shahram. 2008. *Young and Defiant in Tehran*. Philadelphia: University of Pennsylvania Press.

———. 2009. "Gender and Ethnicity Among Iranian Men in Sweden." *Journal of Iranian Studies* 42, 4: 591–609.

———. 2010. "*'Illegal' Traveller: An Auto-Ethnography of Borders*. Basingstoke: Palgrave Macmillan.

———. 2014. "Writing Iranian Culture." *Archivio Antropologico Mediterraneo* 16, 2: 25–32.

Kleinman, Arthur. 2014. "How We Endure." *The Lancet* 383: 119–20.

Krige, Detlev. 2010. "The Meaning of Pyramid Schemes in the Popular Economies." Paper presented at Local Economies Workshop of the Popular Economies and Citizen Expectations Research Group, WISER, Wits University, 15 September 2010.

Ladier-Fouladi, Marie. 2012. "Sociodemographic Changes in the Family and Their Impact on the Sociopolitical Behavior of the Youth in Postrevolutionary Iran." In Negin Navabi, ed., *Iran: From Theocracy to the Green Movement*. Basingstoke: Palgrave Macmillan, 137–65.

Lash, Scott, and Celia Lury. 2007. *Global Culture Industry: The Mediation of Things*. Cambridge: Polity.

Lee, Doreen. 2013. "'Anybody Can Do It': Aesthetic Empowerment, Urban Citizenship, and the Naturalization of Indonesian Graffiti and Street Art." *City & Society* 25, 3: 304–27.

Lefebvre, Henri. 2003. *The Urban Revolution*. Trans. Robert Bononno. Minneapolis: University of Minnesota Press.

Lorey, Isabell. 2011. "Governmental Precarization." *Transversal*, http://eipcp.net/transversal/0811/lorey/en, accessed 26 May 2015.

Lotfalian, Mazyar. 2013. "Aestheticized Politics, Visual Culture, and Emergent Forms of Digital Practice." *International Journal of Communication* 7: 1371–90.

Mahdavi, Pardis. 2009. *Passionate Uprisings: Iran's Sexual Revolution*. Stanford, Calif.: Stanford University Press.

Mains, Daniel. 2007. "Neoliberal Times: Progress, Boredom, and Shame Among Young Men in Urban Ethiopia." *American Ethnologist* 34, 4: 659–73.

———. 2012. *Hope Is Cut: Youth, Unemployment, and the Future in Urban Ethiopia*. Philadelphia: Temple University Press.

Malik, Nadeem. 2004. "Waiting for Imam Mehdi and Development: The Case of Pakistan." In Ghassan Hage, ed., *Waiting*. Carlton South: Melbourne University Press, 54–65.

Malinowski, Bronisław. 1922. *Argonauts of the Western Pacific: An Account of Native Enterprise and Adventure in the Archipelagoes of Melanesian New Guinea*. London: Routledge and Kegan Paul.

Mannheim, Karl. 1952. "The Problem of Generations." In *Essays on the Sociology of Knowledge*. London: Routledge and Kegan Paul, 276–322.

Massey, Doreen. 1993. "Politics and Space/Time." In M. Keith and S. Pile, eds., *Place and the Politics of Identity*. London: Routledge, 141–61.

Mather, Yassamine. 2009. "The Latest Economic Crisis in Iran and the Continued Threat of War." *Critique* 37, 1: 67–79.

Mehregan, Omid. 1388/2009. *Tafakor ezterari*. Tehran: Gaam Nou.

Menashri, David. 2001. *Post-Revolutionary Politics in Iran: Religion, Society, and Power*. London: Frank Cass.

Menoret, Pascal. 2014. *Joyriding in Riyadh: Oil, Urbanism, and Road Revolt*. Cambridge: Cambridge University Press.

Merton, Robert K. 1968. *Social Theory and Social Structure*. New York: Free Press.

Mickler, Michael. 2009. "*Jumong*: A Window into Korean and Unification Culture." *Journal of Unification Studies* 10: 51–72.

Millar, Kathleen. 2014. "The Precarious Present: Wageless Labor and Disrupted Life in Rio De Janeiro, Brazil." *Cultural Anthropology* 29, 1: 32–35.

Mirzoeff, Nicholas. 2011. *The Right to Look: A Counterhistory of Visuality*. Durham, N.C.: Duke University Press.

Miyazaki, Hirokazu. 2004. *The Method of Hope: Anthropology, Philosophy, and Fijian Knowledge*. Stanford, Calif.: Stanford University Press.

Moafian, Ghasem, Mohammad Reza Aghabeigi, Seyed Taghi Heydari, Amin Hoseinzadeh, Kamran Bagheri Lankarani, and Yaser Sarikhani. 2013. "An Epidemiologic Survey of Road Traffic Accidents in Iran: Analysis of Driver-Related Factors." *Chinese Journal of Traumatology* 16, 3:140–44.

Moaveni, Azadeh. 2005. *Lipstick Jihad: A Memoir of Growing Up Iranian in America and American in Iran*. New York: Public Affairs.

Moazami, Shahla. 1382/2003. *Farare dokhtaran, chera?* Tehran: Nashre Gerayesh.

———. 1383/2004. "Hamsar koshi, parkhashgari, va jenayat." *Maghlat-e hamaheshe Meli Asiybhaye ejtemai dar Iran*. Tehran: Agah, 207–32.

Moazami, Shahla, and Mohammad Ashouri. 1384/2005. *Hamsarkoshi va angizehaye an*. Tehran: Dadgostar.

Moghadas, Ali Asghar, and Zekiyeh Sharfi. 1388/2009. "Barrasi avamele barangizande gerayesh be mohajerathaye beinolmelali javanan 18–30 sale sharhaye Shiraz va Arsanjan." *Majale jameshenasi Iran* 10, 1: 162–90.

Mohammadi, Ali. 1995. "Cultural Imperialism and Cultural Identity." In J. Downing, A. Mohammadi, and A. Sreberny-Mohammadi, eds., *Questioning the Media: A Critical Introduction*. London: Sage, 362–378.

Mohammadi, Buik. 1388/2009. *Zanzalil*. Tehran: Vazheara.

Mohebali, Mahsa. 1390/2011. *Negaran Nabash*. Tehran: Cheshmeh.

Molé, Noelle J. 2012. *Labor Disorders in Neoliberal Italy: Mobbing, Well-Being, and the Workplace*. Indianapolis: Indiana University Press.

Monroe, Kristin V. 2011. "Being Mobile in Beirut." *City & Society* 23, 1: 91–111.

Moradi, Ali, and Khaled Rahmani. 1393/2014. "Trend of Traffic Accidents and Fatalities in Iran over 20 years (1993–2013)." *Majale Daneshgah Olom Pezeshki Mazandaran* 24, 118: 186–97.

Mottahedeh, Negar. 2015. *#iranelection: Hashtag Solidarity and the Transformation of Online Life*, Stanford: Stanford University Press.

Naficy, Hamid. 1995. "Mediating the Other: American Pop Culture Representation of Postrevolutionary Iran." In Y. Kamalipour, ed., *The US Media and the Middle East: Image and Perception*. Westport, Conn.: Greenwood, 73–89.

———. 2011. *A Social History of Iranian Cinema*, vol. 2. Durham, N.C.: Duke University Press.

Neilson, Brett, and Ned Rossiter. 2005. "From Precarity to Precariousness and Back

Again: Labour, Life and Unstable Networks." *Fibreculture Journal* 5. http://five.fibreculturejournal.org, 1 April 2016.

Norouzi, Ehsan. 1386/2007. *Betallaat*. Tehran: Cheshmeh.

Osanloo, Aezoo. 2012. "What Focus on 'Family' Means in the Islamic Republic of Iran." In M. Voorhoeve, ed., *Family Law in Islam: Divorce, Marriage and Women in the Muslim World*. London: Tauris, 56–76.

Peacock, James L. 1968. *Rites of Modernization: Symbolic and Social Aspects of Indonesian Proletarian Drama*. Chicago: University of Chicago Press.

Penglase, Benjamin. 2009. "States of Insecurity: Everyday Emergencies, Public Secrets and Drug Trafficker Power in a Brazilian Favela." *PoLAR: Political and Legal Anthropology Review* 32, 1: 407–23.

Peteet, Julie. 1996. "The Writing on the Walls: The Graffiti of the Intifada." *Cultural Anthropology* 112: 139–59.

Peterson, Mark Allen. 2011. *Connected in Cairo: Growing Up Cosmopolitan in the Modern Middle East*. Bloomington: Indiana University Press

Petryna, Adriana. 2002. *Life Exposed: Biological Citizens After Chernobyl*. Princeton, N.J.: Princeton University Press.

Piot, Charles. 2010. *Nostalgia for the Future: West Africa After the Cold War*. Chicago: University of Chicago Press.

Putnam, Robert. 1995. "Bowling Alone: America's Declining Social Capital." *Journal of Democracy* 6, 1: 65–78.

Rahimi, Mostafa. 1369/1990. *Trazhedi va ghodrat dar Shahnameh* [Tragedy and Power in Shahnameh]. Tehran: Nilofar Publishers.

Rahnema, Ali. 2011. *Superstition as Ideology in Iranian Politics: From Majlesi to Ahmadinejad*. Cambridge: Cambridge University Press.

Ralph, Michael. 2008. "Killing Time." *Social Text* 26, 4: 1–29.

Ramezani, Rouhollah. 1980. "Constitution of the Islamic Republic of Iran." *Middle East Journal* 34, 2: 181–206.

Rancière, Jacques. 1999. *Disagreement: Politics and Philosophy*. Trans. Julie Rose. Minneapolis: University of Minnesota Press.

———. 2004. *The Politics of Aesthetics: The Distribution of the Sensible*. Trans. Gabriel Rockhill. London: Continuum.

———. 2010. *Dissensus: On Politics and Aesthetics*. London: Continuum.

Rejali, Darius M. 1994. *Torture and Modernity: Self, Society, and State in Modern Iran*. Boulder, Colo.: Westview.

Robben, Antonius. 2011. "Ethnographic Imagination at a Distance." In A. Robben, ed., *Iraq at a Distance: What Anthropologists Can Teach Us About the War*. Philadelphia: University of Pennsylvania Press, 1–20.

Rose, Nikolas. 1999. *Powers of Freedom: Reframing Political Thought*. New York: Cambridge University Press.

Roudi-Fahimi, Farzaneh. 2002. *Iran's Family Planning Program: Responding to a Nation's Needs*. Washington, D.C.: Population Reference Bureau.

Sadeghi, Fatemeh. 2012. "The Green Movement: A Struggle Against Islamist Patriarchy?" In N. Navabi, ed., *Iran: From Theocracy to the Green Movement*. Basingstoke: Palgrave Macmillan, 123–35.

Sadr, Mahbobeh T. 1392/2013. *Zendegi javanan dar shahr*. Tehran: Tissa.

Saghafi, Morad. 2009. "Saghar Daeeri." In Sam Bardaouil, cur., *Iran, Inside Out: Influences of Homeland and Diaspora on the Artistic Language of Contemporary Iranian Artists*. New York: Chelsea Art Museum, 138–139.

Salehi-Isfahani, Djavad. 2010. "Iranian Youth in Times of Economic Crisis." Dubai Initiative Working Paper 3. Dubai: Dubai School of Government / Cambridge, Mass.: Belfer Center for Science and International Affairs, Harvard Kennedy School.

Salehi-Isfahani, Djavad, and Daniel Egel. 2007. "Youth Exclusion in Iran: The State of Education, Employment and Family Formation." Working Paper e07-2. Virginia Polytechnic Institute and State University, Department of Economics.

Salehi-Isfahani, Djavad, and Daniel Egel. 2009. "Beyond Statism: Towards a New Social Contract for Iranian Youth." In Navtej Dhillon and Tarik Yousef, eds., *Generation in Waiting: The Unfulfilled Promises of Young People in the Middle East*. Washington, D.C.: Brookings Institution Press.

Schielke, Samuli, and Jessica Winegar. 2012. "The Writing on the Walls of Egypt." *Middle East Report*, 265: 13–17.

Schmitt, Carl. 1985. *Political Theology: Four Chapters on the Concept of Sovereignty*. Trans. George Schwab. Cambridge, Mass.: MIT Press. First published in 1934.

Schubert, Violeta Duklevska. 2009. "Out of 'Turn,' Out of Sync: Waiting for Marriage in Macedonia." In Ghassan Hage, ed., *Waiting*. Carlton South: Melbourne University Press, 107–20.

Schwartz, Barry. 1974. "Waiting, Exchange, and Power: The Distribution of Time in Social Systems." *American Journal of Sociology* 79, 4: 841–70.

———. 1975. *Queuing and Waiting: Studies in the Social Organization of Access and Delay*. Chicago: University of Chicago Press.

Shahrokni, Nazanin, and Parastou Dokouhaki. 2012. "A Separation at Iranian Universities." *MERIP* Online, http://www.merip.org/mero/mero101812, accessed 26 May 2015.

Shahsavari, Mohammadhassan. 1388/2009. *Shahb-e momken*. Tehran: Cheshmeh

Shields, Rob. 1994. "Fancy Footwork: Walter Benjamin's Note on *Flânerie*." In Keith Tester, ed., *The Flâneur*. London: Routledge, 61–80.

Shiyani, Maliheh, and Mohammad Ali Mohammadi. 1386/2007. "Tahlil jameshenakhti ehsase anomi eghtesadi dar miyan-e javanan." *Faslnameh elmi pazhohesh-ye refah ejtemaie* 6, 25: 11–37.

Simon, Jonathan. 2007. *Governing Through Crime: How the War on Crime Transformed American Democracy and Created a Culture of Fear*. New York: Oxford University Press.

Simone, A. AbdouMaliq. 2010. *City Life from Jakarta to Dakar: Movements at the Crossroads*. New York: Routledge.

Singhal, Arvind, and Kant Udornpim. 1997. "Cultural Shareability, Archetypes, and Television Soaps: 'Oshindrome' in Thailand." *Gazette* 59, 3: 171–88.

Sluka, Jeffrey A. 1992. "The Politics of Painting: Political Murals in Northern Ireland." In Carolyn Nordstrom and JoAnn Martin, eds., *The Paths to Domination, Resistance, and Terror*. Berkeley: University of California Press, 190–215.

Smith, Daniel Jordan. 2007. *Culture of Corruption*. Princeton, N.J.: Princeton University Press.

Sohrabzadeh, Mehran. 1388/2009. "Moghayes-ye zehniyat nasli va bein-e nasli dar naslha-ye daneshgahi pas az enghlab eslami." *Faslnameh Tahghighat Farhangi* 2, 8: 294–63.

Sontag, Susan. 2003. *Regarding the Pain of Others*. New York: Picador.

Spacks, Patricia Meyer. 1995. *Boredom: The Literary History of a State of Mind*. Chicago: University of Chicago Press.

Sreberny-Mohammadi, Annabelle, and Ali Mohammadi. 1994. *Small Media, Big Revolution: Communication, Culture, and the Iranian Revolution*. Minneapolis: University of Minnesota Press.

Stam, Robert. 1992. *Subversive Pleasures: Bakhtin, Cultural Criticism, and Film*. Baltimore: Johns Hopkins University Press.

Standing, Guy. 2011. *The Precariat: The New Dangerous Class*. London: Bloomsbury.

Statistical Center of Iran 1391/2012. *Gozideye natayeje sarshomari omomi va maskan 1390*. Tehran: Markaz Amar Iran.

Strickland, Ronald. 2002. "Introduction: What's Left of Modernity?" In R. Strickland, ed., *Growing Up Postmodern: Neoliberalism and the War on the Young*. New York: Rowman and Littlefield, 1–14.

Sutton, Rebecca, Darshan Vigneswaran, and Harry Wels. 2011. "Waiting in Liminal Space: Migrants' Queuing for Home Affairs in South Africa." *Anthropology Southern Africa* 34, 1 and 2: 30–37.

Taussig, Michael. 1986. *Shamanism, Colonialism, and the Wild Man: A Study in Terror and Healing*. Chicago: University of Chicago Press.

———. 1992. *The Nervous System*. New York: Routledge.

Tehrani, Amir. 1394/2015. *Hakemiyat taradod dar shahr*. Tehran: Rokhdadtaze. http://meidaan.com/archive/7821.

Tizro, Zahra. 2012. *Domestic Violence in Iran: Women, Marriage and Islam*. London: Routledge.

Torbat, Akbar. 2002. "The Brain Drain from Iran to the United States." *Middle East Journal* 56, 2: 272–95.

Turner, Victor. 1969. *The Ritual Process: Structure and Anti-Structure*. Chicago: Aldine.

United Nations Office on Drugs and Crime (UNODC). 2010. *World Drug Report (2010)*, Vienna: United Nations.

Urry, John. 2004. "The 'System' of Automobility." *Theory, Culture and Society* 21, 4/5: 25–39.

Waite, Louise. 2008. "A Place and Space for a Critical Geography of Precarity?" *Geography Compass* 3, 1: 412–33.

Warner, Michael. 2002. *Publics and Counterpublics*. New York: Zone.

Weizman, Eyal. 2015. *The Roundabout Revolutions*. Berlin: Sternberg Press.

Whitlock, Gillian. 2007. *Soft Weapons: Autobiography in Transit*. Chicago: University of Chicago Press.

Yarmohammadi, Anita. 1393/2014. *Bazdam*. Tehran: Ghoghnos.

Yuval-Davis, Nira. 1992. "Fundamentalism, Multiculturalism and Women in Britain." In James Donald and Ali Rattansi, eds., *"Race," Culture and Difference*. London: Sage, 278–91.

INDEX

Abazari, Yousef, 30, 104, 139

Abu-Lughod, Lila, 200, 202, 203, 204, 212, 214, 215

adulthood: delayed, 33, 73–74, 220; transition to, 5, 16, 18, 55, 60, 77–78, 88, 137

Afghans, as stigmatized group: Afghan-Iranians, 1, 2, 42, 166, 168, 223, 226

Agamben, Georgio, 3, 6, 16, 102

alienation, 5, 13, 69, 72, 180, 203, 212, 222, 230

Allison, Anne, 4–5, 9, 11, 57, 220–22, 227, 231, 244

anomie, 13, 69, 71–72, 138, 141; "sexual anomie," 29, 52, 97; *arazel owbash* (thugs), 16, 97, 104–20, 138, 148, 166, 201–2, 212, 222, 226, 228, 230, 233, 235, 245. See also *biband o bari*

Arendt, Hannah, 4, 111, 128, 171

art: depiction of youth's precarity, 84, 102–3, 141, 216; making a parody of masculinity, 68; official murals, 24, 31, 174–75, 177, 180, 182–84, 187–90; representation of women, 70–71, 141, 152; state intervention into the private, 143; street art, 173, 177–90

Asabani nistam (film), 67, 221

Asb heyvan-e najibi ast (film), 92, 156

automobility, 16, 155–64, 171, 219, 221, 245

Auyero, Javier, 9, 79, 80–82

Bakhtiari, 8, 17, 18, 23, 76, 172, 206, 223, 225, 227

Bakhtin, Mikhail, 23, 128, 130

Bayat, Asef, 16–17, 131, 133–34, 163, 169, 171, 187

Bazdam (Anita Yarmohammadi), 72–73

belataklifi, 78, 82–89, 151, 160, 170, 186, 218–19, 221, 233–34, 243, 245

Benjamin, Walter, 14, 22–23, 126, 152, 235

Betallaat (Ehsan Norouzi), 84

biband o bari (licentiousness), 52, 68–67, 70–72, 99. See also anomie

Bloch, Ernst, 1, 14, 25, 152, 188, 221, 243–45

Boghz (film), 67

boredom, 82–84, 88, 160, 186, 222

Bourdieu, Pierre, 14, 71, 81, 89, 112

bullying, 2, 20, 94, 101–3, 110, 118–19, 166–68, 171, 181, 201, 211, 219, 221, 226, 228. See also mobbing

cinema: depiction of *belataklifi*, 6, 78, 156; depiction of generational conflict, 66–67, 221; and family crisis, 201; and migration, 47

citizenship: act of, 4, 15, 17, 19, 50, 135, 143, 170; citizenship rights, 50, 60, 102, 118, 135, 140–41, 165, 223, 225–26; quasi-citizen, 4, 221, 223, 226

civility, 19, 135–37, 163, 169, 230, 244; political, 135–37; "sly civility," 129–30, 142

coffee shops: as site for new urban practice, 16, 170; as public sphere, 23, 126; youth culture, 17, 83, 144–55; waiting in, 146, 221, 224

corruption: academic, 242; financial, 10, 13, 208, 238, 241; institutionalized, 19, 23–25, 71, 81, 86, 131, 137, 163, 165, 236, 241–42

Countdown (film), 32

"cultural crime," 90–91, 159

"cultural invasion," 46, 54, 89, 91, 153, 196

debt, 48, 215; to private moneylenders, 48, 189, 218, 238

denizen/denization, 4, 226

ACKNOWLEDGMENTS

Writing this book has been torture. Not only the suffering of reading and re-reading my own texts; writing and writing again the whole manuscript; facing difficulties doing fieldwork in Iran; writing in a language I do not master; hearing and thinking about precarious lives, but also the creeping fear of the eventual consequences of my writing for me and my family in Iran, all in all have made me a nervous, distracted, and quiet husband, father, friend, and colleague. I am deeply sorry. Many people, however, helped me bear the unbearable. I thank you all. I am deeply indebted to all those Iranians who generously shared their stories with me. I also thank Mazyar Lotfalian, Narges Erami, Targol Mesbah, Paul Stoller, Michael Fischer, Mahmoud Keshavarz, Golrokh Mosayebi, Mina Keshavarz, Amin Parsa, Behzad Khosravi-Noori, Sepideh Karami, Jinoos Taghizadeh, Amirali Ghasemi, Mona Hajin, and Paolo Favero for long and inspiring intellectual conversation. I am also thankful to the anonymous reviewers for the insightful feedbacks. I am grateful to Peter Agree at the University of Pennsylvania for his patience and kindness. I thank also my editor Alison Anderson who helped me as I made the final push to get this book done. Thank you to Lina Lorentz for editorial assistance. Above all, I am grateful to my wife Maryam Omrani and to my children Maryam and Kian for their endless support and love. Some of the material in Chapter 5 has been published in *Anthropology Now* 5, 1 (2013).